RJ STARR

The Psychology of Grey's Anatomy

Trauma, Identity, and Healing at Seattle Grace

First edition

This book was professionally typeset on Reedsy.
Find out more at reedsy.com

For those who study the mind and those who live its contradictions. For the ones who saw a version of themselves in the traumas, transformations, and tenacity of Seattle Grace. And for the writers, actors, and creators who gave us characters real enough to analyze, feel for, and learn from.

We don't just watch characters heal—we watch them fall apart, rebuild, and try again. That's the real story: not perfection, but persistence. In every operating room, every elevator, every quiet hallway, we see pieces of ourselves—flawed, afraid, resilient. "Grey's Anatomy" isn't just about medicine. It's about what it means to survive feeling everything and still choose to stay.

- RJ Starr

Contents

Preface

I've spent a great deal of my life studying human behavior—not from behind a clinician's desk, but in classrooms, conversations, journals, and long pauses. I'm a professor by profession, but a student of people by nature. Psychology, for me, has never been confined to diagnostic criteria or theory. It lives in the ways we break, hide, show up, and try again. It lives in the contradictions we carry, the defenses we inherit, and the moments when something cracks open just enough to let the light in.

Television, at its best, can be more than entertainment. It can serve as an emotional rehearsal space, a kind of simulated self-reflection chamber. It gives us language for what we've felt but couldn't name. It lets us try on identities, feel through someone else's grief, and see ourselves not only as we are but as we might become.

Grey's Anatomy is one of the richest of those spaces.

In writing this book, I'm not simply dissecting plotlines or offering psychological trivia about fictional people. I'm exploring emotional patterns that are deeply real, rendered with care by a cast and creative team who gave these characters dimensionality, contradiction, and evolution. My aim is to use *Grey's Anatomy* as a map of human psychology—not to explain it away, but to explore what it means to keep going, to try again, to love imperfectly, and to survive what almost breaks us.

Before this book, I wrote *The Psychology of Gilmore Girls* and *The Psychology of Dawson's Creek*, each project rooted in the same driving belief: that the stories we grow up watching can become part of our emotional DNA. These are more than shows. They're textured emotional archives of growing up, losing people, choosing who we want to be, and stumbling through it all with a kind of raw, unfinished grace.

Gilmore Girls invited me to examine the quiet costs of perfectionism, the ache of emotional repression, and the longing for unconditional love. *Dawson's Creek* opened up the inner life of adolescence—the shame, the yearning, the unformed truths about who we are. But *Grey's Anatomy*—this is where adulthood lives. Not the performance of adulthood, but the messy, wounded, hopeful, often terrifying truth of it. This is where trauma meets responsibility, where attachment styles play out in surgical wings and scrub rooms, and where every emotional rupture is sutured or left to scar.

It's not just the big events—the shootings, the plane crashes, the deaths—that shape the psychological landscape of the series. It's the quiet conversations in hallways, the repeated decisions to stay or go, the ways grief settles in the corners of a character's posture. It's Meredith's voiceovers, Cristina's evasions, Bailey's burden, Karev's sudden tenderness. Every emotional thread weaves into something recognizable. Something human.

This book is for psychology students who want to see real-world application of theory through narrative. It's for practitioners who recognize that media can offer insight into how people think, relate, cope, and grow. But it's also for anyone who's ever been drawn to the complexity of the human condition. You don't need a degree in psychology to understand what it means to be hurt, to heal, or to hesitate when love gets too close. You just need to have lived.

Each chapter of this book focuses on a major character or theme. I explore their backstories, behaviors, defenses, relationships, and the emotional transformations—or tragedies—that shape their journey. I ground each analysis in psychological theory, but I write it the way I teach: with clarity, with empathy, and always with the hope that understanding leads to compassion.

I do not know the writers or creators of *Grey's Anatomy*. I do not have any affiliation with Shondaland or ABC. This book is not a product of the studio or anyone involved in the show's production. But I owe a deep and abiding respect to the people who brought this world to life. To the writers who gave us scenes that made us ache or breathe easier. To the actors who played these roles with such emotional precision that we felt known through them. To the producers, directors, editors, and crew who built Seattle Grace not just as a set, but as an emotional ecosystem—we felt it. We still feel it.

Thank you.

I know it takes more than great dialogue to create a character that lingers. It takes understanding. *Grey's Anatomy* has always understood people—not just as story mechanisms, but as emotionally alive, beautifully flawed human beings trying to make sense of their lives in real time. It dared to ask: What happens when the thing you love hurts you? What happens when you want closeness but don't know how to receive it? What happens when you survive something that should have destroyed you?

These are psychological questions. And they are also deeply personal ones.

In a time when so many of us are overwhelmed, overextended, and emotionally fractured, stories like *Grey's Anatomy* help us remember what matters. That we're all trying. That we all have wounds. That we all, in our own ways, are trying to stay.

This book is my offering—a synthesis of character, theory, and heart. It's not a definitive answer to who these characters are, but an invitation to look more closely at who we are through them.

Thank you for picking it up. I hope it gives you something—insight, maybe. Language, hopefully. And perhaps, more than anything, the feeling that you're not alone in the ways you've tried to make sense of your own story.

We all bleed a little in the name of becoming.

And sometimes, it's the fiction that helps us heal.

—RJ Starr

* * *

Introduction

A Psychological Case Study Disguised as a Primetime Drama

The premise of *Grey's Anatomy* is deceptively simple: a group of surgical interns begin their medical careers at Seattle Grace Hospital. What unfolds over the next two decades is far more than a hospital procedural. It is a serialized emotional landscape of trauma, identity, loss, connection, defense, survival, and growth. In psychological terms, the show is not just a drama—it's an evolving case study in human behavior.

From its earliest episodes, *Grey's Anatomy* framed its narrative around emotional conflict, not just clinical crisis. Its voiceovers invited introspection, its storylines mirrored internal battles, and its characters were rarely allowed to remain static. The result is a show that provides a remarkably sustained exploration of what it means to develop psychologically over time—especially while working, living, and grieving inside a high-stakes professional setting.

This book treats *Grey's Anatomy* not as a guilty pleasure or long-running soap opera, but as a cultural artifact rich with psychological data. It examines how the show portrays trauma responses, attachment styles, identity formation, coping mechanisms, and the emotional residue of loss. It asks not just what happened to the characters—but what those arcs reveal about how human beings navigate pain, closeness, ambition, and healing.

While it would be easy to dismiss long-running television series as emotionally indulgent or narratively inconsistent, that misses the point. Human development is not tidy. People regress. Stories loop. Healing is nonlinear. If anything, the show's occasional chaos mirrors the very nature of the psyche it portrays. The emotional realism of *Grey's Anatomy* lies not in its plot mechanics, but in its psychological accuracy.

This book is divided into four parts:

- **Part I** examines origin stories, childhood trauma, and the shaping of early attachment. Characters like Meredith Grey, Cristina Yang, and Alex Karev carry the residue of neglect, abandonment, or parental pressure into every relationship they attempt. We look at how foundational emotional injuries inform future intimacy, self-protection, and career drive.
- **Part II** centers around love, loss, and the complexity of adult attachment. Relationships in *Grey's Anatomy* are often intense, fractured, and illuminating. Rather than framing them as romantic subplots, we investigate them as living demonstrations of how people cope with connection, fear, dependency, and identity within partnership.
- **Part III** turns to trauma, death, and moral fatigue. As the series evolves, characters are exposed to extreme loss: shootings, plane crashes, career failure, and the deaths of partners, friends, and patients. This section explores how the show depicts trauma responses—dissociation, hypervigilance, guilt, and emotional shutdown—as well as the resilience and repair that follow.
- **Part IV** steps back to consider broader psychological and cultural dynamics: race and representation, mental health visibility, professional identity, and the hospital itself as a metaphor for inner life. These thematic essays move beyond character to ask what the show teaches us about systemic and symbolic layers of the psyche.

Each chapter begins with a character- or theme-focused introduction, followed by three psychologically distinct sections. These may explore theoretical frameworks (such as attachment theory, identity development, grief psychology, or trauma science), analyze patterns of behavior across the character's arc, and assess whether transformation, rupture, or resignation defines their psychological conclusion.

The goal is not to retroactively pathologize fictional people. It is to use fictional lives as case illustrations of real psychological principles.

This methodology is not new. For decades, clinicians, researchers, and educators have used narrative as a tool to teach psychological insight. Stories offer abstraction, safety, and emotional distance—while still illuminating core truths. Carl Jung explored mythology and archetype. Viktor Frankl saw meaning as the psychological lifeline that runs through suffering. More recently, narrative therapy has invited clients to reshape their personal stories. Media, too, serves as narrative rehearsal. We watch others navigate choices we haven't yet faced. We cry for characters as a way of touching something buried in ourselves.

That is precisely what *Grey's Anatomy* allows.

It gives us a stage for feelings we've suppressed. It lets us observe grief, connection, rupture, and repair with emotional investment—but also with enough distance to reflect. The show doesn't just depict psychological patterns—it replays them, sometimes over years, letting us observe emotional mechanisms from multiple angles.

Consider Meredith Grey. In early seasons, her emotional unavailability and self-sabotaging intimacy patterns are textbook symptoms of fearful-avoidant attachment. But unlike a single-episode character study, Meredith evolves. She begins to trust. She becomes a mother. She grieves. She stays. Her arc is one of slow psychological integration. Similarly, Cristina Yang's brilliant avoidance—her need for autonomy, her ambivalence about love—is never "fixed" but honored. Her decision to leave isn't a failure of development; it is the most honest act of self-preservation she could perform.

Even more than its characters, *Grey's Anatomy* excels in portraying trauma. And not just acute trauma, but cumulative trauma—what psychologists refer to as complex trauma. The plane crash. The shooting. Derek's death. George's death. Lexie's death. April and Jackson's loss of their son. The emotional cost of working in high-intensity caregiving environments. Through it all, the show never sanitizes the psychological consequences. It lets people fall apart. It gives grief a long tail. It recognizes that trauma lives in the body and the mind—and that it takes time, and often repetition, to even begin healing.

That's not to say the show gets everything right. No fictional series can.

But what it gets right, it gets deeply right. Its emotional truth eclipses any narrative imperfections. And its willingness to center vulnerability as a core human experience makes it unusually well-suited for psychological exploration.

This book is not just for fans of the show. It is for anyone who studies the mind, teaches the emotional life, or walks through the world with a psychological lens. It is for students learning to identify patterns. For professionals looking to deepen their understanding of emotional nuance. And for viewers—especially long-time ones—who have found themselves unexpectedly cracked open by something a character said, did, or survived.

It is also for the emotionally curious. The ones who pause a scene because it felt too familiar. The ones who rewatch because something in the story feels unfinished—not just on screen, but inside themselves.

Importantly, this book also recognizes the extraordinary creative labor behind *Grey's Anatomy*. I am not affiliated with the writers, producers, or actors. I claim no ownership or authority over their work. But I hold it in deep respect. What they created—a twenty-season narrative arc exploring grief, love, trauma, identity, and meaning—is a towering emotional achievement. They did not create a perfect world. They created a human one. And that is what matters most in psychology.

In the pages ahead, we will not look for diagnoses. We will look for understanding. For patterns. For motives. For meaning.

We will ask not only "what happened" to these characters, but "why did it matter?" and "what can we learn from it?"

Because if we listen closely, we'll realize: the stories we tell about fictional people are often the stories we're afraid to tell about ourselves.

* * *

I

Origins, Attachment, and the Search for Belonging

Before they became surgeons, they were sons, daughters, dreamers, and survivors—shaped by loss, longing, and the people who left too soon or stayed too little. In these early character studies, we examine how childhood wounds, attachment styles, and identity formation lay the groundwork for every future connection. Belonging isn't just a theme in Grey's Anatomy—it's the emotional engine behind every choice they make.

1

Meredith Grey – From Abandonment to Emotional Authority

The Girl Who Belonged to No One

Before she became the voice of *Grey's Anatomy*, Meredith Grey was a shadow of herself. When we first meet her, she's emotionally flat, relationally avoidant, and wholly uninvested in explaining her inner world. Her tone is guarded, her posture defensive. Her humor, clinical. She introduces herself in the same breath as she distances herself: "I'm just a girl in a bar." But the truth is, she's not just anyone—she is the emotional nucleus of the series, and her evolution sets the emotional pace for the entire show.

Meredith is the daughter of Ellis Grey, a celebrated surgeon who was both professionally brilliant and emotionally cruel. Her father abandoned her. Her mother belittled her. Her childhood was a cocktail of brilliance and neglect, leaving her relationally stunted, deeply mistrusting, and emotionally armored. And yet, beneath that detachment is something raw and aching—something human and unfinished. Meredith is not unfeeling. She is protecting something she was never taught to hold.

Her trajectory over the course of the show is one of the most sustained psychological evolutions in television. Over nearly two decades of narrative, Meredith transitions from emotionally unavailable and self-sabotaging to stable, open, grounded, and deeply connected to those around her. But this transformation is not romanticized. It is slow. It is painful. It is punctuated by loss after loss, rupture after rupture. It is, in short, exactly what real emotional growth looks like.

Meredith's early relationships—especially with Derek Shepherd—are defined by her ambivalence. She wants closeness but recoils from it. She reaches for love and then retreats when it gets too real. She dismisses her needs before anyone else can reject them. This isn't indecision. It's survival. Her attachment style, a mix of anxious longing and avoidant withdrawal, reflects someone who has never had consistent emotional safety. She was not taught how to trust love, only how to endure its loss.

Yet something about Meredith compels loyalty. Cristina, Alex, George, Izzie—these people anchor her, even when she resists being anchored. There is a quiet magnetism in her fragility, a kind of rawness that others instinctively want to protect. But Meredith is not interested in being saved. She's interested in surviving on her own terms. Her challenge is not only to let others in, but to recognize that love is not synonymous with abandonment.

As the series progresses, Meredith encounters death, motherhood, betrayal, and the loss of nearly every person she's ever loved. These events do not crush her. They shape her. Grief does not make her more closed—it softens her edges. Each loss becomes a strange kind of teacher, nudging her toward emotional presence. The trauma remains, but she stops letting it dictate who she can become.

Meredith's journey is not about becoming unbroken. It's about becoming whole. She does not shed her darkness. She integrates it. She stops fearing that her "dark and twisty" parts make her unlovable and starts recognizing that they are part of her truth. This shift—from self-protection to self-possession—is not dramatic. It happens in increments. In hallway conversations. In parenting decisions. In friendships that deepen instead of dissolve.

By the time we see her mentoring new interns and raising her children alone, she is no longer the girl in the bar. She is the lighthouse. She is the one who stays. She is the one others turn to. She has moved from emotional scarcity to quiet, earned authority.

What makes Meredith Grey such a rich subject for psychological exploration is not just her pain. It's her pattern. Her arc. Her slow, believable undoing of inherited emotional defenses. She demonstrates what happens when someone who never felt safe in love begins to trust it—not because the world suddenly became kinder, but because she finally believed she could survive it.

In this chapter, we'll examine Meredith's early emotional blueprint through the lens of attachment theory and childhood trauma. We'll look at how her emotional defenses play out in her romantic relationships, her friendships, and her approach to work. And finally, we'll trace the evolution of her emotional regulation and presence—not as a return to innocence, but as a deliberate act of emotional authorship.

Meredith Grey doesn't simply grow up. She grows inward. And in doing so, she offers one of the most emotionally intelligent arcs in television history—not because she becomes perfect, but because she finally becomes real.

Raised by Absence - The Psychology of Emotional Withholding

Before Meredith Grey ever set foot inside Seattle Grace, before she met Cristina, or Derek, or made the decision to survive the wreckage of her early life, she was already someone who had learned not to need. That's the real root of her emotional patterning—not avoidance by choice, but avoidance by necessity. She was raised in an environment that taught her to survive without comfort, without consistent love, and without emotional safety. Her armor was not built in adulthood. It was forged in childhood, in the cold and clinical world of Ellis Grey.

To understand Meredith's psychology, we must start with her mother—not as a villain, but as a portrait of intergenerational trauma and narcissistic parenting. Ellis Grey was brilliant, ambitious, and emotionally inaccessible.

Her presence in Meredith's life was marked not by warmth but by judgment, not by safety but by control. She oscillated between hyper-criticism and complete detachment, offering Meredith a blueprint that equated love with conditional performance and identity with invisibility.

This kind of parent-child dynamic often produces what attachment theorists describe as a fearful-avoidant attachment style. Also called disorganized attachment, it arises when a child experiences the caregiver as both a source of fear and the only potential source of comfort. The result is a deep internal conflict: the child wants to move toward the caregiver but instinctively pulls away. Love feels unsafe. Closeness feels threatening. Over time, the child learns to suppress their own needs because they fear those needs will go unmet—or worse, punished.

Meredith exhibits this exact dynamic from the beginning of the series. She wants connection but flinches from it. She longs for intimacy but shields herself with sarcasm, dismissiveness, and detachment. Her one-night stand with Derek is not simply a spontaneous act of liberation—it's an emotionally low-stakes entry point. He's a stranger. He doesn't know her mother. He doesn't expect anything. She can be momentarily seen without the risk of being fully known. That's the pattern: exposure without vulnerability.

In a household where love was rationed or weaponized, Meredith learned early to expect nothing. This is what emotional withholding does to a developing psyche. It conditions the child to internalize not just neglect, but self-abandonment. Meredith's sense of identity was shaped by what she lacked. There was no one to reflect back to her that she was lovable simply for existing. She was raised to perform, to achieve, to endure—but not to attach.

This is evident in how she moves through her early professional life. She's competent but disconnected, brilliant but emotionally opaque. Her validation comes not from relationships but from her capacity to endure stress, to outwork everyone, and to suppress emotion in favor of function. In trauma psychology, this is sometimes referred to as a functional freeze response—a survival strategy where emotional expression is limited to ensure safety and predictability. Meredith doesn't feel because feeling, in her world, was dangerous.

The absence of her father adds another layer. Thatcher Grey did not die. He left. And that absence is arguably more psychologically corrosive because it implies choice. A parent who dies is mourned. A parent who abandons is internalized as rejection. Meredith is not just dealing with a mother who belittled her—she's dealing with a father who erased her. This double abandonment reinforces a core schema: *you are not enough to stay for.*

In schema therapy, core beliefs formed in childhood are called early maladaptive schemas. They become the unspoken assumptions that guide how we interpret the world. For Meredith, one such schema is *defectiveness/shame*—the belief that she is fundamentally flawed and that if anyone gets too close, they will discover the truth and leave. Another is *emotional deprivation*—the assumption that her needs for empathy, warmth, and care will never be met. Together, these beliefs shape how she sees others, how she sees herself, and how she protects her inner life.

This is why she clings so tightly to her identity as a surgeon. It's not just career ambition. It's existential scaffolding. Surgery is where Meredith can be competent without being emotionally exposed. The rules are clear. The outcomes are measurable. There is structure, hierarchy, and skill. The OR becomes a place where she can exert control in a world that, emotionally, has always felt unmanageable.

But even in the surgical world, Meredith's psychological wounds bleed through. She takes risks. She's drawn to chaos. She often uses adrenaline as a stand-in for connection. In early seasons, we see her repeatedly sabotage moments of intimacy, pulling away just as others begin to lean in. When Derek wants to know her, she panics. When friends try to care for her, she deflects. This is not arrogance or aloofness—it is the terrified reflex of someone who never learned to trust love.

Her famous "pick me, choose me, love me" moment—so often parodied—is psychologically revealing. It's one of the few times Meredith lets herself plead. She breaks her pattern of aloofness and asks to be loved, to be chosen. But even in that moment, there's a desperation that reveals just how emotionally starved she is. She's not asking to be met in love—she's asking to be rescued from the belief that she's inherently unlovable. That's not romantic. That's trauma.

It's easy to pathologize Meredith's emotional coolness, but what she displays is a common psychological strategy among adults who were raised in emotionally barren homes: *protective disconnection*. She doesn't know how to need others safely, so she structures her world around not needing at all. But need doesn't disappear just because it's repressed. It festers. It erupts. And in Meredith's case, it slowly begins to surface through her relationships with people who don't leave—Cristina, Bailey, eventually Derek, and even Alex.

These relationships are not just plot devices. They are therapeutic in the truest sense. Through them, Meredith begins to receive emotional mirroring. She is seen, challenged, comforted. And slowly, her early schema—*you are alone, you are too much, you are not enough*—starts to loosen. It doesn't vanish. But it no longer controls her every move.

Meredith's healing is not clean. There is no singular breakthrough. But this, too, is accurate. Real psychological healing happens in repetition. In repaired rupture. In someone saying, *I see you*—and not leaving. It happens in ordinary moments where the emotional script is rewritten, just slightly, enough to feel safer the next time.

By the time we reach the midpoint of her arc, Meredith is no longer governed entirely by absence. She still fears loss. She still grieves deeply. But she no longer assumes that closeness will destroy her. She has built new emotional muscle—one that allows her to tolerate intimacy without panic, to trust without collapse, and to stay present even in the face of goodbye.

Her transformation begins not when she falls in love, but when she begins to believe she is not unlovable.

And that is the difference between surviving and healing.

Holding Back to Survive - Intimacy, Trust, and the Fear of Being Seen

Meredith Grey is not emotionally distant because she wants to be. She is distant because closeness, to her, has always been dangerous. That's the central tension in her early character arc—she craves connection but cannot tolerate the vulnerability it requires. She builds her life with clear relational limits: physically present, emotionally disengaged. Her body may be in the room, her wit sharp, her mind on point—but her inner world remains locked behind a door even she rarely opens.

In the world of trauma-informed psychology, this kind of behavior reflects what's known as protective inhibition—the impulse to self-conceal as a strategy for emotional survival. For those who grew up in emotionally invalidating environments, openness becomes a liability. If expressing need once led to rejection or ridicule, the nervous system begins to associate intimacy with threat. Meredith doesn't mistrust people arbitrarily. She mistrusts them as a matter of emotional conditioning.

That conditioning is most visible in her early relationship with Derek Shepherd. Their initial connection is easy, almost impulsive. It's casual enough to bypass her defenses. But once feelings begin to deepen, we see Meredith flinch. She pulls back, turns cold, evades meaningful conversation. When Derek presses, she deflects with humor, defiance, or silence. These are not quirks. They are survival reflexes. Meredith has learned to maintain control by never allowing anyone full emotional access. The closer Derek gets, the more Meredith reverts to emotional minimalism.

And yet, she doesn't want to lose him. That's the paradox of her attachment style. Psychologists call it fearful-avoidant—a mix of anxious longing and avoidant distancing. These individuals want connection desperately but believe it's inevitably unsafe or fleeting. So they create push-pull dynamics, initiating closeness and then withdrawing from it, creating confusion in partners and emotional exhaustion in themselves. Meredith illustrates this beautifully. She's not simply a woman who's hard to read. She's someone whose entire nervous system has been trained to expect that closeness will cost her more than it gives.

What's most compelling about Meredith's defense mechanisms is how nuanced they are. She's not overtly guarded. She's funny, warm in small doses, quick to comfort others. She's capable of deep empathy, particularly with patients. But she compartmentalizes that empathy. She offers it to those who cannot threaten her emotionally. With patients, she can be present. With peers, she chooses carefully. With Derek, she is a fortress with shifting gates—sometimes open, sometimes shut, always testing whether she can be loved without being consumed.

Nowhere is this more evident than in her friendship with Cristina Yang. Their bond is one of the most emotionally significant relationships in the series, precisely because it exists outside of the romantic or familial. With Cristina, Meredith allows more of herself to be visible. She lets her guard down not through dramatic disclosure but through constancy. They don't need to explain themselves to one another. They are understood. And for someone like Meredith—who has spent a lifetime feeling misunderstood—that kind of recognition is both rare and reparative.

Cristina never tries to fix Meredith. She never demands emotional availability. She offers space, loyalty, and a kind of intellectual intimacy that feels safe. This kind of non-romantic secure bond provides Meredith with a template for closeness without threat. It's not therapy, but it's therapeutic. Cristina becomes a co-regulator—someone whose steady presence helps Meredith learn that closeness doesn't always lead to abandonment.

In trauma recovery, these are known as corrective emotional experiences—interactions that contradict old emotional scripts and begin to rewrite them. Cristina doesn't leave. She doesn't punish vulnerability. She doesn't demand Meredith become someone different. She accepts her as she is, and that, paradoxically, becomes the doorway through which Meredith begins to change.

Meredith's other early friendships—with George, Izzie, and eventually Bailey—also serve this purpose, though less directly. With George, she plays out a familiar pattern: someone wants her, and she panics. Her rejection of him is not cruel, but it is clumsy and emotionally unprocessed. She struggles to be emotionally present when it matters most, because presence requires confronting her own fear. Izzie's openness is foreign to her. Bailey's strength, however, provides something Meredith both respects and quietly needs—external structure and emotional clarity.

It is important to note that Meredith's emotional withholding is not only reactive. It is also strategic. She uses it to maintain control. In emotionally chaotic lives, control is the closest thing to safety. Meredith controls what she says, who gets in, when she reveals vulnerability. She is not emotionally repressed in the traditional sense—she feels deeply—but she regulates that feeling through detachment. The surgical environment is ideal for this. It allows her to channel emotion into technical precision. Blood and chaos surround her, but within the rules of the operating room, she knows her place. She performs not only surgery, but emotional discipline.

This is also why intimacy with Derek is so difficult. Love has no rulebook. It is ambiguous, volatile, unpredictable. The closer they grow, the less Meredith is able to rely on performance as protection. Derek sees her. He pushes for more. And at times, that pressure backfires. His need for clarity collides with her need for space. He wants her to speak. She wants him to intuit. And when he fails to meet her unspoken needs, it confirms her belief: you cannot count on people to stay.

What makes their dynamic so compelling is that it never fully resolves into an easy romance. Even in its best moments, it is layered with psychological tension. Meredith wants to be chosen, but she also wants to be untouched. She wants to be known, but only partially. And that ambivalence is real. Many people who carry attachment injuries experience intimacy not as a destination but as a dilemma.

Yet there is movement. Slow, halting, nonlinear—but real. We begin to see moments when Meredith doesn't flee. When she tells the truth. When she lets someone hold her pain. These moments don't announce themselves. They sneak in. A hand held in silence. A look of acceptance. A decision not to run. And each one adds a new thread to her internal sense of safety.

Meredith begins to realize that safety isn't the absence of loss—it's the presence of people who don't flinch when she's hurting. That realization reshapes her approach to love, to friendship, to herself. She learns not to disappear. She learns to speak. She learns to let others help.

And still, the fear never vanishes. But it no longer rules her.

This is what healing often looks like—not the eradication of fear, but the growth of tolerance. The ability to stay present even when your body wants to retreat. The willingness to trust again, even if trust has failed you before. Meredith's journey through intimacy and trust is not one of romantic triumph. It is one of psychological courage. To feel love and not leave—that is her victory.

In the next section, we will examine the arc of Meredith's emotional growth in greater detail, tracing the transition from protective withdrawal to grounded presence. Not as a fairytale ending, but as a hard-won process of integration. Meredith Grey doesn't just fall in love. She learns how to exist in it.

Becoming the Lighthouse - Healing Through Presence and Purpose

Meredith Grey's psychological journey does not follow the arc of recovery so much as the rhythm of reclamation. She doesn't resolve her past, nor does she transcend it. What she does—slowly, imperfectly, and often with great emotional cost—is learn to live with it. To make room for it. To stop fighting her wounds and instead integrate them into the fuller story of who she is becoming.

In the early seasons, Meredith is defined by her fear of emotional engulfment. Her relationships, even those she cares deeply about, are filtered through a deep and often unspoken question: how close can I get before I lose myself? The question isn't intellectual. It's somatic. Her body anticipates loss before it occurs. Her tone, posture, even her gaze carries the weight of someone who has already rehearsed your absence.

But grief is what changes her. Not just one loss, but many. Derek. Lexie. George. Her mother. Her stepmother. The accumulation of departures does not break Meredith—it transforms her. She learns, through repeated emotional devastation, that survival is not the same as numbing. That staying is not only possible, but necessary. That love, when allowed to flow without control, may hurt—but that hurt is not a verdict. It is evidence of aliveness.

Meredith's turning point is not easy to date. It's not the moment she confesses her love to Derek or the moment she holds her child for the first time. It's the gradual unfolding of someone who has decided—consciously or not—that she wants to be more present in her own life. That she no longer wants to live under the shadow of past abandonment. That while fear still exists, it no longer has executive power.

Grief, in many psychological frameworks, is not simply a reaction to loss. It's an emotional process of reorganizing one's identity. After Derek's death, Meredith is not only mourning her husband—she is rebuilding her inner landscape. She goes away for a while, literally and figuratively. She disappears, not as a relapse into avoidance, but as an act of regrouping. She gives herself distance. And when she returns, she is quieter. Still intense, still guarded—but less fragmented. Something has settled.

This is what maturity often looks like: less drama, more discernment. Meredith doesn't explain her transformation. She embodies it. Her responses slow down. Her gaze lingers. She begins to teach more than she critiques. She becomes, in essence, a lighthouse—steady, grounded, and emotionally available in a way she never was before.

The metaphor is deliberate. A lighthouse is not frantic. It is not aggressive or demanding. It simply shines. It offers orientation in the storm. And that is what Meredith becomes for others. For her children. For her interns. For Alex, for Bailey, even for Jo. She no longer needs to prove her intelligence or worth. Her presence, shaped by pain and persistence, speaks for itself.

This shift is not only emotional—it's existential. Meredith begins to operate from a different place within herself. Where once her choices were driven by fear, she begins making decisions anchored in clarity. She chooses to stay in relationships, not because she's dependent on them, but because she's present in them. She doesn't need saving. She doesn't need chaos. She doesn't need to be the most brilliant in the room. She knows who she is. And more importantly, she's no longer afraid of what that means.

We can see this most clearly in how she parents. Meredith does not replicate Ellis Grey's coldness. She is warm, protective, attuned. She is not perfect, but she is present. She answers her children's questions. She holds their grief with grace. She admits when she is overwhelmed. She models emotional regulation not through perfection but through participation. She shows up. She stays. And in doing so, she repairs the intergenerational rupture that defined her own early life.

This is perhaps the most significant element of Meredith's arc. She becomes the kind of parent she never had. She gives her children what she was denied—not just safety, but emotional availability. In developmental psychology, this is called earned security—the process by which an adult with an insecure or disorganized attachment history creates a new internal model of attachment through reflective work, consistent relationships, and self-awareness. Meredith does not inherit emotional safety. She builds it.

Her growth also redefines her professional identity. She no longer uses surgery as an escape from feeling. Instead, she sees it as an extension of presence. She mentors, she collaborates, she leads with measured confidence. She no longer needs to be dramatic to be effective. She doesn't need to win every argument or hold every grudge. She has become someone others can rely on—not because she is infallible, but because she is real.

This is not a triumphal transformation. Meredith still has moments of retreat. She still deflects. She still loses people. But what changes is her capacity to metabolize pain. To feel it without being destroyed by it. To respond, not just react. Her nervous system, once tuned to anticipate abandonment, is now more resilient. She can weather emotion without shutting down. She can love without collapsing. She can grieve without vanishing.

This is not something we often see in television. Character arcs typically end with a resolution or a redemption. Meredith's doesn't. It continues. It evolves. Her healing is never finished. But it is deeply integrated. She no longer fears being known. She no longer confuses vulnerability with weakness. And she no longer believes that being "dark and twisty" means being unworthy of love.

If anything, Meredith's arc teaches us that healing is not about becoming someone new. It's about reclaiming the parts of yourself you buried to survive. It's about letting go of the belief that closeness is a liability. It's about choosing presence—not because it's easy, but because it's honest.

By the later seasons, Meredith Grey is no longer the emotionally shutdown intern hoping no one sees how lost she feels. She is still grieving, still learning, still holding contradictions. But she is also open. She is rooted. She is safe enough to be soft.

And for viewers—especially those who have loved and lost, those who have struggled with abandonment, those who have learned to protect themselves at the cost of connection—her story offers more than hope. It offers instruction. It says: you can learn to stay. You can learn to trust. You can build a life where presence is no longer a threat, but a gift.

That's the quiet power of her arc.

She became the thing she never had.

And she stayed.

* * *

2

Cristina Yang – The Avoidant Achiever

Love Is Not the Prize

Cristina Yang does not enter the hospital looking for love. She enters to win. From her first scenes in *Grey's Anatomy*, she makes it clear that she is there to be the best, not to be liked. Where Meredith is emotionally withdrawn but hesitant, Cristina is controlled, competitive, and unapologetically driven. She is the embodiment of mastery as defense—someone whose emotional restraint is not just habit, but strategy. Her brilliance is not simply intellectual. It is a wall.

To call Cristina emotionally unavailable would be technically accurate but conceptually incomplete. What she displays is not the absence of feeling, but the meticulous management of it. Her emotional life is not vacant—it is guarded, filed, and buried beneath layers of surgical precision and professional ambition. Cristina doesn't resist vulnerability because she's cold. She resists it because vulnerability has never felt safe.

Her character is a living case study in avoidant attachment. Early in life, those with this pattern learn that expressing emotion is either irrelevant or met with rejection. As a result, they adapt by minimizing emotional expression, relying on themselves, and keeping others at a distance. In Cristina, this manifests as self-containment, sarcasm, and what seems like a contempt for emotional display. But beneath that surface is something deeper: fear of being consumed, controlled, or emotionally eclipsed.

Cristina's background is never fully unpacked in the series, but what we do know offers important clues. Her father died when she was young—a traumatic loss that likely intensified her emotional self-reliance. Her mother is portrayed as image-conscious and superficial, often dismissive of Cristina's desires or professional identity. We're given the impression that Cristina learned early on that approval was conditional, and authenticity was inconvenient. Her response? To cultivate an identity that could not be questioned: the best, the smartest, the most focused.

This is a common psychological pattern in what some theorists call "high-achieving avoidants." These individuals channel emotional needs into performance. If connection feels unpredictable or unsafe, they seek mastery instead. Validation is earned through skill. Worth is tied to output. And control becomes the primary mode of relating—to work, to people, to themselves.

Cristina's relationship with surgery is not just about ambition. It is about safety. The OR is where she is most fully herself—precise, competent, in control. Unlike relationships, which are full of ambiguity and unmet expectations, surgery is clear. It rewards discipline. It doesn't ask for emotional exposure. It demands skill, not softness. In many ways, surgery becomes Cristina's primary attachment. It's where she channels her identity, her drive, her need for order in a chaotic world.

But no amount of precision can prevent emotional life from intruding. And as the show progresses, Cristina's attempts to manage her inner world through work begin to strain. Her relationship with Burke introduces her to a new kind of vulnerability—the terror of needing someone. And it is, in many ways, a destabilizing force. Burke wants intimacy. He wants connection. Cristina wants autonomy. Their dynamic is not simply a mismatch of personalities—it's a clash of attachment systems. Cristina feels suffocated by the very closeness Burke craves. She interprets his emotional demands not as love, but as threat.

When Burke leaves her at the altar, it is both a heartbreak and a strange relief. The emotional exposure required of that relationship was nearly intolerable for her. And yet, it leaves a mark. Cristina may appear to bounce back, but we see her deepen in subtle ways. She begins to question—not just relationships, but what it means to share her life at all.

Her friendship with Meredith remains her one steady emotional anchor. Like Meredith, Cristina trusts few. But in Meredith, she finds a kind of emotional safe zone. There is no pressure to be different. No demand to change. Cristina can be brilliant, blunt, avoidant, and messy—and still belong. Their bond is not therapeutic in the traditional sense, but it is profoundly regulating. With Meredith, Cristina doesn't have to explain herself. And for someone whose life has been built on managing others' expectations, that freedom is rare.

Cristina's relationship with Owen Hunt introduces a more volatile emotional dynamic. Unlike Burke, Owen is himself a trauma survivor. He is emotionally intense, sometimes dysregulated, and frequently triggered. This challenges Cristina in a different way—not to open up, but to stay steady in the face of someone else's instability. At first, she tries. But over time, Owen's trauma begins to replicate the kind of emotional unpredictability she has spent her life avoiding.

Their conflict over children becomes a crucible moment for Cristina's arc. She is clear: she does not want to be a mother. Not now, not ever. But Owen refuses to hear that. He wants her to become someone else—to choose a version of adulthood that fits his narrative of family. The result is one of the most psychologically significant decisions in the series: Cristina chooses to leave. Not in anger. Not in rupture. But in clarity. She will not become emotionally compromised to preserve a relationship that demands her erasure.

This is often misunderstood as selfishness. But from a psychological perspective, it is integrity. Cristina knows who she is. And while she is not perfect, she is honest. She does not pretend to want what she doesn't. She does not martyr herself in the name of love. Her departure from Seattle is not an act of abandonment. It is an act of self-protection. She leaves because staying would require a disconnection from self that she has spent her life fighting against.

Cristina Yang's story is not about transformation. It is about self-definition. She does not evolve into someone more emotionally expressive. She evolves into someone more fully aligned with her own truth. Her arc challenges the idea that healing always looks like softness. Sometimes, healing looks like boundaries. Like leaving. Like refusing to perform intimacy that does not feel safe.

In a culture that often equates emotional health with openness, Cristina's character complicates the narrative. She reminds us that emotional intelligence is not one-size-fits-all. That not everyone wants to be saved. That some people, especially those with deep attachment wounds, feel most alive not in emotional vulnerability—but in mastery, clarity, and independence.

Cristina does not need to be rewritten. She needs to be understood.

In the following sections, we'll explore how avoidant attachment operates in high-functioning adults, how Cristina's career serves as both shield and sanctuary, and how her final choice to leave was not a failure of love—but a triumph of self-awareness.

She did not break open. She held her shape.

And in doing so, she showed us that healing can look like holding firm.

Productivity as Armor – Avoidant Attachment in High Performers

Cristina Yang doesn't ask you to like her. That's part of her brilliance—and part of her defense. While other characters in *Grey's Anatomy* attempt to balance vulnerability with ambition, Cristina moves through the world with a singular mission: to be exceptional. She does not flirt. She does not soften. She does not perform likability for comfort. Her focus is clinical, even surgical, and it is that same approach she applies to her emotional life. When something feels threatening, she cuts it out.

To understand Cristina's emotional architecture, we must consider how high performance can function as psychological armor. For individuals with avoidant attachment patterns, achievement offers something emotional closeness never could: predictability, control, and personal validation that does not require intimacy. Where insecurely attached individuals might seek reassurance through connection, the avoidantly attached seek reassurance through mastery. Productivity becomes proof of worth.

Cristina is this model in motion. She does not ask for love. She demonstrates competence. She does not rely on emotional disclosure. She offers results. Her validation is earned, not assumed. She is not reckless with her reputation. She is precise. Every step she takes is calculated, every accolade another layer in her protective shell.

This is not narcissism. It is survival.

Avoidant attachment often originates in childhood environments where independence was necessary and emotional need was either discouraged or unsafe. In these contexts, children learn to regulate their distress alone. They stop turning toward caregivers because experience has taught them that such bids are ignored, invalidated, or met with contempt. Over time, this develops into an internal working model that says: it is better to depend on no one. Feelings are a liability. Attachment is a risk.

Cristina exemplifies this from her first days at Seattle Grace. She establishes herself quickly as competitive, brilliant, and emotionally disengaged. She is clear about her goals and unapologetic about her drive. There is no room in her worldview for softness. If she shares anything personal, it's usually embedded in sarcasm or buried in procedural commentary. And when she does form relationships, she enters them on her own terms—with clear, if unspoken, boundaries.

Her romance with Burke is one of the first cracks in her emotional defense system. Not because she becomes needy, but because she is forced to navigate a world where emotional proximity comes with expectation. Burke wants access. He wants ritual. He wants Cristina to fit into his version of what intimacy should look like. And Cristina tries—for a while. She moves in. She meets his mother. She accepts the ring. But every step toward traditional romantic integration feels like erosion. She is not growing in love. She is disappearing inside of it.

This is where Cristina's avoidant attachment manifests most clearly. She begins to shrink to accommodate what love appears to demand. Her voice gets quieter. Her energy dims. The sharpness that defines her fades into compliance. By the time Burke leaves her at the altar, she is emotionally gutted—but what hurts more than the abandonment is the realization that she betrayed herself trying to belong to someone else's story.

This is an essential point. Avoidantly attached individuals are not afraid of love. They are afraid of annihilation within it. They fear that emotional closeness will require the suppression of self. For Cristina, this fear is not abstract—it's confirmed by experience. She did what she thought she was supposed to do. She tried to be the girlfriend, the fiancée, the daughter-in-law. And in the end, she was left—not because she wasn't loving enough, but because the template she was asked to fit never matched the shape of who she actually was.

In the aftermath, Cristina doubles down on what has always felt safe: her work. She throws herself back into surgery, research, and competition. She rejects the narrative that emotional vulnerability is necessary for a meaningful life. She recommits to the operating room as both a profession and a psychological refuge. And in doing so, she begins to reclaim a truth that got buried in her effort to belong: her autonomy is not a flaw. It is part of her emotional integrity.

Cristina's emotional journey is not linear. Like many avoidant personalities, she oscillates between moments of openness and retreat. Her relationship with Owen is more emotionally intense, but also more fraught. Unlike Burke, Owen carries his own trauma. He is volatile, sometimes explosive, and often triggered. This creates a dynamic in which Cristina, who has spent her life avoiding emotional chaos, must learn to tolerate unpredictability from someone she loves.

She tries. But even her best effort to stay steady is strained by Owen's inability to self-regulate. Their relationship becomes a tug-of-war between closeness and containment. Owen wants emotional transparency. Cristina wants emotional boundaries. He sees her restraint as detachment. She sees his intensity as intrusion. And neither is fully wrong. But the relationship exposes the limits of Cristina's emotional tolerance. She does not know how to absorb another person's pain without losing her footing.

It's tempting to interpret this as a failure of emotional growth. But that's a misreading of her arc. Cristina's attachment system is not broken. It's calibrated for safety. What she reveals across seasons is not a resistance to love, but a refusal to collapse inside of it. And this refusal is not pathology—it's self-preservation.

Her avoidance is nuanced. She's not unfeeling. She loves deeply—in her own way. She is loyal, protective, and attuned to the needs of those she respects. Her friendship with Meredith is proof of that. What makes their bond work is that it is neither demanding nor performative. It is secure. Meredith doesn't ask Cristina to be different. And Cristina doesn't have to choose between love and selfhood. In their friendship, she finds what avoidantly attached individuals rarely do: a relationship that respects boundaries without abandoning intimacy.

Over time, Cristina's growth is not marked by a radical change in personality, but by a deepening of discernment. She becomes clearer about what she can offer and what she cannot. She stops trying to fit into emotional templates that feel foreign. She accepts that her way of relating—direct, reserved, fiercely independent—is not lesser. It is simply hers.

By the time she decides to leave Seattle, it is not an act of evasion. It is an act of truth. She chooses a life that reflects her values, her boundaries, and her need for freedom. She does not choose marriage. She does not choose motherhood. She chooses a vision of selfhood that includes excellence, solitude, and space.

And in doing so, she models an often overlooked form of psychological health: the capacity to hold your own shape even in the presence of love.

Cristina Yang is not broken. She is whole in a way many people never dare to be.

Surgical Precision, Emotional Distance – The Cost of Self-Containment

Cristina Yang is a study in control. Her movements are precise, her words sharp, her reactions restrained. In the operating room, she is unstoppable. Her focus is absolute. Her hands rarely tremble. She is, in many ways, the ideal surgeon—emotionally neutral, unshaken by chaos, able to compartmentalize fear and function under pressure. But this precision, so vital to her professional identity, is also how she copes with the unpredictability of emotional life. It is not just a skill. It is a defense.

Cristina's emotional distance is not the absence of feeling. It is the presence of overwhelming emotion that has no place to go. People often mistake emotional containment for coldness, especially in women. But what Cristina demonstrates is not apathy—it is vigilance. She cannot afford to feel too much because feeling, for her, is unsafe. It is disorganizing. And anything disorganizing threatens the internal system she's built to survive.

From the beginning, Cristina uses surgical excellence as her anchor. It is the one realm where she does not have to negotiate vulnerability, where the rules are clear and outcomes are measurable. In a world where connection feels murky and potentially destabilizing, surgery offers clarity. It rewards certainty. It doesn't require emotional interpretation. And for Cristina, that is a kind of sanctuary.

But what she cannot fully control is the emotional residue of her own containment. Holding everything in comes at a cost. Her identity is so intertwined with her profession that she struggles to define herself outside of it. When her ability to perform is challenged—whether by external events, trauma, or emotional conflict—she begins to unravel. Not loudly, not dramatically. But in the quiet erosion of her certainty.

One of the clearest illustrations of this comes after the shooting at Seattle Grace. Cristina is held at gunpoint, forced to operate on Derek with a weapon inches from her face. She performs the surgery flawlessly, but something changes afterward. Her confidence collapses. Her hands, once steady and instinctual, now hesitate. For the first time, her emotional world overtakes her professional identity. And she doesn't know how to integrate it.

She quits surgery. Not because she stops caring, but because she no longer feels safe inside her own body. The trauma has disrupted her nervous system, and her usual strategy—emotional suppression through productivity—no longer works. She is flooded, disoriented, and ashamed. This is not the unraveling of someone fragile. It is the temporary disintegration of someone who has never been allowed to break.

Cristina's reaction to trauma is clinically consistent with dissociative shutdown, a common response in individuals who have relied on control to manage emotional threat. She does not rage or collapse publicly. She disappears. She becomes numb, disengaged. Her disconnection is both physiological and psychological—a reflection of what happens when the emotional container finally overflows.

And yet, even in this unraveling, she remains composed. She does not seek comfort. She does not cry in front of her friends. She hides. She minimizes. She tries to will herself back into competence. Because in Cristina's world, emotional expression is synonymous with exposure. And exposure has never ended well.

Over time, Cristina does return to surgery. But she is not the same. Something has shifted—not just in her skill set, but in her sense of self. The trauma has pierced her emotional insulation. And though she rebuilds her confidence, she never quite returns to the untouchable precision of her earlier days. There is more awareness now. More gravity. She no longer believes she can outwork or out-intellect her inner life. She begins, in subtle ways, to acknowledge that emotional integrity might be just as important as surgical skill.

But this realization brings new conflict, especially in her relationship with Owen. He wants more from her than she is wired to give. He wants softness. He wants surrender. And Cristina resists—not out of cruelty, but out of necessity. For her, maintaining a clear boundary around the self is essential. She cannot merge identities. She cannot lose herself in partnership. And when those boundaries are threatened—by Owen's volatility, by his desire for children, by his attempts to domesticate their life—Cristina's nervous system flares with alarm.

This is the core of her emotional distance. It is not emotional laziness or a fear of commitment. It is the deep, embodied knowledge that intimacy can become erasure. That to be truly close to someone may require her to diminish herself. And Cristina will not do that—not again.

What's striking is that she's not afraid to be alone. That's one of the most psychologically mature aspects of her character. She does not use relationships to fill voids or distract from herself. She is capable of being alone without being lonely. And in a culture that often defines a woman's growth through her willingness to soften or sacrifice, Cristina's refusal to do so is radical. She holds the line, even when it costs her.

And yet, she is not emotionally unreachable. She loves. Deeply. Fiercely. But she loves in ways that don't always align with cultural expectations. Her love is protective, private, loyal. It is not demonstrative. It does not beg. It does not collapse. She will operate on your heart, save your life, and then refuse to say "I love you" until she means it so fully that saying it feels like a risk.

Cristina's emotional containment is her power—and her burden. It gives her clarity but costs her comfort. It makes her excellent but isolates her. She is rarely misread, but often misunderstood. People project coldness onto her where there is actually discipline. They see ego where there is actually integrity. But Cristina knows who she is. And for the most part, that is enough.

The cost of self-containment, however, becomes more visible as the series progresses. We see her longing, though she rarely admits it. We see the toll of holding everything in—the fatigue, the friction, the unspoken sorrow. Her body begins to carry what her voice won't express. She sleeps less. She eats in snatches. She works until she breaks. And still, she does not ask for help. Because asking would mean needing. And needing, for Cristina, is the most dangerous position of all.

Often noted in trauma recovery research, particularly among those with complex PTSD, this is referred to as functional hyper-independence. It is a common adaptation in people who learned that dependence invites disappointment or control. It is not about pride. It is about survival. Cristina does not believe the world will catch her if she falls. So she never lets herself fall.

And yet, by the time she leaves Seattle, there is a softness—not in her behavior, but in her clarity. She is more grounded. More discerning. She knows what she can handle and what she cannot. She no longer views emotional life as a distraction. She simply knows that it must be managed on her terms.

In the end, Cristina's precision remains. But it is no longer about hiding. It is about choice. She does not open herself to everyone. But when she does, it is real. She offers not emotional performance, but presence. She is not warm in the traditional sense. But she is fiercely present in the moments that count. And that, in its own way, is a kind of intimacy.

She never stops being surgical. She simply becomes more whole.

Choosing the Exit – Integrity Over Intimacy

Cristina Yang leaves quietly. Not with a breakdown, not in a flurry of romantic drama or sudden trauma, but with certainty. Her exit is deliberate, considered, and emotionally coherent. It is not a rejection of others—it is a reclamation of self. For a character so often described as emotionally avoidant, Cristina's final act is one of the most emotionally mature decisions we see across the entire series. She doesn't collapse into love. She doesn't stay out of obligation. She leaves because she knows who she is—and who she is cannot exist fully within the life she has built in Seattle.

Television dramas often depict character departures as emotional crises. Cristina's departure defies that. It is a case study in psychological integrity. Not integrity in the moral sense, but integrity in the structural sense—alignment between one's internal values and one's external choices. She does not pretend to want something she doesn't. She does not fake readiness for a life she never chose. She does not compromise who she is for the comfort of others.

What makes this act so powerful is that it runs counter to the dominant narrative arc so often expected of women in long-running television series. In many shows, the emotionally distant woman eventually "learns to love," softens her edges, and settles into a version of relational contentment defined by partnership or family. Cristina refuses this script. She does not "heal" into conformity. Her growth is not a journey toward intimacy for its own sake. It is a journey toward clarity. And clarity tells her: this is not the life I want.

Her relationship with Owen Hunt brings this into sharp focus. Their connection is real. Their love is intense. But intensity does not equal sustainability. They are fundamentally incompatible—not because they don't care, but because their values are misaligned. Owen wants children. Cristina does not. This difference is not negotiable. It's not a phase. It's not fear. It is a truth. And when Owen tries to override that truth, Cristina makes the only psychologically sound decision she can: she walks away.

This decision is not cold. It's excruciating. We see her hesitate. We see her reflect. But in the end, she chooses herself—not as an act of selfishness, but as an act of respect. Respect for Owen. Respect for their history. And most importantly, respect for the life she has spent building—one that is rooted in autonomy, mastery, and choice.

In psychological terms, this is the opposite of emotional avoidance. This is emotional authorship. Cristina is not fleeing intimacy. She is setting a boundary within it. She knows the cost of staying would be internal erosion. It would mean slowly compromising until she becomes unrecognizable to herself. And she has already done that once. She will not do it again.

There is a moment in her final episode where Meredith asks if she's sure. Cristina, without hesitation, replies, "Yes." That certainty is not bravado. It is earned. It is the result of years of internal work—quiet, private, invisible to most. Cristina has spent season after season confronting the ways in which the world asked her to be different. Softer. More open. More willing to bend. She tried. Sometimes sincerely. Sometimes with resentment. But what she discovered, again and again, is that what the world wanted from her was not expansion—it was dilution.

Cristina's exit is a refusal to be diluted.

This is why her arc is so emotionally resonant, especially for viewers who have struggled to hold their own shape in relationships, institutions, or systems that reward conformity. Cristina reminds us that growth does not always mean softening. That love is not always the answer. That sometimes the most emotionally intelligent act is to know when to walk away.

In attachment theory, we often place a premium on "earned secure" attachment—the idea that through insight, healing, and experience, people can shift from insecure patterns to secure ones. But security does not always look like merging. It does not always result in a picture-perfect partnership. Sometimes, security is knowing what you need and being able to tolerate the discomfort of not being fully understood.

Cristina's departure is a secure act. It is not reactive. It is not panicked. It is not designed to hurt anyone or prove anything. It is rooted in self-awareness. She knows that if she stays, she will be asked—explicitly or implicitly—to compromise something essential. And she knows she cannot do that without consequence.

This clarity, however, is not devoid of emotion. Cristina is not detached from the people she's leaving. Her farewell with Meredith is one of the most emotionally grounded scenes in the series. There are no dramatic speeches. No begging or bargaining. Just a quiet acknowledgment of what they've meant to each other. Meredith, for once, does not ask Cristina to stay. And Cristina, for once, allows herself to say what is often left unsaid. It is not a breakup. It is a benediction.

And in that moment, we see the full arc of their relationship: two women who anchored each other not through constant emotional expression, but through presence. Through respect. Through knowing when to hold on and when to let go. Cristina and Meredith were not co-dependent. They were co-regulators. They gave each other space to grow, space to be fully themselves, and space to leave when the time came.

Cristina Yang leaves not to escape—but to expand.

She does not need a partner to define her. She does not need applause to validate her. She does not need to explain herself in ways that diminish her. Her departure is not an ending. It is an arrival. A movement toward a life that fits her internal landscape. A life where she can remain whole.

For viewers, this kind of ending can be bittersweet. We want resolution. We want reunion. But Cristina's arc resists that. Her story does not tie itself in a bow. It closes with truth, not closure. And that, psychologically, is often more powerful.

Not everyone who grows becomes softer.

Some become clearer.

Some become quieter.

Some leave—not to vanish, but to fully appear in a life that was waiting for them beyond the frame.

Cristina's story teaches us that emotional maturity is not about learning how to stay in every relationship. Sometimes, it's about learning when not to.

And in a world that often demands we choose intimacy over integrity, her choice stands as something rare and essential.

A woman who knew what she wanted.

And didn't apologize for leaving to go get it.

* * *

3

Alex Karev – Wounded Healer with a Guarded Heart

Punch First, Feel Later

When Alex Karev first appears on screen, he is abrasive, arrogant, and emotionally unfiltered. He talks too loudly, smirks too often, and treats connection like a sport to be won or dismissed. To the untrained eye, he reads as unlikable—another ego in a sea of surgical ambition. But even in his earliest scenes, there is something else at work. Something jagged beneath the bravado. Something raw. Alex is not simply cocky. He is covering. And what he is covering is pain.

Unlike Meredith or Cristina, who protect themselves through withdrawal or detachment, Alex protects himself through offense. He pushes before he can be pushed. He wounds before he can be wounded. He weaponizes crudeness as a kind of emotional decoy—daring people to reject him so he doesn't have to wait for the inevitable disappointment. His early persona is a shell—a survival construct. And it works. At first.

But over time, that construct begins to fracture.

Alex Karev is one of the show's most complex psychological studies because his transformation is not immediate, linear, or easily explained. He does not have a singular turning point. He is not "fixed" by love. He is not softened by friendship overnight. His evolution happens gradually, through repeated experiences of being allowed to stay. Through people choosing not to give up on him. Through moments when his capacity for care overwhelms his instinct for protection.

Alex grew up in an abusive, unstable household. His father was violent. His mother struggled with mental illness. He was placed in foster care. He became the caretaker of his younger siblings at an age when most children are still learning how to be cared for themselves. This history is not incidental—it is central. Alex's early environment taught him that trust is dangerous, that vulnerability is a liability, and that emotional safety is not something you wait for—it's something you build by never needing anyone.

These lessons do not fade with age. They become baked into personality. The young adult version of Alex has internalized a worldview where every connection carries risk. His relationships are transactional or guarded. His tone is defensive, even when he's being sincere. He expects betrayal. He expects judgment. So he preempts it by being difficult, brash, and often cruel.

And yet, beneath all of that, there is an unrelenting drive to protect. That drive is often misdirected—into control, aggression, jealousy—but it is there. And it is real. Alex does not push people away because he lacks feeling. He pushes them away because he feels too much. Because caring threatens the emotional scaffolding that has kept him upright since childhood. Because care, in his experience, always ends in loss.

What makes Alex's arc so significant is that the show never tries to make him anyone but himself. He doesn't become charming. He doesn't become verbally eloquent. He doesn't suddenly shed his roughness. What changes is his ability to sit with closeness without destroying it. He begins to learn how to stay—how to be present in love, in friendship, in grief—without lashing out or running. He begins to trust that he can show up emotionally without being obliterated by it.

This transformation is supported, in large part, by the people around him who see past his defenses. Izzie, despite their chaotic relationship, believes in his goodness early on. Meredith becomes a kind of emotional sibling—someone who knows what it means to be both loyal and lost. Arizona challenges him, mentors him, and eventually becomes one of his few true professional allies. Jo becomes his mirror—another survivor, another person trying to figure out how to be loved without losing control.

But these relationships alone do not change him. What changes Alex is repetition. He is given more than one chance. He is forgiven more than once. And slowly, those experiences begin to revise his internal script. They do not erase his trauma, but they rewrite what comes next. He begins to believe, at first tentatively and then with increasing confidence, that he is more than what he survived.

From a psychological standpoint, Alex is a compelling study in reparenting. Reparenting is the process by which adults, especially those with childhood trauma, learn to offer themselves the kind of emotional safety they never received. This doesn't happen through self-talk alone—it happens through lived experience. Through staying in the room when conflict arises. Through not sabotaging closeness when it becomes uncomfortable. Through holding someone else's pain without being crushed by the weight of your own.

Alex does all of this—haltingly, imperfectly, and never without resistance. He makes mistakes. He reverts. He punches when words would suffice. He ghosts people he loves. But over time, those behaviors become less frequent. Less necessary. He starts to regulate instead of react. He starts to name what he feels instead of masking it. And perhaps most importantly, he begins to believe that he is capable of love not just as a provider, but as a person.

What's remarkable is that Alex never loses his edge. He remains direct, irreverent, even harsh when the situation calls for it. But that harshness is no longer a reflex. It becomes a choice. A tool, not a shield. He learns discernment. He becomes capable of both holding boundaries and offering softness—depending on what the moment demands. That's the mark of emotional growth: not becoming someone else, but having access to more versions of yourself, each appropriate to a different kind of relationship or situation.

And yet, even as he grows, the residue of his early life remains. He does not forget what it felt like to be neglected, dismissed, afraid. That memory informs his work with pediatric patients. It informs the way he advocates for the overlooked. It informs the way he holds space for Jo's trauma without demanding more than she can give. His wounds do not define him, but they shape the empathy he brings to others. That empathy, once buried under bluster, becomes his most defining trait.

Alex Karev begins as a boy who punches first and trusts later—if at all. He ends as a man who can be trusted with the most fragile parts of others, because he finally learned how to hold his own.

In the sections that follow, we'll explore the developmental impact of early neglect and abuse, the emotional push-pull in his most formative relationships, and the quiet, controversial choice he makes in the end—a choice that is either a regression or a return, depending on how one sees the shape of healing.

What is clear is this: Alex Karev's arc is not about transformation through redemption. It is about coherence through repetition. He learns, over time, that love can stay. That being known doesn't always end in pain. And that his own rough edges don't make him unworthy of peace.

He does not become someone else.

He becomes someone more fully himself.

Broken Foundations - Childhood Trauma and the Rage-Protective Self

Before Alex Karev was a doctor, before he was a partner, a brother, a friend—he was a boy trying to survive. And not just survive a difficult childhood, but survive a system that taught him early that care was conditional, stability was fragile, and safety was self-created or not at all. When we meet him in season one, those lessons have calcified into behavior: belligerent, sarcastic, flirtatious in a hollow sort of way. But none of this is incidental. Alex is a character formed by threat. His demeanor is defensive architecture. His personality is armor.

The details of Alex's childhood are revealed sparingly, but what we do know is psychologically potent. His father was abusive and disappeared from his life. His mother suffered from severe mental illness, at times unable to care for herself or her children. Alex was placed in the foster care system and grew up with inconsistent parenting, instability, and the unspoken demand that he step into the role of adult long before his brain or body was ready.

This background points to chronic developmental trauma. Unlike acute trauma, which stems from a single incident, developmental trauma involves prolonged exposure to emotionally unsafe or dysregulated environments during critical periods of identity formation. The damage is relational. The child grows up without consistent co-regulation from a caregiver, which is essential to developing secure attachment, emotional language, and stress management strategies. Instead, the child adapts. They become hyper-independent, emotionally avoidant, or in some cases—like Alex—functionally aggressive.

Aggression becomes a language. Not necessarily because the child is angry, but because anger is safer than fear. Safer than longing. Anger says, "You can't hurt me, because I'm already holding the knife." For Alex, this manifests in the way he interacts with his peers, especially early on. He mocks George. He objectifies women. He gets defensive at the first sign of intimacy. He uses crudeness as a buffer, turning every emotionally vulnerable moment into a joke, a sneer, or a confrontation.

But underneath the bravado, Alex is constantly scanning for threat. And for someone with his history, threat isn't limited to violence—it includes affection, dependency, admiration. Anything that exposes him as emotionally invested feels dangerous. His aggression is not just a tool of intimidation; it is a strategy of preemption. If he alienates people first, they cannot betray him. If he's disliked, he cannot be disappointed. And if no one gets too close, no one can abandon him.

This pattern is most visible in how he handles compliments or care. When others see potential in him, he either dismisses it or rebels against it. When people try to connect emotionally, he shuts down or acts out. It's not that he doesn't want approval—he does. Desperately. But his early life has taught him that praise is a prelude to control, and care is often a setup for disappointment. He does not know how to receive love without suspicion.

The psychological term for this state is defensive reactivity. It is common among adults who grew up in emotionally chaotic environments. Their nervous systems are primed for instability, and as a result, even safe relationships can trigger fear responses. These individuals often feel most comfortable in roles that do not require vulnerability. They may be kind, loyal, even generous—but on their terms, and often with invisible conditions. Alex operates from this space for much of the early series. He wants connection, but only if he can control the emotional terms. He wants respect, but distrusts the people who offer it. He wants love, but fears what it might undo.

There is another layer to Alex's early psychology that deserves attention: the pressure of premature adulthood. Parentified children—those forced to take care of a parent or siblings at a young age—often develop a hyper-responsible outer shell that masks deep emotional depletion. They learn to manage crisis with competence, to suppress their own needs, and to associate worth with usefulness. For Alex, this plays out in his later career, particularly in pediatrics. He is fiercely protective of children, especially those who are ill, neglected, or abandoned. These cases pierce his defenses not because he is soft, but because he knows exactly what it feels like to be the child no one protected.

His aptitude for pediatrics is not just skill—it is identification. He sees himself in his patients. He knows their terror, their shame, their deep sense of being left behind. And unlike many adults in his own life, he shows up for them. This is not just a professional success. It is emotional repair. He becomes the adult he never had. And in doing so, he reclaims some of what was taken from him.

Still, the cost of this reactivity lingers. In his romantic relationships, Alex often replicates early dynamics. He chooses partners who need care or who come with their own instability. His relationship with Izzie, for example, is emotionally charged but fragile. He struggles to trust her love, lashes out when she gets too close, and disappears emotionally when she needs him most. This is not immaturity—it is unresolved trauma. Alex does not know how to be emotionally available without fear of being consumed, used, or rejected.

When his relationships deteriorate, he regresses. This is particularly evident when Izzie leaves. He shuts down. He becomes rigid, bitter, and impulsively cruel. Abandonment does not merely hurt—it confirms his worst fear: that no matter how hard he tries to stay, people will always leave. His grief is not loud. It is withdrawn, masked by increased emotional rigidity. He becomes harder, more disciplined, less willing to open. But over time, this rigidity also becomes unsustainable.

Healing, for Alex, does not come in dramatic catharsis. It comes in repetition. It comes in staying when he wants to run. In choosing to repair rather than punish. In allowing himself to care, even when it terrifies him. Slowly, we begin to see fewer emotional explosions and more emotional regulation. We see apologies—not dramatic, but deliberate. We see loyalty—less performative, more consistent. We see that his reactivity is not gone, but tempered. And perhaps most importantly, we see his ability to remain present, even when the emotional terrain is unfamiliar.

Alex's arc demonstrates what it means to heal from developmental trauma without erasing its imprint. He never becomes someone else. He remains sharp, skeptical, guarded. But those traits are no longer shields. They are part of a fuller emotional range. He gains the ability to modulate, to respond rather than react, to stay without self-sacrifice.

And in doing so, he offers a rare example of trauma-informed growth on television: messy, halting, nonlinear—but real.

In the next section, we'll explore how Alex's guardedness plays out in his romantic and emotional relationships, and how his push-pull dynamic is not about ambivalence, but about fear—fear of being fully seen and then left behind.

Love with Sharp Edges - Trust, Loyalty, and Emotional Push-Pull

Alex Karev doesn't fall in love cleanly. He doesn't arrive in relationships fully formed, emotionally literate, or ready to receive affection. He approaches love with hesitation disguised as arrogance, vulnerability disguised as sarcasm. For most of his early adult life, closeness is a calculation: what will it cost, and how soon will it be taken away?

This is not emotional immaturity. It's protective conditioning. Alex's early life taught him that love could not be trusted—that care was unstable, often conditional, and sometimes even dangerous. His parents were inconsistent or absent. His formative attachments were marked by fear, unpredictability, and survivalism. As a result, adult relationships carry a weight that is often invisible to the people closest to him. What others experience as emotional volatility is, for Alex, a struggle to believe that intimacy won't lead to emotional harm.

This creates a dynamic familiar in attachment theory: the anxious-avoidant trap. Alex wants closeness but fears what it will undo. He needs love but doesn't know how to let it in safely. So he tests it. Pushes it. Pulls away from it. Sometimes he lashes out in advance, hoping to make the other person retreat before he has a chance to be rejected. Other times, he becomes hyper-loyal, clinging too tightly, trying to hold on before love can vanish. Both patterns are rooted in the same fear: abandonment.

His early relationship with Izzie Stevens exemplifies this. At first, he dismisses her. Then he pursues her with charm laced in arrogance. When she shows genuine interest, he becomes inconsistent. He seduces and retreats, offers intimacy and then withdraws. Izzie, who comes with her own emotional history of instability and idealized love, mirrors this intensity—until the inevitable rupture. Their relationship swings between affection and distance, commitment and collapse. When it works, it works fiercely. When it fails, it fails catastrophically.

The reason their connection resonates with viewers is that it never feels fake. It feels familiar—especially to those who have tried to love while still carrying the residue of early relational wounds. Alex and Izzie are two people trying to hold each other while still learning how to hold themselves. They both want safety, but neither knows how to create it.

This dynamic comes to a head when Izzie becomes emotionally overwhelmed after Denny's death. Alex tries to be supportive, but he lacks the emotional vocabulary to hold grief that is both ambiguous and delayed. He needs clarity. Izzie needs containment. Neither can provide what the other truly requires. When Izzie eventually leaves—suddenly, without resolution—it confirms Alex's belief that no matter how hard he tries, people will always leave. The pain is deep, but he doesn't express it with tears. He expresses it by shutting down. By closing the door a little tighter.

This is a pattern that follows him through other relationships. With Rebecca (Ava), he steps into a caregiver role. He rescues her, takes on emotional responsibility for her well-being, and in doing so, reenacts a pattern common among trauma survivors: finding worth through being needed. But caregiving cannot substitute for intimacy, and over time, their relationship erodes under the weight of Alex's need to feel safe and competent, even at the expense of his own emotional truth.

Later, with Jo Wilson, we see a more evolved—but still guarded—version of Alex. Jo, herself a survivor of abandonment and abuse, offers him something he's never fully had: recognition without judgment. She understands the fear, the volatility, the instinct to push away before being hurt. Their relationship is not smooth, but it is sincere. They fight. They regress. But they also repair.

Jo becomes the first person Alex truly lets in—not in moments of grand declaration, but in the slow, cumulative acts of trust. Letting her see his mother. Telling the truth about his past. Admitting when he's wrong. Protecting her not as a reflex, but as a choice. These are the building blocks of relational maturity. Alex doesn't become a different person. He becomes a person capable of deeper presence.

Still, his love remains sharp-edged. He remains capable of cruelty, especially when threatened. When Jo hides her marriage to an abusive ex, Alex reacts with fury. He doesn't process it. He attacks. Not physically, but emotionally. He interprets her secrecy not as fear, but as betrayal. It's only later—after reflection, after space—that he returns, not with flowers or grand gestures, but with responsibility. He tries again. And this, for Alex, is growth. The ability to rupture and repair without emotional annihilation.

The push-pull dynamic that defines his early relationships becomes less pronounced, though never disappears entirely. He learns how to stay, but also when to step back. He learns that love does not require constant vigilance. That people who care for him are not always trying to control him. That vulnerability does not automatically result in loss.

What makes Alex's relational growth so compelling is that it is not framed as romantic achievement. He doesn't "win" love. He becomes someone capable of withstanding it. He stops testing it. He stops resenting it. He begins to believe it. This does not make his relationships easy. But it makes them real.

This shift is particularly visible in his friendships. Early on, Alex is a loner—tolerated by the group but not deeply included. His friendship with Meredith, however, becomes an anchor. It begins without fanfare. There are no emotional confessions, no shared traumas—just a quiet loyalty that builds over time. Meredith sees the parts of Alex that others miss. His steadiness. His compassion. His commitment. And she doesn't demand he change. She lets him unfold.

Their bond becomes a kind of emotional blueprint. With Meredith, Alex learns what it feels like to be trusted. To be relied on. To be accepted not in spite of his wounds, but alongside them. He becomes her person—not by force, but by function. He shows up. Again and again. And slowly, that pattern of showing up begins to define his sense of self more than his fear of being left.

In his relationships with Arizona, Bailey, and eventually Richard Webber, we see this pattern expand. He moves from guarded peer to respected colleague. From volatile presence to stabilizing force. Not perfect. Not fully healed. But anchored. Not in the absence of emotion, but in its regulation.

Alex Karev's love story is not about passion. It's about endurance. About learning how to stay when every instinct tells you to run. About letting someone in even when the fear is still whispering that they'll leave. His love is not smooth, but it is sincere. It is jagged, but it is real.

And in the end, what he offers—both in romance and in friendship—is not ease, but depth. Not predictability, but presence.

He doesn't give you the easy version of himself.

He gives you the one he fought to become.

The Quiet Goodbye - Regressions, Redemptions, and the Pull of Origin

When Alex Karev leaves Grey Sloan Memorial Hospital, he does not give a speech. He does not say goodbye in person. He disappears, and then sends letters. It is, by all surface accounts, an anticlimactic departure for a character whose growth had become one of the emotional pillars of the show. But beneath the disappointment many viewers felt was something psychologically raw, real, and unresolved. His exit wasn't neat because Alex Karev was never neat. His departure was not a betrayal of his arc—it was a return to the question that had always haunted him: what does it mean to go back and finish what you didn't know how to survive?

Alex leaves to be with Izzie. Years after she walked out of his life, he learns she had children—his children—and never told him. And upon discovering this, he doesn't run from it. He runs to it. In doing so, he leaves his marriage, his job, and his closest friends behind. On paper, it looks like regression. Emotionally, it reads like abandonment. But psychologically, it is something more complicated. Something that lives in the gray area between healing and relapse, identity and origin.

To understand Alex's final decision, we must return to his psychological foundation: the wounds of instability, betrayal, and parental failure. He spent his entire life building structures to protect himself from the chaos he once endured. Career, relationship, emotional regulation—all of it was earned, not given. And yet, some part of him always remained tethered to the feeling that something vital had been left unfinished. The family he never had. The father he never became. The question of what it would mean to love not out of repair, but from the very beginning.

So when he learns he has children, something ancient in him stirs. This is not about rekindled romance with Izzie. It's about something more primal—something from the part of him that was once a boy who wasn't protected, now faced with the opportunity to protect. He is not chasing a fantasy. He is responding to a rupture that he did not cause, but cannot ignore.

And yet, the way he leaves hurts. It undoes much of what he built in the eyes of those who knew him best. He leaves Jo without warning. He exits Meredith's life without face-to-face closure. He walks away from the community that helped him grow. There is no defense for how he departs. But what the show captures—perhaps unintentionally—is how deeply unfinished trauma can resurface even after years of emotional work.

In trauma studies, this is called reactivation. It occurs when a present-day experience awakens dormant emotional material from the past—material that was never fully processed, only contained. In Alex's case, the reactivation comes in the form of unexpected fatherhood. Suddenly, he is faced with the chance to give his children what he never had. And that chance eclipses the version of his life that had come to define him.

The psychology here is not tidy. People who have experienced deep abandonment often carry a longing not just to be loved, but to repair love at its root. For Alex, parenting his children is more than responsibility—it's redemption. Not in a grand or moral sense, but in a private, internal way. It allows him to rewrite the story of his own beginnings by being present for someone else's.

This doesn't justify how he leaves. But it explains why he might.

Alex's choice reflects something many trauma survivors wrestle with: the tension between chosen stability and unresolved origin. He built a life with Jo—secure, reciprocal, mature. But when confronted with the chance to revisit and repair the first rupture of his adult life—the loss of Izzie and the imagined family they never became—he is pulled backward, not out of immaturity, but out of unfinished grief.

Grief, after all, is not always loud. Sometimes it lies dormant for years, resurfacing when the right—or wrong—combination of events cracks it open. And in Alex's case, the discovery of his children doesn't just reopen the wound of Izzie's departure. It reopens the wound of his own childhood. His longing to be someone's safe place. His need to end the cycle not just by doing better, but by being there from the start.

In many ways, Alex's departure is not a collapse—it's a return. Not to the person he was, but to the boy who never got to grow up in a home where love stayed. His choice reflects a desire to be that home for someone else, even if it costs him the stability he fought so hard to earn.

Psychologically, it's a controversial arc. Some would argue it erases his growth. Others might say it completes it. The truth likely lives in between. Because healing is not a straight line. It loops. It circles. It revisits. And sometimes, it leads us back to the places we once ran from—not to relive them, but to understand them more fully.

Alex's goodbye is not the one we wanted. But perhaps it is the one that was truest to who he has always been: someone trying to make peace with pain by rewriting what love looks like when it finally has a chance to stay.

The people he left behind grieve his absence. And they should. But the people he ran toward—those children—will grow up with a father who chose them. That matters too. Not as justification. But as complexity. And that is what Alex Karev's story has always been: emotionally complex, sometimes incoherent, always human.

He was not healed. He was healing.

He was not whole. He was trying.

And sometimes, trying looks like staying. Other times, it looks like leaving in the hope that, for once, it means coming home.

* * *

4

George O'Malley – Shame, Sensitivity, and Self-Worth

The Kind One Who Couldn't Hold His Place

In the early chaos of *Grey's Anatomy*, George O'Malley is often the one overlooked. He's not the loudest, the smartest, or the most daring. He doesn't command a room. He hesitates. He apologizes. He blends into the background. Surrounded by personalities who take up space—Meredith with her melancholy, Cristina with her force, Alex with his edge—George is soft. Gentle. Quiet. And in that quiet, we meet one of the most psychologically poignant characters of the early seasons: the boy who is good, but never quite enough.

George O'Malley is a walking study in relational vulnerability. He is kind without being naive, compassionate without being performative. But what makes his character so complex is the emotional undercurrent of shame that seems to follow him. He wants to be respected. He wants to belong. But often, he doubts his place. His presence among the interns feels, at times, tentative—like he's still waiting to be told he deserves to be there. While others assert themselves, George second-guesses. And that hesitation is not born of incompetence. It is born of internalized doubt.

At the heart of George's psychological profile is a subtle but pervasive sense of **defectiveness**—a schema often formed early in life when children grow up feeling that they are somehow fundamentally wrong, inadequate, or unworthy of acceptance. This schema does not always arise from direct abuse or neglect. Sometimes, it comes from chronic misattunement: caregivers who are present but not emotionally responsive, environments where sensitivity is seen as weakness, or family systems where identity is measured by performance rather than presence.

We don't know much about George's childhood, but we know enough to read between the lines. He grew up in a family that valued stereotypical masculinity—toughness, physicality, dominance. George, by contrast, is tender. He leads with empathy. He doesn't fight to be seen—he waits to be invited. And in environments that reward aggression or confidence over care, this temperament can become a liability. What was once sensitivity becomes a source of self-doubt. What was once kindness becomes shame.

This is what makes George's early presence in the hospital so painful to watch. He is competent, even brilliant, but he carries himself like an imposter. He doesn't speak unless spoken to. He doesn't argue when dismissed. He absorbs others' projections—Alex's cruelty, Cristina's condescension, Meredith's confusion—without protest. He becomes the person people go to when they need something, but not the one they protect. He is seen, but not safeguarded.

And yet, George is not passive. He pushes back—just not loudly. His resistance is relational. He shows up for others even when it costs him. He chooses integrity over pride. He listens when no one else does. In a hospital full of brilliance and ego, George becomes the emotional conscience. And like many people in this role, his worth is often recognized only after he's gone.

One of the most psychologically insightful arcs in George's storyline is his relationship with Meredith. He falls for her deeply, genuinely. She does not reciprocate. And when he confesses his feelings, she reacts with ambivalence. Their eventual attempt at intimacy is clumsy and painful—one of the most emotionally awkward scenes in the series. But beneath that discomfort is a psychological truth: people who feel invisible often try to become indispensable. George wants Meredith to see him. He wants her to love him not out of pity, but out of clarity. And when she can't, he feels not just rejected, but confirmed in his fear that he is unlovable.

This dynamic replays across his relationships. With Callie, George is loved more than he is ready to receive. With Izzie, the friendship-turned-romance is full of longing but never rooted in shared stability. He is someone others feel safe around, but rarely someone they believe in as fully as he deserves. And in response, George often becomes self-sacrificing—taking care of others, giving more than he gets, hoping that his goodness will eventually be enough.

But kindness, when not reciprocated or respected, becomes exhaustion. And George begins to unravel not with drama, but with depletion. He starts making impulsive choices. He lashes out in uncharacteristic ways. He searches for something—anything—that will give him a sense of solidity. At one point, this leads him to join the army, a decision that stuns his friends and speaks volumes about his internal state. It is not courage alone that drives him there. It is the aching need to be more than the one everyone forgets.

From a psychological lens, George's story is not about transformation in the traditional sense. He doesn't become hardened or unrecognizable. He doesn't shed his sensitivity. Instead, his arc is a quiet exploration of what happens to men who are emotionally open in systems that reward detachment. His masculinity is never toxic. It is tender, unsure, searching. And in a series full of bold personalities, George becomes a kind of emotional litmus test: how others treat him reveals who they are beneath the surface.

When George dies—suddenly, heroically, and almost anonymously—it is not only a loss to the characters. It is a loss to the emotional fabric of the show. His death is one of the most shocking moments in *Grey's Anatomy*, in part because it reflects how often the quiet ones are overlooked until it is too late. He dies saving a stranger. Not for attention. Not for glory. But because it is who he is. His final act is one of pure integrity.

And therein lies the tragedy and triumph of George O'Malley. He was never the star. Never the one with the soaring speeches or dramatic monologues. But he was the soul. The one who reminded us that goodness is not loud. That courage can look like staying soft in a world that hardens everyone. That shame can be survived, even if it's never entirely erased.

In the sections that follow, we'll examine George's patterns of self-doubt, the cultural expectations around masculinity that shaped his sense of self, and the quiet dignity of a character whose worth was never in question—except in his own mind.

He wasn't perfect.

But he was good.

And in a world where that isn't always enough, he made it matter anyway.

The Psychology of Invisibility – When Niceness Masks Need

George O'Malley is the kind of person who is easy to underestimate. He is affable, respectful, quick to help, and rarely the center of attention. In any workplace or social dynamic, someone like George often becomes the emotional glue—the one who softens tension, fills in gaps, and carries emotional weight without ever being asked. But this kind of role, while admirable on the surface, comes with a hidden cost. It often conceals unspoken needs, and when left unacknowledged, it can erode a person's sense of self.

From the first episodes of *Grey's Anatomy*, George is cast in this role. He's "the nice one." The one who fumbles in surgery but shows up for everyone else without question. The one who is teased, overlooked, and routinely underestimated, yet continues to show loyalty and kindness even in the face of dismissal. His demeanor is easygoing, but underneath it lives something heavier: a quiet desperation to be taken seriously.

This is the heart of George's psychological struggle—not incompetence, not immaturity, but chronic emotional invisibility. He is not unaware of how others perceive him. In fact, he's painfully attuned to it. He knows he's not seen as dominant or commanding. He knows his sensitivity makes him a target in a culture that equates competence with confidence and leadership with volume. And because he knows these things, he tries to compensate—not by becoming louder, but by becoming more agreeable. More helpful. More indispensable.

This is what psychologists often refer to as adaptive submission—a pattern in which individuals attempt to gain safety or belonging by minimizing their own needs and maximizing their availability to others. These individuals learn, often early in life, that overt self-expression leads to rejection, ridicule, or conflict. So they suppress. They smile. They nod. They serve. And they do so hoping that, eventually, their worth will be recognized not through demand, but through quiet reliability.

George plays this role to perfection. He listens when others vent. He comforts when others cry. He volunteers for tasks others avoid. He steps in, time and again, as the emotional support system for those around him. But beneath that supportiveness is a growing resentment—a sense that he is always the helper, never the helped. Always the friend, never the choice. Always present, but never truly seen.

We see this most clearly in his relationship with Meredith. George falls for her with a kind of quiet ache. He doesn't say anything at first, because he doesn't want to disrupt the friendship. But the longing is there—in the way he looks at her, the way he steps in when she's hurting, the way he carries her secrets. When he finally confesses his feelings, Meredith is surprised, even confused. Not because George lacks value, but because she never saw him that way. And that's precisely the point.

George has made himself so emotionally available that he has disappeared into the background. He has been so accommodating, so safe, so non-threatening, that his identity has blurred. And while Meredith's rejection isn't cruel, it confirms a deeper wound in George: that being good is not the same as being chosen. That kindness does not automatically earn connection. That invisibility, even when well-meaning, is still invisibility.

This dynamic is not unique to George, nor to fiction. Many emotionally attuned men—especially those raised in environments that devalue sensitivity—learn to suppress their needs in exchange for social acceptance.

They become caretakers, listeners, helpers. But often, they internalize a belief that their emotional expression is unwanted or excessive. So they wait. They hope someone will notice what they're not saying. And when no one does, the shame deepens.

Shame, for George, is a persistent undercurrent. It shows up in the way he apologizes before speaking. In the way he defers to authority, even when he knows he's right. In the way he doubts himself after making sound decisions. This shame is not irrational—it is embedded. Shame thrives in silence. It grows in the absence of reflection. And for George, that silence is loud. He is surrounded by people who feel everything out loud, while he internalizes, rationalizes, and minimizes.

There's a scene early in the series when George performs his first solo surgery. The build-up is intense—his colleagues tease him, his confidence wavers, and the pressure to perform becomes overwhelming. And yet, he succeeds. He does the procedure. He saves the patient. And for a moment, he stands in his own success. But even in that triumph, he is not celebrated in the way others might be. The reaction is muted. The applause is delayed. And the message, though unspoken, is familiar: George is capable, but still somehow not commanding.

This pattern continues in his relationships. With Callie, George is initially resistant. Not because he doesn't like her, but because he doesn't believe someone could genuinely want him. When he eventually accepts her affection, he does so with caution. But once married, he realizes that love built on insecurity is fragile. Their marriage collapses not just from infidelity, but from a lack of emotional foundation. George didn't know how to be loved. He knew how to be needed, how to be helpful, how to be present. But being truly seen? That was unfamiliar territory.

The problem with chronic niceness is that it often prevents emotional truth. When a person suppresses conflict, defers opinions, or hides their pain in the name of harmony, what they are really doing is erasing themselves. George does this repeatedly. And though it's rarely acknowledged on screen, the psychological toll is significant. Over time, he becomes more impulsive. He makes erratic decisions. He tries to assert control in ways that feel out of character. These are not betrayals of his personality—they are expressions of a self that has been neglected for too long.

The kindness that once defined George becomes a burden. Not because kindness is wrong, but because it was never balanced with permission to need, to express, to want. Niceness without boundaries is self-abandonment. And George, for much of his time on the show, abandons himself quietly, consistently, and with increasing emotional cost.

And yet, even in this erosion, he remains good. Not performatively good. Not strategically good. But deeply, painfully, quietly good. He keeps showing up. Even when it hurts. Even when he's dismissed. Even when the people he loves don't know how to love him back.

George's invisibility is not a character flaw. It is a reflection of what happens to people who are taught to disappear in the name of being agreeable. His arc reminds us that emotional presence is not the same as emotional agency. That being there for others does not guarantee others will be there for you. And that kindness, to be sustainable, must be reciprocal.

In the sections that follow, we will explore how George navigates masculinity, shame, and emotional dignity—and how, in the end, his quiet strength becomes his greatest legacy.

Masculinity in Conflict - Yearning, Hesitation, and Silent Crises

George O'Malley is not the kind of man television typically celebrates. He isn't assertive in the traditional sense. He doesn't dominate conversations or operate with the swagger often reserved for male leads in high-stakes environments. In the high-adrenaline world of surgery, he is not the one who kicks down doors. He hesitates. He listens. He reflects. And because of that, he is often perceived as less masculine—not by the audience, but by many of the characters within the show's narrative world.

This perception is not incidental. It is structural. From the start, George is contrasted with other male characters who more closely embody conventional traits of male dominance—Derek's confidence, Burke's authority,

Alex's aggression. George is different. He is emotionally available, gentle, relational. He seeks affirmation through connection rather than competition. And in a professional culture that prizes decisiveness and bravado, his presence becomes a kind of resistance—though not one he fully owns.

Instead, George internalizes the idea that his way of being a man is less than. Not outwardly. He doesn't rant or rail against it. But inwardly, he doubts. He second-guesses. He carries a quiet, corrosive sense of failure—not because he isn't capable, but because he isn't loud about it. This inner tension plays out in the small, painful moments: the missed promotions, the miscommunications, the failed relationships. Not because George lacks substance, but because the shape of his masculinity doesn't match the mold he's been handed.

This psychological conflict is common for men who grow up sensitive in environments that reward stoicism. These boys are often praised for being helpful but teased for being emotional. They are told to speak up but also to toughen up. They receive mixed signals that confuse authenticity with weakness and pressure them into silence. Over time, they may develop a form of muted yearning—the deep desire to be seen for who they are, coupled with the chronic fear that doing so will make them unlovable.

George embodies this completely. His longing for connection is palpable, but so is his fear of being misunderstood. He wants to be chosen—for Meredith, for respect among his peers, for a leadership role—but he doesn't know how to demand it. His instincts are relational, not transactional. And because of this, he is often outpaced by those who self-promote more effectively, even if they are less emotionally aware.

His masculinity becomes a negotiation. He doesn't reject it outright. He tries, at various points, to fit the mold. He joins the army, hoping for a sense of structure and valor. He marries Callie, attempting to claim a traditional role that others might recognize as adult, stable, legitimate. But in both cases, the fit is off. George is not made for posturing. His power is quiet, and when he tries to wear someone else's identity, it falls apart—not catastrophically, but quietly. A series of small unravelings.

And yet, he keeps trying. Not because he wants to conform, but because he wants to be worthy. That is the emotional engine underneath his choices—the yearning to be worthy of love, of respect, of presence. This is not an uncommon psychological arc for men who don't relate to dominant masculine norms. They want to be accepted without erasure. They want to belong without betrayal of self. And when that belonging doesn't come, they often assume it's because they failed to be enough.

This self-perception is compounded by how others treat him. Cristina dismisses him. Alex mocks him. Even Meredith, despite her fondness for him, doesn't truly see him in the early seasons. George becomes what many emotionally intelligent men become in patriarchal spaces: the backup plan, the second choice, the friend zone. And while those terms have often been co-opted to express entitlement, in George's case, they reflect something more existential. He doesn't believe he's owed anything—but he aches, quietly, for something he rarely gets: to be seen as powerful, not in spite of his gentleness, but because of it.

One of the most painful dynamics he navigates is the one with Callie. She loves him. He marries her. But the relationship always feels unbalanced. George wants to want her in the way she wants to be wanted. But emotionally, he is still chasing a fantasy of validation that cannot be fulfilled through partnership alone. He marries to prove something—perhaps to himself, perhaps to others. And when the reality of marriage sets in, it becomes clear that Callie is not the resolution to his crisis of identity. She is a mirror to it.

And then there's Izzie—a relationship born of proximity, shared pain, and emotional confusion. When George sleeps with Izzie while still married to Callie, it is not just betrayal—it is disorientation. A desperate grasping at clarity, at recognition, at something that feels right in a life that increasingly feels false. The fallout is, of course, devastating. But again, it is not drama for the sake of plot. It is the emotional wreckage of a man who never learned to say what he needs until he's already caused harm trying to get it indirectly.

George's masculinity is never toxic. It is hesitant. It is searching. And at times, it is hidden under layers of shame that are never fully spoken aloud. This silence is perhaps his deepest wound. Not his failed relationships, not his missed career opportunities—but the chronic self-doubt that keeps him from standing fully in his own emotional power.

And yet, his masculinity is a quiet revolution. He is not aggressive. He is not domineering. But he is brave in ways that are rarely celebrated. He comforts patients when others cannot. He shows up for friends when others retreat. He acts from principle, not performance. And in the end, he sacrifices his life for a stranger—not because he wants to be a hero, but because that's who he is.

George's final act is not loud. It's not designed for recognition. It's consistent with the way he lived: doing the right thing, even when no one is watching. And in that act, his masculinity becomes something rare—something defined not by dominance, but by dignity. Not by performance, but by presence. Not by how many people remember him, but by the quiet, indelible mark he leaves behind.

In the final section, we'll explore the emotional cost of being the overlooked one, the toll of persistent shame, and the slow, steady strength of George O'Malley's presence as the moral heart of the early seasons.

The One They Didn't Protect - Legacy, Loss, and Emotional Dignity

When George O'Malley dies, no one recognizes him.

Not at first.

Not even Meredith, who knew him best.

He arrives at the hospital unconscious, unrecognizable, having thrown himself in front of a bus to save a stranger's life. He is broken, bloodied, speechless—and yet still trying to communicate. It is a haunting metaphor, almost too perfect. George, the quiet one, the overlooked one, the one who spent his life doing for others without demanding much in return, makes his final act a pure expression of everything he was. And in the end, he is not recognized. Not until it is nearly too late.

This moment captures, with devastating precision, what George's entire arc was about: being present without being seen, being good without being remembered, being essential without ever fully taking up space.

His death is not simply tragic. It is emblematic of the psychological cost of invisibility. It shows us what happens when the person who has spent their life minimizing themselves is finally gone—and how suddenly, in their absence, the weight of their presence is fully felt.

For much of his time on the show, George was the emotional scaffold for others. He carried others' pain, soothed others' chaos, and served as the sounding board for his more volatile peers. Meredith's spirals, Izzie's grief, Alex's rage, Callie's yearning, even Bailey's burdens—all found, at one point or another, an outlet in George. But what makes his role so emotionally painful to watch is that his own needs were often unspoken. Not because he didn't have them, but because he didn't believe they mattered.

This is the heart of his psychological wound: the belief that he must earn his place through service, that being seen must be purchased with perfection or compliance, that worth is conditional. And when that belief is baked into one's emotional core, it is almost impossible to name your own pain, let alone ask others to tend to it.

George's dignity was often confused with passivity. His emotional availability mistaken for weakness. But as his arc unfolds, it becomes increasingly clear that he is not lacking strength—he is carrying more than most. He feels more. Absorbs more. Processes more. And he does it quietly, without spectacle. His way of loving is not dramatic. It is consistent. Unyielding. Steady. And in a culture that rewards loudness, this kind of constancy is easily overlooked.

That, perhaps, is why his death lands with such emotional violence. It is not just that he dies young. It's that he dies still becoming. Still struggling to claim his space. Still trying to believe that who he is—soft, thoughtful, unsure—is enough.

And yet, there is profound meaning in the way he goes. George doesn't die in a surgical accident, or a moment of reckless emotion. He dies choosing to protect a stranger. It is an instinct, not a decision. Reflexive, not calculated. And that, in itself, is a revelation. Because for all the doubt he carried, all the shame, all the quiet pain of feeling like he didn't measure up, when the moment called for courage, he didn't hesitate.

That act—throwing himself in front of a bus—is not just heroism. It is the fullest expression of who George O'Malley had always been, even when no one noticed. And that is what makes his legacy so powerful. Not that he died saving someone. But that he lived always trying to.

In psychological terms, George's life and death expose a central human contradiction: we can be deeply loved and still feel unworthy. We can be essential and still feel invisible. We can be surrounded by people and still die with words in our throat, unheard. And that is what makes George's story so hard to watch—and so necessary to witness.

He represents those among us who give everything and ask for nothing. The ones who hold the room together without needing to center themselves in it. The ones whose emotional labor goes unnamed, unpaid, unpraised. And he reminds us, painfully, that people do not need to be loud to be vital. That sometimes the person you barely register is the one keeping everything intact.

After his death, the people who knew him are shattered. Meredith, in particular, carries the weight of his loss with quiet devastation. She realizes, too late, what so many of us realize too late: that the people who never demanded your attention were often the ones most deserving of it. That the friend who always listened might have needed someone to ask how he was doing. That the one who showed up at every crisis might have been quietly weathering his own.

This is the emotional truth at the core of George O'Malley's legacy. He lived in the background, but he held the foundation. He doubted himself, but never others. He gave, even when depleted. And when he died, it was not for recognition. It was for someone he didn't even know.

In many ways, his death is the ultimate act of emotional dignity. Not just because of the sacrifice, but because of the integrity. He didn't become someone else before he died. He didn't change himself to fit expectations. He didn't chase a spotlight. He simply lived—flawed, hesitant, good—and then he was gone.

And yet, what lingers is not just the loss. It's the echo. The realization, for those left behind, that George mattered. That he had always mattered. That the love he gave was not soft—it was strong. That the space he held was not small—it was sacred.

For those of us watching, George's story becomes an invitation. To look more closely at the people we might be overlooking. To listen more deeply to the voices that don't interrupt. To ask the quiet ones what they need—not just what they can offer. To remember that emotional strength doesn't always come wrapped in charisma or certainty. Sometimes, it's wrapped in humility.

George O'Malley was not the best surgeon, or the most confident, or the most magnetic. But he was the kindest. The most willing to show up. The one who kept trying, even when it hurt. And in a hospital full of brilliance and trauma, that made him irreplaceable.

He was not the one they protected.

But in the end, he was the one who did the protecting.

And that is a legacy worth holding.

* * *

5

Izzie Stevens – Idealism, Abandonment, and the Longing to Be Chosen

Love as Proof of Worth

From the beginning, Izzie Stevens wants to matter. Not just in medicine, not just to her patients, but to the people around her. She wants to be seen. Valued. Chosen. Her energy is bright, her presence unmistakable, her heart on display. But beneath her warmth and idealism is a more complex emotional terrain—one shaped by deep abandonment, relational hypervigilance, and a longing to secure identity through emotional significance.

Izzie is often remembered for her romantic entanglements, her idealistic passion for her patients, or her sometimes impulsive decisions. But these plot points, while dramatic, are symptoms of something deeper. At her core, Izzie is a psychological study in attachment anxiety. She doesn't just want love—she needs it to prove she's not disposable. And when that love is threatened, she fights, clings, or collapses in ways that reflect an inner life structured around uncertainty.

Raised in poverty and forced to give up a child as a teenager, Izzie enters adulthood with a fractured sense of continuity. She is familiar with loss, but refuses to be defined by it. Instead, she builds an identity around her capacity to give—her care for patients, her loyalty to friends, her romantic devotion. Her kindness is not performative, but it is purposeful. She wants to be needed, not for control, but for permanence. If she is needed, she cannot be forgotten. If she is loved, she cannot be left.

This orientation toward others is both her greatest strength and her most painful vulnerability. She pours herself into relationships and then struggles when the return doesn't match her emotional investment. She expects that love should look like rescue. That loyalty should look like permanence. That kindness, given freely, should come back in equal measure. When it doesn't, her responses can seem extreme—jealousy, impulsivity, moral outrage—but these are the reactions of someone who is terrified of being abandoned again.

Her relationship with Denny Duquette is the clearest expression of this dynamic. She meets him as a patient—dying, charming, in need—and she gives herself fully to the hope that their connection might defy death. She isn't naïve. She knows the odds. But she needs the story to work. She needs it to end differently than hers did. Denny represents not just love, but redemption. The chance to save someone and be loved for it. The chance to hold on when everything else in her life has been taken away.

Her decision to cut his LVAD wire is not just about passion. It's about desperation. It's an ethically catastrophic act born from the psychological logic of someone who cannot tolerate another loss. She risks her career, her friendships, and her future—not because she believes in magic, but because she cannot bear another ending she didn't choose. Her moral transgression is inseparable from her emotional history. It is an act of attachment panic disguised as romantic sacrifice.

When Denny dies, Izzie's grief is profound, not just because she lost someone she loved, but because she believed—truly believed—that love, this time, would be enough to change the outcome. That belief, so core to her personality, begins to unravel. Her idealism, once a source of hope, begins to collapse under the weight of reality. And this shift marks the beginning of her more erratic behavior—emotional detachment, impulsive decisions, and eventually, a quiet withdrawal from the life she worked so hard to build.

Izzie's relationships with her friends—especially Meredith, George, and Alex—are similarly shaped by emotional intensity and unspoken expectations. She gives deeply, sometimes overwhelmingly. She shows up with food, with tears, with fierce loyalty. But she also expects the same in return. And when she doesn't get it—when Meredith confides more in Cristina, when George marries Callie, when Alex pulls away—she feels betrayed, even if no betrayal was intended.

This is the bind of the anxious-preoccupied attachment style. The world is filtered through a relational lens: am I safe? Am I still loved? Am I being replaced? The threat of abandonment never fully disappears, and every shift in closeness feels like a warning. Izzie doesn't mean to overreact. But her nervous system is constantly preparing for loss. And that preparation often takes the form of heightened emotion, control attempts, or withdrawal as protest.

Her identity is deeply relational. She defines herself by how she is received. And when that reception changes—when she is no longer the center of someone's attention or affection—she flails. Her sense of self is so enmeshed with how others see her that rejection, real or perceived, becomes a kind of psychological annihilation. It doesn't just hurt. It confirms what she already suspects: that she is not enough.

And yet, Izzie is not weak. She survives, again and again. She works her way into a competitive surgical program after modeling to pay her way. She stands up for her patients when no one else will. She chooses her own moral compass, even when it costs her. Her fragility is not a lack of strength. It is the residue of too much loss. And her emotional expression, while sometimes overwhelming, is authentic. She cares. Too much, maybe. But never too little.

What makes her arc so emotionally difficult to watch is that it lacks closure. Her departure from the series is abrupt, unceremonious. She leaves without the fanfare or emotional reckoning we expect from someone so emotionally embedded in the show. And in many ways, this ending mirrors her psychological fear: to be forgotten. To be left. To become someone others once loved but no longer mention.

But if we look deeper, Izzie's story is not a failure. It is an exploration of how people who were once abandoned try to live lives of meaning. How they fight to be more than what they were handed. How they love not because it is safe, but because they believe it might save them anyway.

In the sections that follow, we'll examine the link between Izzie's past and her professional identity, how love becomes both salvation and sabotage, and what her departure means for the people she left behind—and for the woman she was still becoming.

She was not always easy to love.

But she was never indifferent.

And in a world that too often confuses guardedness with strength, Izzie Stevens gave us a different map: one where caring too much is not a flaw, but a scar from loving in a world that didn't always hold her back.

Left Before She Could Stay - Early Loss, Idealism, and Emotional Risk

Izzie Stevens enters *Grey's Anatomy* with bright energy, big emotions, and a deeply romantic view of the world. But beneath her optimism and warmth lies something more raw: a wound shaped by early abandonment, and a coping strategy that centers around hope, idealization, and relentless emotional generosity. What often appears on the surface as impulsivity or naiveté is, in truth, the high-wire act of someone who is constantly trying to build a life that contradicts her beginnings.

We know early on that Izzie gave up a child for adoption in her teenage years. We know she grew up in poverty. We know that she used her physical appearance—specifically, modeling—to pay for medical school, a detail that becomes a point of both pride and shame depending on who's asking. But these facts are just the scaffolding. Psychologically, Izzie's foundational experience is not just loss. It's unprotected loss. Loss without buffer. Loss without scaffolding. And that kind of experience leaves a deep imprint.

Children who experience abandonment—whether through adoption, neglect, or inconsistent caregiving—often internalize a core belief: love is conditional. You may be wanted, but only if you meet certain expectations. You may be safe, but only temporarily. You may be enough, but only until someone better arrives. This belief becomes part of their attachment framework, shaping how they relate to others, to love, and to themselves.

For Izzie, this shows up in the way she gives love: fiercely, immediately, and often with a kind of urgency that reads as romantic intensity but is more accurately described as attachment anxiety. She does not ease into relationships—she leaps. She doesn't flirt with affection—she declares it. She doesn't wait to be chosen—she tries to become indispensable. Because if she is needed, she believes she won't be left again.

This is why her idealism is not weakness. It is strategy. Hope, for Izzie, is armor. If she can believe—really believe—that love will last this time, that someone will stay this time, that care will not collapse again, she can continue living in a world that once failed her. Her belief in the best-case scenario isn't naïve; it's defiant. It's a way of reclaiming emotional agency in a world where, for a long time, she had none.

Her early relationships with her patients reveal this. She becomes emotionally involved, invested, protective. She crosses lines—not recklessly, but because she believes she is doing what is right. And when others caution her, she listens, but rarely changes course. Her need to connect emotionally is not limited to romance—it is part of how she builds meaning. Part of how she repairs her own emotional losses by helping others avoid theirs.

But when these attachments don't hold—when patients die, when friends choose others over her, when love feels shaky—her reactions become more extreme. Not because she is unstable, but because she is emotionally overinvested. She puts too much of her identity into being loved, and when that love wavers, she feels not just sadness, but threat. The loss is not a moment. It is a reactivation of every past loss she has already survived.

Her relationship with Denny Duquette is the most vivid illustration of this pattern. She falls hard. And fast. And completely. Denny is dying, which means he is already half gone. But Izzie refuses to see it that way. She believes her love can sustain him. That her presence can rewrite the ending. That if she just stays—fully, loyally, unflinchingly—she can finally undo the narrative of being left. She can be the one who saves.

This is a common emotional pattern for adults with abandonment trauma: they are drawn to situations where love feels precarious, because it matches the emotional tone of their earliest experiences. The hope is that, this time, they can hold on. That this time, they can control the outcome. That this time, staying will be enough.

But it never is. And when Denny dies, Izzie's world collapses—not just because he is gone, but because she believed, with everything she had, that he wouldn't be. Her grief is not only heartbreak—it is shame. Shame that she believed so fully. Shame that she risked everything—her career, her reputation, her future—on love. And shame, especially when rooted in early trauma, is not something people simply recover from. It shapes identity. It marks the emotional blueprint.

After Denny's death, Izzie becomes less grounded. Her decisions become more erratic. Her optimism, once radiant, becomes forced. She returns to the hospital, but not fully. She drifts. She tests people. She overcorrects. And all of it points to the same internal rupture: the loss wasn't just of a person. It was of a worldview. A belief system that had held her together since she was a teenager.

This loss reverberates in her friendships. She becomes more jealous. More reactive. She struggles to tolerate ambiguity. When people don't behave the way she expects, she doesn't adjust—she panics. Because ambiguity, for Izzie, is dangerous. It's the space in which abandonment hides. If she doesn't know where she stands, she assumes she's already been left. And that assumption is devastating—not because she lacks strength, but because she has always needed love to be clear, visible, and guaranteed.

But the truth is, love is rarely guaranteed. And that reality sits uncomfortably inside Izzie's psyche. She wants permanence, but life keeps offering unpredictability. She wants emotional safety, but she only seems to recognize it when it is dramatic. She wants to be loved, but struggles to trust it unless it comes with a grand gesture or a risk. Quiet, stable love feels foreign. Unconvincing.

This is the cost of idealism born from trauma: it offers hope, but at a price.

The price is constant emotional risk. The price is the inability to rest inside love without trying to prove it. The price is the slow erosion of self-worth every time someone leaves—because every departure feels like a personal failing, not a circumstantial event.

And yet, Izzie's capacity for love never fades. Even when she leaves the hospital. Even when she says goodbye. Even when she disappears. Her story is not one of failure. It is one of survival. She loved people with a kind of urgency that came not from selfishness, but from fear. Fear that she would never again be that needed. That central. That loved.

She gave more than she had, over and over. Because giving was how she told herself she belonged.

In the next section, we will explore how this giving—the caregiving, the romantic over-functioning, the moral urgency—becomes both a source of identity and a trap. Because when you equate being loved with being needed, it becomes very hard to ask for love when you are not performing.

Care as Currency - Overgiving, Romantic Idealization, and the Need to Matter

Izzie Stevens doesn't just care—she *gives*. She gives her time, her emotional energy, her focus, her heart. When someone around her is in pain, she doesn't wait to be asked. She intervenes. She shows up with food, with unsolicited advice, with a relentless determination to make things better. But her care, though genuine, is not always clean. It is tangled up with identity, with a longing to be valued, with the psychological belief that being useful is the closest thing to being safe.

People who have experienced abandonment—particularly in formative years—often grow up believing that their value is transactional. If they are helpful, they are lovable. If they are accommodating, they are wanted. If they anticipate others' needs, they will not be left. This emotional template doesn't always produce outward submissiveness; in Izzie's case, it produces high-functioning overgiving. She is active, assertive, involved—but often in ways that exceed what is asked of her.

At the hospital, this shows up in how she treats her patients. She doesn't just attend to their medical needs. She bonds. She listens. She brings in homemade cupcakes or sits with them long after her shift is over. It's endearing, but also risky. She crosses lines—not maliciously, but compulsively. She can't quite separate compassion from personal responsibility. She doesn't just want patients to get better. She wants them to feel loved. And if they die, she grieves as if she failed them. Because for Izzie, caregiving is not just a job—it is a form of emotional tethering.

This tethering is even more pronounced in her romantic relationships. Izzie loves in technicolor. She romanticizes, idealizes, and commits with an intensity that outpaces reality. She projects not because she's foolish, but because she is hungry—for connection, for permanence, for reassurance that she will not be discarded again. When she loves someone, she wraps her life around them—not in a controlling way, but in a way that makes it difficult to distinguish where her concern ends and her identity begins.

Her relationship with Denny is the most obvious example of this. It's not just that she loves him—it's that she needs to save him. She needs their love to succeed because it proves something to her: that if she stays, someone won't leave. That if she believes hard enough, the story will end differently. Her devotion is fierce, and in many ways, beautiful. But it is also built on a fantasy. One where her love can suspend mortality, fix a broken heart, and give her back the stability life once stole.

When Denny dies, her devastation is layered. It is not simply grief—it is disorientation. The act of overgiving, in her mind, was supposed to guarantee a different outcome. And when it doesn't, she doesn't just mourn Denny—she questions the emotional logic she's lived by. If love doesn't protect her, if care doesn't save her, then what does?

This question haunts her as she tries to reenter normal life. She throws herself into friendships, into baking, into declarations of affection. But there is a desperation beneath it—a need to regain the emotional power she once thought came from being indispensable. The tragedy is that Izzie often gives more than she has. She burns herself out emotionally. She pours herself into others not just out of kindness, but out of fear: that if she stops giving, she will be forgotten.

In psychology, this is sometimes referred to as "care as currency." It's a dynamic where people, often those with insecure attachment histories, use caregiving to buy emotional safety. They give, not with strings attached, but with unspoken hopes: that they'll be prioritized in return. That they'll be irreplaceable. That their care will bind others to them. But this dynamic is precarious, because it relies on emotional reciprocity that may never fully arrive.

We see this in her relationship with George. Their friendship is real, rooted in trust and shared experience. But Izzie leans hard into emotional closeness—sometimes crossing boundaries, sometimes inserting herself where George doesn't ask her to. When he begins to pull away—especially during his relationship with Callie—she reacts not with distance, but with increased investment. She bakes. She questions. She protests. She can't understand why George choosing someone else feels so personal. But the truth is, Izzie has come to define her importance by how central she is to others. George stepping away is not just a shift in friendship—it is a challenge to her identity.

When they eventually sleep together, it is not lust that drives it. It is emotional desperation. Two people who feel unseen, unloved, emotionally frayed—reaching for each other not because of compatibility, but because of pain. The aftermath is messy, not because of the act itself, but because neither of them knows how to make sense of what they were trying to solve. For Izzie, it's another moment where emotional investment becomes emotional chaos. Where caregiving morphs into over-involvement. Where love becomes entangled with guilt, with shame, with a need to make things right.

Her relationship with Alex offers another emotional mirror. He is guarded, reluctant, often cruel. But Izzie sees something in him—vulnerability, maybe, or the same ache she carries. She invests. She nurtures. She becomes the emotional laborer in the relationship, often absorbing his detachment as something to fix. Their connection, while real, is asymmetrical. She gives more. And when he finally begins to meet her where she is, she is already emotionally fatigued. Their timing rarely aligns. Because for Izzie, love is not ease. It is effort.

This is one of the saddest contradictions in her arc: she gives to be chosen, but the more she gives, the less centered she becomes. The more emotional labor she takes on, the less capacity she has to receive. And when the giving is not reciprocated, she doesn't get angry—she gets smaller. Quieter. She questions her worth, not others' behavior. This is the hidden cost of romantic over-functioning: it feels like purpose, but eventually becomes depletion.

And yet, Izzie never stops trying. That's what makes her story both frustrating and deeply moving. Even when she is left, even when she is broken, even when she walks away—there is always love in her. A belief, however faint, that maybe next time will be different. That she can care again. That love can still mean something.

In the next section, we'll look at how Izzie's eventual withdrawal from her life at Seattle Grace reflects not just character fatigue, but emotional collapse—the kind that occurs when someone who has built their identity through connection finds themselves untethered. We'll explore whether her departure is regression, freedom, or a quiet surrender to a life she no longer knows how to hold.

Fantasy as Coping - Escapes, Endings, and Emotional Withdrawal

For Izzie Stevens, reality is negotiable. Not in the clinical sense, but in the deeply human way many people use hope, imagination, and narrative control to survive a life they never felt prepared for. Izzie's use of fantasy is not delusional—it's strategic. When pain is unbearable, she doesn't deny it. She just rewrites it. Or tries to. Fantasy becomes her coping mechanism of choice, and for a long time, it works. Until it doesn't.

At first glance, Izzie appears to be simply optimistic, even idealistic. But optimism implies a belief in good outcomes based on logic or experience. Izzie's version is more emotionally constructed. It stems not from experience, but from longing—a longing so intense that the story she needs to be true often overtakes the story that actually is. In clinical terms, this is a form of magical thinking: the belief that emotional intensity can influence or even rewrite objective outcomes. For Izzie, love isn't just powerful. It's redemptive. And if she loves hard enough, stays loyal enough, gives enough—then death can be avoided, abandonment reversed, mistakes erased.

This emotional worldview is seductive because it offers temporary relief from the powerlessness she felt growing up. When she gave up her baby as a teenager, she wasn't just losing a child—she was losing control over her own narrative. She didn't get to keep the person she created. She didn't get to choose how the story ended. So as an adult, she tries to exert control in the only way she knows: by rewriting the narrative as it unfolds.

The Denny storyline is the most vivid expression of this. Izzie falls in love with a man who is dying—and yet, she does not emotionally orient to his terminal diagnosis. She orients to the fantasy that she can save him through devotion, through presence, through the power of love itself. When she cuts his LVAD wire, it's not just an impulsive act. It is the ultimate expression of her psychological need to believe that love can triumph over biology. That care can outrun chaos. That her story will not end like it did before.

When Denny dies anyway, her grief fractures more than her heart. It fractures her entire internal framework. The emotional system she used to keep reality tolerable—hope, love, control through care—collapses. And she doesn't rebuild it. She floats.

This floating becomes evident in her behavior post-Denny. She becomes unmoored. Her emotional expressions become sharper, more unpredictable. Her sense of connection to others becomes erratic—over-involved one moment, withdrawn the next. This is not randomness. This is coping. When reality becomes too painful, the body protects itself through numbing, through denial, through distraction. But Izzie doesn't disengage through cynicism—she retreats into yet another story.

She tries to revive her sense of purpose through over-giving, through baking for everyone, through infusing her life with performative hope. But these actions don't ground her. They mask her. What she longs for isn't domestic routine—it's emotional anchoring. And she can't find it, not even in herself.

When she begins a relationship with Alex again, she seems ready to try reality again. He's flawed. He's difficult. But he's there. He stays. And when she gets diagnosed with cancer, her world contracts. Now, she's the one who is sick. Now, she's the one others might lose. And she tries, at first, to fight. To stay rooted. To stay visible. But even this story—cancer survivor, love redeemer, comeback narrative—doesn't hold. Because the emotional weight beneath her illness is heavier than even her fantasy can support.

Her behavior after treatment is sporadic. She leaves, comes back, leaves again. This is not flightiness—it's fragmentation. She cannot sustain emotional continuity because her coping mechanism—magical thinking—is no longer working. She cannot will herself into being okay. She cannot love herself into certainty. And instead of rebuilding a new framework, she quietly withdraws.

Psychologically, what we're witnessing is a form of dissociative self-protection—not in the clinical dissociative identity sense, but in the more relatable sense of psychic distancing. When emotional reality becomes too threatening, some people leave physically, some emotionally, and some narratively. Izzie does all three. She withdraws from Seattle Grace. She pulls away from Alex. And perhaps most poignantly, she stops trying to control the story. She stops explaining.

Her departure feels sudden to others, but it wasn't sudden to her. It was the long, slow build of someone who no longer recognizes herself in her own life. When you've constructed your identity around being needed, being romantic, being brave, and all those identities have failed to keep people close or keep death at bay, what's left? For Izzie, the answer is absence.

Fantasy, for a time, allowed Izzie to override her fear of abandonment. It gave her something to believe in when logic and evidence failed her. But fantasy is exhausting when it isn't rooted in reciprocity. When her efforts weren't met with consistency, when her love didn't save lives, when her emotional labor didn't guarantee connection—she didn't rage. She faded.

Her disappearance from the show mirrors what often happens to people whose primary survival strategy stops working. They don't always crash.

Sometimes, they just go quiet. Not because they stopped caring, but because the cost of staying present was higher than they could emotionally afford.

Izzie's withdrawal was not just from the hospital, or from Alex. It was from a life that no longer made emotional sense to her. And while many viewed this as narrative failure, it was, in fact, a rare and painful reflection of something real: when emotional coping strategies collapse, some people don't rebuild in public. They vanish.

And yet, her vanishing act is not the end of her emotional truth. It is the final chapter of a character who lived through story. She tried to outrun abandonment by becoming indispensable. She tried to outlove death by giving everything she had. And when none of it kept her safe, she did the only thing she hadn't tried—leaving before she could be left again.

Her final legacy isn't in her exit. It's in the way she made love a verb. Even when it hurt. Even when it failed. Even when it wasn't returned.

In the end, Izzie Stevens gave everything she had to the belief that love could save her.

And when that belief broke, she disappeared—not because she was weak, but because she could no longer hold the weight of her own hope.

* * *

II

Love, Loss, and the Anatomy of Attachment

Love at Seattle Grace is never simple—it's tender, tangled, and often tragic. These chapters trace the emotional currents beneath the romances: the pull of longing, the ache of misalignment, and the moments when love isn't enough. From passion to heartbreak, we watch how connection shapes identity, tests boundaries, and forces each character to ask the hardest question of all—how do you stay close without losing who you are?

6

Meredith & Derek - Attachment Anxiety, Avoidance, and the Fantasy of the One

Love That Refuses to Stay Still

From the moment Derek Shepherd appears in Meredith Grey's life, nothing about love stays simple. Their chemistry is immediate, but their connection is laced with contradiction: passion and avoidance, devotion and doubt, closeness and emotional distance. It's easy to romanticize their story—two brilliant surgeons drawn to each other in spite of their flaws, secrets, and traumas. But to watch them through a psychological lens is to see something more complicated and more truthful: the collision of two attachment systems, each shaped by unresolved histories and unrealistic expectations.

Their love doesn't begin cleanly. It begins in a haze of anonymity, a night without names, a spark without story. And for Meredith, that initial ambiguity is safe. There's no risk in loving someone you're not supposed to see again. But when that stranger turns up in the hospital as her new boss, the fantasy fractures—and so begins the long, looping emotional push-pull that defines their relationship.

What unfolds over the following seasons is not just a love story. It's an attachment drama. Meredith, whose formative years were shaped by abandonment, emotional inconsistency, and maternal detachment, brings into adulthood a nervous system primed for loss. She wants love deeply, but she fears it just as much. Her instinct is to retreat before the pain begins, to withdraw before she becomes dependent, to sabotage before she gets left.

Derek, in contrast, presents as secure, charming, and self-possessed. But his own backstory—defined by betrayal, regret, and the wreckage of a failed marriage—reveals a subtle form of avoidant defense. He desires connection, but often idealizes it. He projects permanence onto people before truly seeing them. He wants the fantasy of home, the reassurance of being "the one," but struggles to sit with relational discomfort when things get messy or real.

Together, Meredith and Derek activate each other's unresolved wounds. When she leans in, he often pulls away—insisting she be ready, stable, or open in ways she hasn't yet learned to be. And when he leans in, she flinches—afraid that her emotional neediness will push him away. Their most iconic moments are not their declarations of love, but their missteps: Meredith begging him to choose her. Derek trying to fix her pain with plans and houses. Meredith shutting down. Derek giving up too soon. The pain they cause each other is never cruel, but it is persistent—because neither one truly knows how to be held without bracing for the fall.

Psychologically, they represent a classic anxious-avoidant pairing. Meredith's anxiety shows up in her protest behaviors—emotional outbursts, distancing, pleas for reassurance. Derek's avoidance shows up in his control—his desire to solve Meredith, to have her fit into his vision of what love should be. Neither pattern is pathological. Both are deeply human. But they are mismatched in rhythm and regulation. They love each other, but they are constantly out of sync.

And beneath all of this is the fantasy. The myth of "the one." It haunts them both. For Meredith, it's the fantasy that love can be stronger than trauma—that it can erase the coldness of her childhood, the instability of her mother, the abandonment by her father. For Derek, it's the fantasy that he can find a partner who completes the picture he lost when his marriage collapsed—someone who will step into the home he's been trying to rebuild.

This fantasy gives their relationship shape—but also pressure. When love has to be everything, it becomes brittle. When a person becomes the solution to your emotional past, they eventually become a source of disappointment. And for Meredith and Derek, disappointment arrives not in one dramatic collapse, but in a series of quiet failures to see each other clearly. Derek often tries to fix Meredith rather than understand her. Meredith often tries to prove herself rather than express herself. And in doing so, they miss the vulnerability beneath the other's behavior.

But what makes their arc compelling is not just the tension. It's the work. The repeated efforts to return, to repair, to grow. Meredith eventually begins to regulate her fear of abandonment—not through Derek, but through therapy, through friendship, through motherhood. Derek begins to confront his own need for control—not by changing Meredith, but by learning to live in the uncertainty of her healing. Their most profound moments come not when they are "in love," but when they stop trying to fit each other into a fantasy and begin to meet each other where they actually are.

Even then, though, the fantasy never disappears. It reemerges in symbolic form—in the dream house, in the post-it note wedding, in the belief that love should be grand and permanent and final. And when Derek dies, that fantasy ends—not with closure, but with grief. Meredith is left not only to mourn the man she loved, but to integrate the fantasy she built around him. His death is not just loss. It is psychological rupture—the moment when the imagined future collapses, and the only path forward is a relationship with absence.

In the chapters leading up to this one, we explored how individuals form their identities in the wake of abandonment, survival, and trauma. But here, in Part II, we shift focus. Here, we ask how these identities fare in connection—how love becomes a mirror, a magnifier, a battlefield. Meredith and Derek's relationship is the centerpiece of this inquiry. It is not perfect. But it is illuminating. Because it reveals the fundamental truth of romantic attachment: that we don't fall in love as blank slates—we fall as people shaped by every goodbye we've ever endured, every promise we ever believed, and every part of ourselves we hoped someone else might hold.

In the following sections, we'll examine how attachment patterns play out in their dynamic, how Meredith's anxiety and Derek's avoidance collide and evolve, and how the myth of the soulmate—though seductive—can become a psychological trap when it replaces emotional presence with imagined rescue.

Their love was real.

But it wasn't magic.

And in the end, that may be the most honest story of all.

The Push-Pull of Attachment - Anxiety, Avoidance, and the Dance of Dependency

At the core of Meredith and Derek's love story is a psychological paradox: two people who feel deeply, yet remain emotionally unsynchronized. Their connection is undeniable, but it is rarely steady. It contracts and expands with stress, miscommunication, and personal history. And the more they try to hold onto each other, the more often they find themselves pulled into opposite corners of the room. This is not simply incompatibility. It is an attachment dynamic—one of the most classic, compelling, and frustrating patterns: anxious meets avoidant.

Attachment theory, developed through the work of John Bowlby and Mary Ainsworth, tells us that our early relationships form internal templates—models of what closeness feels like, what we expect from love, and how we regulate proximity and vulnerability. For Meredith and Derek, these templates are not aligned. Meredith, shaped by a childhood of emotional neglect and unpredictable caregiving, leans toward anxious-preoccupied attachment. Derek, emerging from a failed marriage and carrying his own history of betrayal and grief, exhibits a more dismissive-avoidant style. They are drawn to each other, but their instincts often tell them to respond in incompatible ways.

Meredith's anxiety is not loud at first. In the early stages of their relationship, she appears emotionally reserved, even aloof. But this is a defense—what psychologist Dan Siegel might call a "false window of tolerance." She appears regulated, but she is bracing. When she realizes that her one-night stand has become her boss, her reaction is not just about professional awkwardness—it's about vulnerability. Derek becomes real. Accessible. And therefore dangerous.

As their relationship deepens, Meredith's anxiety begins to surface. She becomes emotionally reactive, especially when she senses Derek might leave her. Her protest behaviors—pulling away, acting out, attempting to assert control over uncertainty—are all hallmarks of an attachment system in overdrive. She isn't irrational. She's scared. Not just of losing Derek, but of what that loss would mean about her. About her worth, her safety, her capacity to be loved without being abandoned.

Derek, on the other hand, enters the relationship seeking comfort, but on his own terms. He is charming, emotionally present, and attentive—so long as the connection feels orderly. But when Meredith's pain becomes messy, when she pulls back or demands more than he's ready to give, he withdraws. He becomes critical, prescriptive, controlling. He wants to fix her, not feel with her. And when she doesn't conform to the version of love he envisioned—calm, communicative, resolved—he begins to question her readiness, rather than his own avoidance.

This dynamic unfolds again and again. Meredith pulls him in—pleading, revealing, needing—and Derek pushes her away—retreating, questioning, withholding. Then, just as she begins to close off, he reappears with tenderness and clarity. And so they circle. Not because they don't love each other, but because their attachment systems are out of sync. When one is open, the other is closing. When one is brave, the other is afraid.

This anxious-avoidant loop is well-documented in attachment research. It creates a relationship of intermittent reinforcement—periods of intense closeness followed by emotional distance. The inconsistency itself becomes addictive. Each partner feels perpetually unsatisfied, but also unable to let go. The highs are validating. The lows are devastating. And the brain, wired for attachment, starts to conflate volatility with passion.

For Meredith, this pattern reinforces a core belief: that love must be chased. That stability is a reward for loyalty, effort, and emotional labor.

When Derek distances himself—whether emotionally or by returning to Addison—Meredith's anxiety escalates. She feels rejected, not just in the present, but through the lens of her past. Her mother's emotional absence, her father's detachment, the fragmented nature of her upbringing—all of it resurfaces. Derek becomes not just a partner, but a proxy for every unresolved relationship before him.

For Derek, Meredith becomes a challenge to the tidy image he holds of love. He wants emotional safety, but he expects it to look like predictability. He struggles to accommodate Meredith's emotional intensity because it mirrors the parts of himself he's tried to suppress: his own grief, his own failure, his own messiness. When Meredith is in pain, he tries to soothe her through reason. But love, for Meredith, is not a problem to be solved—it is a wound to be witnessed.

And yet, they return to each other. Again and again. Why? Because despite the mismatch, they offer each other something rare. Meredith offers Derek emotional depth. She shows him what it means to stay, even when it's hard. Derek offers Meredith a vision of home—not the kind she grew up with, but the kind she hoped might still be possible. They don't regulate each other well, but they represent the promise of something they've both been missing: someone who sees them and doesn't run.

Over time, they begin to shift. Meredith learns, slowly, to tolerate ambiguity. She starts therapy. She begins building a life outside of Derek. Her sense of self grows sturdier, less reactive. Derek, for his part, starts to listen more. He softens. He stops prescribing. He learns to hold Meredith without needing her to be fixed. These changes don't erase the push-pull, but they reduce its intensity. The cycle shortens. The rupture becomes easier to repair.

But even as they grow, the fantasy still lingers—the idea that love should be effortless, that the right person should make everything fall into place. This belief, though romantic, becomes a source of pressure. When things go wrong, both of them interpret it as evidence that something is fundamentally broken. That's the burden of "the one"—any sign of incompatibility feels like failure. And in relationships shaped by anxious and avoidant dynamics, failure is not a possibility. It's a fear always waiting at the edge of intimacy.

What Meredith and Derek ultimately teach us is not how to love perfectly, but how to stay through imperfection. How to regulate not just each other, but themselves. How to slowly disarm the defenses that kept them safe but alone. Their push-pull is not a pathology. It's a process. One rooted in old fears, old scripts, and the slow, patient work of emotional rewiring.

In the next section, we will examine the psychological architecture of that fantasy—the myth of the soulmate—and how Meredith and Derek both chase and resist the promise of being "the one" for each other. Because for all their work, one truth remains: when you've been hurt enough times, even love that stays feels like something you can't fully trust.

The Myth of the Soulmate - Fantasy Bonds and the Emotional Refuge of Destiny

To believe in soulmates is to believe that love has a preordained path. That someone out there is meant for you—not because of shared values or hard-won emotional intimacy, but because the universe designed it so. It's a belief rooted not in logic, but in longing. For Meredith Grey and Derek Shepherd, that longing is mutual. Both are deeply intelligent, practical, even cynical in their professional lives. But when it comes to each other, they retreat into something far less rational and far more seductive: the idea that this love, their love, is fated.

From the beginning, their bond is framed with the language of inevitability. They meet by chance, connect instantly, and then discover they're already entangled by circumstance. Rather than take that as a warning, they take it as a sign. And once the seed of destiny is planted, it becomes a refuge—for both of them. Whenever their relationship strains under the weight of distance, doubt, or betrayal, they return to the myth: *we're supposed to be together.* It becomes less of a question and more of a justification.

But what looks like romantic fate is, in psychological terms, a fantasy bond.

A fantasy bond, a concept developed by Dr. Robert Firestone, refers to a subconscious substitute for real emotional connection. Rather than risk the pain of true vulnerability, people in fantasy bonds use roles, rituals, or narratives to simulate closeness. The relationship feels safe because it feels symbolic—something to hold onto, even if it doesn't always offer the real, messy, human connection that intimacy requires.

Meredith and Derek don't just fall in love. They form a symbolic identity together. He is her person. Her dream. Her answer to every version of abandonment she's survived. And she is his second chance. His clean slate. His escape from the pain of betrayal and the failure of his marriage. These roles become so powerful that they begin to supersede reality. Instead of working through their emotional ruptures in real time, they often retreat to the comfort of the narrative: *we're meant to be.*

This is why their relationship is so often unbalanced. Not in love, but in labor. Meredith, early in the relationship, does more emotional lifting. She fights for them. She pleads. She endures. Because for her, being chosen by Derek is not just about romance—it's about rewriting the story of never being chosen at all. Derek, in contrast, often idealizes Meredith but struggles to tolerate her emotional volatility. He wants her, but he wants her composed, ready, healed. He doesn't always know how to love her in her woundedness. And so, when she expresses fear, insecurity, or reactivity, he sometimes disengages—not out of cruelty, but because it disrupts the fantasy.

And fantasy, for both of them, is comforting. Because it feels permanent.

But permanence built on projection cannot hold. Meredith is not only the lost girl needing rescue. She is brilliant, angry, independent, and at times emotionally flooded. Derek is not only the knight in surgical armor. He is controlling, conflict-avoidant, and occasionally self-righteous. The more they try to live out the roles assigned by their romantic myth, the more they deny the full truth of who they are. And that denial leads to disappointment—because when the fantasy fails, they each feel betrayed. Not necessarily by the other person, but by the story they thought they were in.

This is particularly evident when Derek builds the dream house—the house with candles, the house of future children, the house that Meredith doesn't know how to enter. To Derek, the house is love made real. To Meredith, it's a monument to a life she's not sure she can live. The more he invests in the fantasy of "happily ever after," the more her anxiety spikes. Not because she doesn't love him, but because the pressure to *believe in the story* feels overwhelming. She's not rejecting him. She's rejecting the version of herself the fantasy demands her to become.

There's a deeper layer to this conflict: both Meredith and Derek are trying to heal through each other. She wants to be good enough to be chosen by someone who doesn't leave. He wants to love someone who validates the hope that love can be redemptive. But healing is not linear, and it is never achieved through projection. Each time one of them fails to meet the emotional ideal—when Meredith shuts down, when Derek pulls away—the other feels destabilized. Because it's not just about the moment. It's about the myth starting to crack.

The soulmate fantasy becomes a way to avoid emotional complexity. Rather than sit in the discomfort of mistrust, misalignment, or individual pain, they fall back on phrases like *we're meant to be*. But meaning is not a shield. It's not a substitute for emotional presence. And in time, both of them begin to realize that destiny, no matter how romantic, is not a strategy for relational growth.

Real intimacy requires dismantling the myth. Not all at once, but piece by piece. When Meredith begins to own her fear of abandonment—not just act it out—she starts relating to Derek from a place of grounded need, not frantic protest. When Derek stops trying to "fix" Meredith and begins to listen—to truly witness her pain without trying to solve it—he starts relating not to the fantasy, but to the woman herself.

Their eventual marriage is quiet—no vows, no ceremony, just a post-it note. Symbolic, yes, but grounded. It reflects a shift: from performative romance to chosen partnership. From narrative to presence. From destiny to decision. It is, paradoxically, the most romantic thing they ever do—not because it fulfills the fantasy, but because it finally lets it go.

Still, the soulmate myth lingers. When Derek dies, Meredith is devastated—not only by the loss of her husband, but by the collapse of the story they were still writing. The person who anchored her healing journey is suddenly gone. And the grief is not just personal—it is existential. Who is she now, without *him*? Without *them*?

This is the danger of the fantasy bond: when the relationship becomes the center of identity, its loss threatens to unmake the self. But Meredith does not collapse. She mourns. She disappears for a time. But she returns, not to the story, but to herself. Because somewhere along the way, through all the myth and meaning, she learned how to stand. Not because of Derek. But beside him.

In the next section, we'll explore what remains after the myth breaks—how Meredith survives Derek's death, how her attachment wounds don't disappear but transform, and how grief, when metabolized, becomes a form of relational maturity. Because the real love story here isn't just about soulmates.

It's about how you keep becoming when the person you became with is gone.

When the Fantasy Breaks - Grief, Growth, and the Self After the Story Ends

When Derek Shepherd dies, Meredith doesn't scream. She doesn't fall apart in public. She doesn't rail against the universe or insist the world stop spinning. She goes silent. Disappears. And in that disappearance, we see the full psychological gravity of a love story that wasn't just about passion or compatibility—it was about survival.

Derek wasn't just her partner. He was her emotional anchor, her proof that someone could love her and stay. He was the ending to the question that defined her: *Am I too broken to be loved?* When he dies, it is not just a personal loss. It is the collapse of the narrative that had become her home.

This is the kind of grief that destabilizes identity.

When people lose someone with whom they've built not only a life but a self, the grief becomes existential. It's not just, *I lost them.* It's, *I lost who I was with them.* Meredith's reaction isn't numbness—it's disintegration. And in the early aftermath, she does what many attachment-wounded people do when their worst fear comes true: she withdraws. Not because she doesn't feel, but because she feels everything. And has no map for what to do next.

The post-Derek Meredith is not a reinvention. She doesn't become someone new. She becomes someone **stripped**. The scaffolding of her fantasy—the soulmate, the house, the future with a person who would never leave—is gone. And what's left is something quieter, shakier, more real: the task of living with grief not as a wound to be healed, but as a truth to be carried.

Psychologically, this is the rupture point between fantasy and individuation.

Individuation, in Jungian terms, is the process by which a person becomes whole—not by merging with another, but by integrating all aspects of the self, even those shaped by loss. For much of her adult life, Meredith defined herself through the lens of her attachments: to her mother, to Cristina, to Derek. Her sense of identity was relational—understandably so, given her childhood of emotional absence and inconsistency. But Derek's death forces a reckoning. There is no longer someone to orbit. No relationship to hide inside. Only her. And for a time, that emptiness is unbearable.

But what follows is not collapse. It is transformation. Meredith's grief is not linear. She runs, yes. Leaves without explanation. But she also reemerges—not as the same person, but as someone who has accepted that no one is coming to finish her story. It is hers to write now. Not with grand gestures, but with ordinary persistence. She raises her children. She returns to surgery. She continues to love, but differently—without the desperate grip of someone trying to keep a fantasy alive.

There's something radical in how *Grey's Anatomy* treats her grief. It doesn't resolve quickly. It doesn't offer clean lessons. It allows Meredith to drift. To be inconsistent. To carry her pain without forcing it into growth. And eventually, it lets her evolve—not because she's over it, but because she has let the fantasy go.

One of the most powerful aspects of her post-Derek journey is that she doesn't try to replace him. Others appear—Nathan Riggs, for a while—but these relationships aren't framed as destiny. They're framed as choice. And choice, for someone who once believed love had to be fated to be real, is a sign of emotional maturation. Meredith doesn't need a story now. She needs a life. One that can hold both memory and motion. One that honors what was, without freezing her in it.

The grief shifts her, but it does not harden her. She becomes more self-contained, yes—but not closed. Her compassion deepens. Her clarity sharpens. She stops needing people to save her or see her in a certain light. She becomes capable of showing up as she is, not as the version someone else once needed her to be. In this way, Derek's death—while devastating—becomes a psychological threshold. It moves her from romantic attachment to integrated selfhood.

This shift is rarely shown in television. Female characters, especially, are often defined by who they love, who they lose, or who they live for. Meredith was all of these. But then she became something else: someone whole. Someone capable of honoring her grief without making it the center of her identity.

There's no post-it note for this part. No big moment where the narrative ties itself up. There's just slow, continuous effort. There are surgeries. Mornings. Kids. The occasional joy. The occasional breakdown. There is the realization that healing isn't forgetting. It's remembering differently.

This is what makes Meredith Grey's arc not just emotionally rich, but psychologically rare. Her grief is not a detour. It is the road. And as she walks it—alone, uncertain, unstyled—we see the full weight of love that was never about perfection. A love that was real, that ended, and that didn't take her with it.

In the end, Meredith doesn't just survive Derek's death. She outgrows the story that he was the only place she could belong.

And that is the quiet triumph of her emotional life: not that she found the one, but that she learned to stay standing when the one was gone.

* * *

7

Callie Torres - Identity, Sexuality, and Reclaiming Self

Becoming Who You Already Were

Callie Torres enters the world of *Grey's Anatomy* with swagger. She's bold, confident, flirtatious—a striking figure in both physical presence and professional command. But like many characters on the show, her outer armor tells only half the story. Beneath the sarcasm and sexual energy is a woman quietly negotiating some of life's deepest psychological questions: Who am I allowed to be? What happens when I am rejected for being it? And how do I live with fullness in a world that keeps asking me to shrink?

Callie's arc is one of the most profound evolutions in the series—not because she transforms completely, but because she stops pretending that she has to. The woman she becomes by the end is not unrecognizable from the one we met in the hospital hallway. She is simply more rooted, more self-authored, more free. Her journey isn't about reinvention. It's about return. Not to childhood, not to family, but to truth—the kind of truth we spend years avoiding, silencing, or bending to fit the roles handed to us.

From the start, Callie is "too much" in all the ways society loves to punish.

She's too loud, too sexual, too muscular, too assertive, too smart, too emotional. She isn't demure. She doesn't ask for space—she takes it. And yet, despite all this apparent confidence, she is also deeply conditioned to seek approval. To please. To mold herself into something more palatable—especially for her parents, her partners, and the cultural scripts she grew up with. This tension—between self-possession and self-erasure—becomes the psychological terrain she must navigate.

We learn early on that Callie comes from a conservative background, one that holds traditional beliefs about gender, sexuality, and respectability. Her success as an orthopedic surgeon may be impressive, but it isn't enough to insulate her from the expectations of her upbringing. She's expected to marry well, look appropriate, follow the rules. And for a time, she does. Her early relationship with George is not just about love—it's about conformity. About ticking the boxes. About being "normal" in a way that will make her family proud.

But Callie is not normal. She is extraordinary. And that extraordinariness doesn't come without cost.

The psychological rupture begins when she falls for Erica Hahn, another female surgeon. The realization that she is attracted to women destabilizes her—not because it feels wrong, but because she doesn't yet know how to hold it in her identity. The language for this part of herself isn't yet formed. And so, she turns to others—friends, partners, even strangers—to help her name it. To help her understand what this means about who she is.

This is a critical moment in identity development. For many queer individuals, the process of self-recognition isn't instantaneous. It unfolds over time, through emotional resonance, through trial and error, through relationships that awaken parts of the self that had previously been silent. Callie's bisexuality is not a plot twist. It is a reclamation. A letting in of what was always there.

But the moment she begins to integrate this truth, the world pushes back. Her father disowns her. Her faith community, implied through dialogue and tone, becomes a source of rejection. Even within the hospital—a relatively progressive space—she encounters skepticism, confusion, and erasure.

People want her to pick a side. To clarify. To simplify her truth into something more binary. But Callie, by nature, is complex. And that complexity becomes her emotional battleground.

Her relationships become crucibles for this work. Erica, Arizona, even Mark Sloan—all serve as mirrors through which she tries to see herself more clearly. With Erica, she feels raw recognition, but also emotional rigidity. With Arizona, she experiences joy, parenthood, and devastation. With Mark, she finds unexpected tenderness and a sense of safety that is more familial than romantic. Each relationship is real. Each one is formative. But none of them define her. They help her see herself, but they do not complete her.

This is the heart of Callie's psychological journey: moving from being defined by relationships to being defined in relationship. She doesn't stop loving. She doesn't become guarded. But she stops outsourcing her identity. She begins to speak with authority—not just as a surgeon, but as a person. She stops apologizing for being complicated. For being bisexual. For being Latina. For being a mother who co-parents with her ex, who coexists with her ex's wife, who makes choices that others don't always understand. She stops needing to explain her life. She starts living it.

There is immense power in this shift. For women, especially women of color and queer women, the pressure to explain, justify, and soften oneself for others' comfort is relentless. Callie's refusal to do so—especially as the series progresses—is not just personal growth. It is political. It is cultural. It is psychological emancipation.

But she doesn't arrive there easily. Her growth is punctuated by heartbreak, professional humiliation, physical trauma, and deep loss. She is injured. She is abandoned. She is divorced. She is challenged in court for the right to raise her own daughter. And through it all, she remains tender. She never loses her capacity for intimacy, even when intimacy has betrayed her.

That is perhaps the most radical thing about Callie Torres: her capacity to remain open. She keeps choosing love. She keeps choosing truth. And eventually, she chooses herself.

In the sections that follow, we will explore how Callie's sexuality and cultural background shape her early struggle with belonging; how her confidence was, at times, a performance to mask rejection; and how, through heartbreak and healing, she became the kind of woman who no longer asked for permission to exist.

She wasn't becoming someone new.

She was finally becoming who she already was.

Permission to Exist – Sexual Identity and Family Shame

For Callie Torres, coming out isn't a triumphant announcement. It's not a banner moment. It's a slow unraveling of assumptions—hers, her family's, her culture's. She doesn't declare her identity so much as discover it, piece by piece, as though her life up until that point had been written in one language and she's only now learning to translate it. The experience isn't just about understanding her sexuality. It's about finding the courage to exist in the truth of it, even when that truth makes her unrecognizable to the people who say they love her.

Sexual identity doesn't emerge in a vacuum. For Callie, the process is inseparable from her upbringing—steeped in religious, familial, and cultural expectations. She is the daughter of a wealthy, conservative Latino family. She has a trust fund. A name. A pedigree. And with that comes a tightly bound set of rules about what makes a life respectable. Heterosexuality is assumed. Femininity is expected. Marriage to a man—preferably with status—is a foregone conclusion. And so, when Callie begins to feel something different, something that doesn't fit that story, the shame begins.

It is not the shame of wrongdoing, but of disruption. Of letting people down. Of stepping outside the roles that kept her connected to her family, even if those connections were conditional. The shame Callie experiences is not rooted in self-hatred; it is rooted in fear. Fear that if she lives truthfully, she will lose everything—her father's love, her cultural belonging, her spiritual legitimacy. And for a time, that fear keeps her quiet. Keeps her grasping at relationships with men—George, Mark, even Alex—not because they fit, but because they make her legible.

When she falls for Erica Hahn, it's not framed as a grand awakening. It's a whisper. A look. A softness. Something that feels emotionally right before it makes intellectual sense. And that's what destabilizes her. Not that she's attracted to a woman, but that she's never allowed herself to consider the possibility. That her emotional world might be more expansive than she had been taught. That she might want something different than what she was raised to pursue.

This realization is not met with celebration. It's met with confusion, silence, and resistance—even from herself. She doesn't yet have the language for bisexuality, or for the fluid, evolving experience of identity. And in this absence of language, shame grows. Because when you can't name who you are, you can't defend it. You can't explain it. You can't demand that others respect it.

Her attempt to come out to her father is one of the most painful and revealing moments in her story. He doesn't yell. He doesn't argue. He simply withdraws. Disowns her. As if her truth is too incompatible with the image he's held of her. This rejection cuts deeper than disapproval. It confirms what Callie has long feared—that her identity is conditional. That love, even from a parent, can be revoked.

For a woman like Callie, who is fierce and accomplished and seemingly unshakable, this rejection isn't just personal—it's existential. She's been taught to carry herself with pride, to be confident, to take up space. But when your own family erases you for being yourself, confidence becomes theater. It becomes a mask you wear while you quietly question whether you belong anywhere at all.

Callie's experience is emblematic of a larger truth: for many LGBTQ+ individuals, especially those raised in conservative or religious households, coming out is not just a revelation—it's a confrontation. It forces a reckoning with the systems that once offered safety, purpose, and place. Faith, family, and tradition become battlegrounds. And even when someone finds acceptance later, the early rejection often lingers, encoded into the nervous system as a kind of permanent vigilance: *Will I be safe if I'm seen?*

This internalized fear doesn't disappear when others accept her. Even as she finds affirmation through friends, lovers, and eventually colleagues,

Callie continues to brace. She expects loss. She expects to be questioned. Her defiance—her insistence on being open about her sexuality, her refusal to apologize—is both strength and scar tissue. It's the confidence of someone who has been punished for being honest and chose not to go quiet again.

But there's nuance in her defiance. Callie is not aggressive in her queerness. She's tender. She still wants connection. She still hopes for reconciliation. She doesn't write her father off immediately. She holds space for the possibility of his return—not because she needs his approval, but because she still longs to be known by him. This longing is not weakness. It's human. To want love from the people who first gave it to you is not regression. It is part of the lifelong work of identity integration: trying to hold your truth without losing your place in the world you came from.

Eventually, her father does return—not with full understanding, but with willingness. He meets Arizona. He listens. He chooses relationship over rigidity. And while the reconciliation is not perfect, it is healing. Not because everything is fixed, but because Callie no longer needs him to fully get it in order to be whole. She's not waiting to be re-included. She's not waiting for permission. She's already living her truth. His return is not a beginning. It's an acknowledgment of how far she's come without him.

This section of Callie's story is a psychological portrait of shame as exile—and pride as return. Not pride as in celebration, but pride as in refusal. A refusal to be smaller. A refusal to collapse into silence just to preserve someone else's comfort. A refusal to participate in her own erasure.

Callie does not perform queerness to educate others. She lives it to survive. And in doing so, she grants herself the one thing she was never offered at the start: permission to exist, exactly as she is.

Perfection, People-Pleasing, and the Performance of Confidence

Callie Torres moves through the halls of Seattle Grace with an energy that commands attention. She is bold. Direct. Physically powerful and professionally respected. She flirts without apology. She makes jokes in moments of tension. She stands tall, even when she's falling apart. But beneath this confidence is a far more complex psychological system—one fueled not just by strength, but by performance. One that relies on perfection and people-pleasing as strategies to stay safe in a world that has made her earn her place at every turn.

To understand Callie's confidence, you have to understand the labor behind it. Confidence, in her case, is not simply a trait. It is a coping mechanism. It is the well-practiced mask worn by someone who has spent her life being told that she was both too much and not enough. Her sexuality was too disruptive. Her cultural identity too loud. Her body too muscular. Her emotions too visible. Her ambition too intimidating. The message wasn't just "change"—it was *perform better.* Be impressive enough, agreeable enough, extraordinary enough to offset the discomfort your authenticity creates.

And so, she learns to outperform rejection. If she can be charming enough, competent enough, accommodating enough, maybe she won't be dismissed. Maybe she won't be left. This is the psychological contract that underlies perfectionism—not a desire for excellence, but a fear of disconnection. If everything on the outside looks secure, no one will question the instability beneath.

This tension becomes particularly visible in her romantic relationships. With George, she tries to mold herself into the ideal wife. She tones herself down, tries to match his emotional bandwidth, tries to meet his friends halfway—even when they make it clear she's not what they pictured for him. When he cheats on her, the betrayal confirms her deepest fear: that she can follow all the rules and still not be enough. That people-pleasing doesn't guarantee protection. That love, even when earned, can still leave.

Instead of folding inward, Callie doubles down. She reasserts her power, but in a way that still hinges on external validation. She rushes into decisions—relationships, housing arrangements, even a Vegas wedding—because stability feels urgent. If she can just build a life that looks solid, maybe she'll stop feeling like she's standing on emotional quicksand.

Her relationship with Arizona eventually offers her something different: a space where her queerness is not questioned, where her confidence is met rather than managed. But even then, her perfectionism persists. She wants to be the perfect mother, the perfect partner, the perfect co-parent with Mark, the perfect surgical innovator. And when any of these identities wobble, she blames herself. Her instinct is to over-function, to take on more, to hold it all together with a smile.

This is classic people-pleasing behavior—what psychologists sometimes refer to as fawn response. In moments of relational stress or perceived threat, some individuals move toward others instead of away. They appease. They accommodate. They anticipate needs. Not because they're weak, but because this was once a strategy for emotional survival. For Callie, whose coming out was met with rejection, whose relationships have been fractured by betrayal, whose confidence was once undermined by shame, people-pleasing becomes a way to guard against further abandonment.

But people-pleasing has a cost. Over time, it breeds resentment. Callie begins to lose track of her own needs, her own boundaries, her own voice. She says yes when she wants to say no. She extends grace to people who don't always offer it back. She makes herself palatable in spaces that should already be safe. And underneath it all is a fatigue—a psychological exhaustion from being "on" all the time.

This performance of confidence eventually cracks. The most notable rupture comes during her custody battle with Arizona. Callie, who has long prided herself on being accommodating and emotionally generous, is pushed to her limit. The legal conflict strips away her ability to perform. It exposes how much she has given up in her pursuit of approval—how much she has deferred, compromised, and internalized in order to make things work. And when the court rules against her, it doesn't just take her daughter's full custody. It takes the narrative she's built about who she is: the stable one, the good one, the strong one.

But in that collapse, something honest begins. The mask slips. The perfect posture softens. And Callie starts telling the truth—not just to others, but to herself. She begins to separate confidence from control, strength from performance, generosity from over-functioning. She doesn't stop being powerful. She stops pretending that power means perfection.

This shift is slow, but transformative. We see it in her later choices—not just the people she dates, but the way she shows up in those relationships. She's no longer trying to prove her worth through flawless execution. She begins to expect reciprocity. She begins to say no. She begins to trust that being imperfect doesn't make her unlovable.

What Callie ultimately models is not the erasure of confidence, but the evolution of it. The move from performative to integrated. From something she uses to protect herself to something she carries because she knows who she is. The shift from confidence as armor to confidence as embodiment.

This is what makes her so psychologically compelling. Not that she starts strong and stays strong, but that she stops needing strength to mean sameness. That she stops performing for inclusion and starts living with integrity.

Self-Definition After Heartbreak – When Identity Is Reconstructed, Not Chosen

Heartbreak, when deep enough, doesn't just hurt. It unmakes us. It leaves us standing in the rubble of an identity that once felt stable, certain, shared. For Callie Torres, heartbreak doesn't just arrive as a personal wound. It arrives as a psychological disruption—of role, of identity, of who she thought she was becoming. Her relationship with Arizona Robbins was never simple, but it was foundational. It shaped her adulthood. It gave her the vocabulary for queerness, for family, for parenthood. And when it ends, it takes more than love with it. It takes the self she had been living inside.

Callie does not fall apart dramatically. She doesn't implode. She adapts. She tries to move on, find new rhythms, build a new life. But the emotional residue is thick. The grief is not linear. And the version of herself she once curated—proud, ambitious, loving, maternal, settled—no longer fits. This is the quiet rupture we rarely see on screen, but one *Grey's Anatomy* allows to unfold: the slow, painful realization that when a long-term relationship ends, the real loss isn't just the other person—it's the self you were in their presence.

Psychologically, this is the work of identity reconstruction. It is what happens when we stop trying to "return to ourselves" and start asking, *Who am I now?*

When Arizona leaves, Callie doesn't just lose her partner. She loses the imagined future. The stability of co-parenting. The ease of having someone who already knows your rhythms. And, perhaps most jarringly, she loses the validation that came with being part of a beloved couple. Their love had weight. Visibility. Cultural resonance. They weren't just in a relationship—they were a symbol. A reminder that queerness could be complex, joyful, messy, and enduring. When that ends, the symbolic loss hits just as hard as the emotional one.

Callie's next chapter isn't defined by bitterness. It's defined by quiet perseverance. She keeps showing up—for her daughter, for her patients, for herself. But she no longer operates with the same urgency to be understood. The performance fades. She stops contorting herself to be the good ex, the perfect co-parent, the constant peacemaker. The people-pleasing we saw in earlier seasons softens. And in its place emerges something harder to name, but unmistakable: self-definition without external agreement.

This shift is most visible in the custody battle over Sofia. What begins as a logistical disagreement spirals into a legal and emotional war—a war in which Callie loses. But what she regains, over time, is a different kind of power. The loss forces her to ask questions she's avoided: Where do I draw the line between compromise and self-erasure? What does it mean to fight for something you believe in when the cost is steep? What happens when doing your best still isn't enough?

The answers don't arrive cleanly. But they arrive. In the silence after court. In the ache of distance from her daughter. In the quiet dignity of not turning her pain into performance. This isn't the Callie we met seasons ago—the one who tried to hold everything together with charm and effort. This is a Callie who understands the value of restraint. Of discernment. Of letting people misunderstand you if it means not abandoning yourself.

Her eventual decision to leave Seattle Grace is not an escape. It is an act of reclamation. A declaration that her identity can exist outside of the hospital, outside of her relationships, outside of the institution that both affirmed and constrained her. It's a risk. But it's also a reset. A moment where she chooses a future not built around fixing or proving or pleasing, but around integration. She takes her daughter. She takes her story. She takes herself.

This kind of identity reconstruction is subtle, and often invisible. It doesn't come with grand speeches or clear markers. It comes with a shift in posture. A deeper breath. A steadier voice. A quiet refusal to perform the old roles. In psychological terms, this is post-traumatic growth—not just the ability to survive pain, but to let pain reorient you to truth. Callie doesn't become someone else. She becomes someone more fully herself. Not despite the heartbreak. Because of it.

And this is what makes her arc so emotionally resonant. Many characters on *Grey's Anatomy* experience love. Many experience loss. But Callie's story reminds us that identity is not just discovered. It is assembled. Reassembled. Lived into. And that becoming yourself isn't always about revelation. Sometimes it's about surviving what dismantles you, and finding that the pieces still hold—even when the picture looks different than you imagined.

Her final scenes in the series are not defined by reunion or redemption. They are defined by choice. She chooses a different life. Not to run. Not to hide. But to build something that fits her. Something not dictated by obligation or performance. Something that doesn't require her to be perfect, or palatable, or easily explained.

In the end, Callie Torres is not the same woman we met years before. She is softer in some ways, firmer in others. She no longer tries to convince anyone she belongs. She simply lives like someone who knows she does.

* * *

8

Arizona Robbins - Trauma, Disability, and Control

The Good in the Middle of the Storm

Arizona Robbins entered Grey's Anatomy like a gust of fresh air—confident, charming, and skating down hospital corridors with light-up sneakers and an easy grin. Her energy was disarming in a place so often shrouded in death, intensity, and trauma. She exuded warmth and a kind of moral clarity that made her instantly likable. But as with most characters who carry brightness into the darkest rooms, that light was doing more than illuminating others—it was often shielding her from having to confront the shadows in herself. Over the seasons, Arizona's storyline would unravel into something far more complex than her early appearances suggested. She would become one of the show's most nuanced portrayals of trauma, bodily loss, and the lifelong project of learning to live differently—when the life you had planned is suddenly gone.

Arizona's arc is one of paradox. She is introduced as pediatric royalty, the golden child of a military family, a woman who wins over Callie Torres with her confidence and spark, who seems to possess the rare skill of balancing professionalism with personal joy. Yet underneath that polished surface is a tightly wound need for control. This becomes more visible the deeper we go—her resistance to parenting at first, her forceful stance on certain medical decisions, and ultimately, her response to losing her leg in the plane crash that alters everything. Arizona isn't just navigating trauma. She is navigating how to be in a body that no longer feels like her own, how to reinhabit a life that no longer fits the blueprint she had drawn up in her head. And unlike some of the other characters whose damage is emotional or relational, Arizona's wound becomes physical, visible, and deeply tied to her identity.

In psychology, trauma is often defined not by the event itself, but by how the event reorganizes the internal world of the person who experiences it. For Arizona, the plane crash doesn't just break her leg; it breaks her sense of safety, predictability, and selfhood. It turns her from a surgeon into a patient, from a caregiver into someone who now needs care. And crucially, it forces her into a loss of autonomy—something that had always been central to how she moved through the world. This is one of the core psychological threads we will explore in this chapter: how trauma, particularly trauma that manifests through disability or bodily change, destabilizes the illusion of control, and what it takes to rebuild a self that feels whole even in the presence of permanent loss.

But Arizona is not just a portrait of trauma. She is also a portrait of resilience, and of the complicated ways that people try to reestablish control when they've lost it. In psychological terms, her behavior post-amputation is consistent with what trauma theorist Bessel van der Kolk describes as an attempt to "restore ownership of the body and mind." Her mood swings, outbursts, denial, and even infidelity are not evidence of moral failing—they are evidence of someone in profound distress, trying to reassert mastery in a world that no longer feels safe or navigable. In this way, Arizona's arc challenges the viewer to reframe disability and trauma not as something that breaks a person, but as something that pushes them into a more honest, sometimes painful, and ultimately more expansive sense of who they are.

There's a moment in Season 9 when Arizona says she is "alive," and that should be enough. And yet, it isn't. This is a psychologically resonant statement, because survival after trauma is often romanticized, but rarely interrogated. What does it mean to survive in a way that feels meaningful? To live in a body that feels foreign? To maintain relationships when you no longer recognize yourself? Arizona's story explores the complexity of survival—not just as a biological state, but as an emotional and relational project. Her journey is not about returning to who she was, but about creating a version of herself that can hold what she's lost, without being defined by it.

The interplay between Arizona and Callie also forms an emotional axis for this chapter. While Callie undergoes her own struggles in this period, Arizona's reaction to the aftermath of the crash drives much of the relationship's volatility. It becomes a study in mismatched grieving—Callie wanting to fix and move forward, Arizona needing space to rage, retreat, and reclaim her autonomy on her own terms. This dynamic offers a psychologically rich exploration of how trauma can isolate not just individuals, but couples. It reminds us that healing often happens at different paces and in different languages, and that attempts to help can sometimes land as further violations of the very agency the traumatized person is trying to recover.

Throughout this chapter, we'll also explore how Arizona's earlier persona—the bright, enthusiastic doctor with a gift for connecting to children—was not a façade, but a functional part of her psychological defense structure. That charm, that optimism, was real. But it was also a way of creating emotional safety. It allowed her to connect with others without showing her own vulnerabilities. When she loses her leg, she can no longer perform that version of herself. And the collapse of that identity is part of what makes her story so profound. She doesn't get to hide anymore, not even from herself. And what she eventually builds in the ruins of that collapse is not the return of the old Arizona, but the emergence of a more integrated one.

The question at the heart of Arizona's narrative is not just about how to recover from loss. It's about how to become someone new, while still loving who you were. It's about learning to inhabit a body that no longer matches your sense of self, and finding a way to extend compassion to yourself in that dissonance. It's about rebuilding trust—not just with others, but within the self, in a way that allows for both acceptance and agency.

Charm as a Defense – Attachment Through Safety and Sparkle

Arizona Robbins entered Grey Sloan Memorial Hospital with a disarming confidence. She glided down pediatric hallways with brightly colored sneakers and a glowing smile, the very image of a doctor children could trust. But beneath that sparkle was something far more complex. Her ability to charm—her warmth, her lightness, her playfulness—was not just personality. It was strategy. It was protection. It was control dressed up as charisma.

Psychologically speaking, charm can be a defense mechanism. It functions as a way to regulate emotional proximity: to bring others close enough to feel safe, but not so close that they see the vulnerable self beneath. For Arizona, whose identity was shaped in part by her role as the daughter of a military hero and by her own climb through the surgical ranks, charm became a way to manage her environment. In children's wards filled with fear, parents wrought with anxiety, and fellow doctors burdened by their own trauma, Arizona's lightness became an organizing principle. She was, as one might say in psychological terms, an adaptive performer—someone who learned to generate emotional safety in others as a means of regulating her own inner world.

From attachment theory, we know that people develop relational patterns based on how safe or unsafe they felt in early relationships. While the show does not give us a deep dive into Arizona's childhood, we are offered glimpses—her father's military background, her assertion that she was "raised to be a good man in a storm." These details suggest a context where composure, loyalty, and strength were prioritized, and where feelings may not have been freely explored or validated. In such environments, children often learn to equate worth with performance. For Arizona, that meant being cheerful, competent, and above reproach. Her charm, then, can be seen not just as a way to win people over, but as a deeply internalized survival strategy rooted in anxious-preoccupied attachment.

There is a subtle, telling moment early in her relationship with Callie Torres when Arizona pulls back from emotional intensity. She enjoys the thrill of connection, the flirtation, the warmth—but when real vulnerability emerges, she hesitates. She's more comfortable managing emotion than expressing her own. This pattern persists throughout her early seasons: she supports, she soothes, she holds. But she rarely cracks. Her capacity to be present for others' pain often outpaces her willingness to reveal her own. This, too, is a hallmark of relational defense—an outward warmth masking inward containment.

What's important to recognize here is that none of this is fake. Arizona's kindness is real. Her empathy with children, her passion for medicine, her dedication to doing the right thing—these are not manufactured traits. But they are also not the full story. In psychological language, we might say that Arizona has a high-functioning persona that obscures an underdeveloped internal permission to be messy. She's not manipulative; she's guarded. And that distinction matters. Because when trauma eventually cracks through that surface, what we see is not the unraveling of a false self, but the confrontation of a self that was never given the space to fully emerge.

Another notable layer of Arizona's charm is her almost compulsive need to smooth things over. This is particularly evident in high-stakes situations—when tensions rise, she defaults to positivity, to making things palatable. In psychological terms, this is often a signal of a person who fears disconnection. Her charm, again, functions as a glue—keeping relationships intact, avoiding rupture, making things feel okay even when they aren't. But as any psychologist will tell you, avoiding rupture is not the same as building resilience. At some point, reality has to be faced.

This is where Arizona's storyline becomes especially interesting. Her charm becomes unsustainable. The scaffolding of her defense begins to collapse under the weight of real trauma. And once the plane crash occurs, the system she's built for managing emotion—charm, sparkle, cheer—is rendered almost useless. She is no longer the one bringing comfort. She is now the one in pain, the one afraid, the one grieving a part of herself she can never get back. Her previous strategies of emotional regulation—brightening the room, creating safety for others—cannot be turned inward. And this is a fundamental psychological inflection point: when our defenses no longer serve us, we are forced into either deeper denial or deeper transformation.

Even in the immediate aftermath of the crash, Arizona attempts to cling to her performative traits. She tries to be upbeat. She tries to reassure. But this quickly gives way to anger, avoidance, and withdrawal. The failure of her charm-based coping reveals how incomplete that mechanism was for the internal work she now needs to do. And it sets the stage for the second act of her arc—the confrontation with loss, embodiment, and identity that we will explore in the next section.

To understand Arizona's early behavior as mere cheerfulness is to miss the richness of her psychology. What Grey's Anatomy does so well with her character is show how people who seem emotionally intact can still be deeply defended. Arizona didn't just show up happy—she *had* to be. It was her way of managing a world that felt unpredictable, especially in medicine and in relationships. Her sparkle was armor. Her kindness was a boundary. And her ability to soothe others was, in part, a way of ensuring she wouldn't be abandoned for being too much.

These are all classic dynamics of relational anxiety dressed in professional success. We see this often in high-functioning people, especially women, especially caregivers. They become experts at creating emotional safety for others, while never really developing the internal infrastructure for their own. Arizona's story is the slow, often painful process of shifting from emotional performance to emotional honesty. And while that journey is messy, it is also profoundly human.

The Leg That Changed Everything - PTSD, Identity, and Embodiment

There is a point in trauma when the story you had been living in suddenly ceases to apply. For Arizona Robbins, that moment is marked by the amputation of her leg—a singular, violent rupture in the continuity of self. It is not just a bodily loss. It is a collapse of identity, a disorientation of everything she once knew about who she was, how she moved through the world, and what she could count on. The psychological fallout is not only expected but profound, as it shatters the illusion of control she had always carried, and forces her into a new, unfamiliar relationship with her own body, her sense of agency, and her very existence.

Trauma, when experienced as bodily invasion or alteration, registers not only cognitively but somatically. Bessel van der Kolk, in *The Body Keeps the Score*, underscores how trauma lives in the body, how it marks and transforms it. For Arizona, the trauma is not metaphorical—it is surgically precise. The leg she loses is not merely a limb; it is a symbolic casualty of her independence, her mobility, her self-concept. She cannot escape its absence. She cannot bypass her grief. Every movement is a reminder. Every pain flare, every prosthetic strap, every limitation forces her to reckon not just with what happened, but with who she is now in the aftermath.

In those early episodes following the crash, the viewer witnesses a dramatic shift in Arizona's psychological presentation. Gone is the buoyant energy, the social ease. In its place is a storm of rage, volatility, avoidance, and shame. These are not overreactions. They are classic trauma responses. Post-traumatic stress disorder, particularly when linked with bodily harm and medical trauma, often manifests through emotional lability, hypervigilance, detachment, and disorientation. Arizona cycles through all of these, not because she has become someone else, but because her internal regulatory systems—previously supported by control, cheer, and competence—have been dismantled. Her nervous system is unmoored.

What Grey's Anatomy portrays with surprising psychological accuracy is the non-linear nature of Arizona's response. She does not get "better" on a schedule. She does not immediately see a therapist and begin to heal in a neatly charted arc. Instead, she lashes out at Callie. She retreats from intimacy. She oscillates between self-loathing and denial. These behaviors, though painful to watch, are textbook illustrations of someone coping with traumatic loss without sufficient emotional scaffolding in place. The amputation is not just an injury. It is a complete interruption of self-narrative—and what follows is the effort to survive not only physically, but psychologically, inside that rupture.

One of the more harrowing aspects of Arizona's journey is her fractured relationship with embodiment. To be embodied means to be at home in one's physical form—to feel integrated, safe, whole. After the loss of her leg, Arizona becomes estranged from her body. She resents it. She hides it. She avoids touch. This alienation is not just about the missing limb. It is about the entire nervous system response to trauma: the shutdown of sensation, the hyperawareness of defect, the fragmentation of self into "before" and "after." She no longer inhabits her body as a source of pride or competence. She sees it as a betrayal.

The loss of her leg also shatters Arizona's perception of control—a trait that previously allowed her to navigate the chaos of the hospital, the unpredictability of pediatric trauma, and the complexities of romantic partnership. Control had always been her anchor. It kept her polished, prepared, and emotionally protected. After the crash, she is no longer in control of anything: not her body, not her moods, not her reactions, not even her intimacy with Callie. Her arc becomes a visceral illustration of what it means to lose not only what you had, but who you thought you were. It is in this sense that trauma experts speak of identity disintegration—not just a crack in the narrative, but a total collapse.

What deepens Arizona's psychological fracture is the layered betrayal she experiences at the hands of her wife. Callie, acting from a place of desperation and survival, makes the decision to amputate Arizona's leg to save her life. The fact that Arizona is unconscious, unable to consent, and awakes to a permanent, life-altering change made by someone she loves, introduces an ethical and relational trauma on top of the physical one. This compounds the emotional injury. Arizona is not only grieving her leg; she is grieving her autonomy. And for someone whose identity was built around strength and choice, this loss of agency cuts even deeper.

In trauma psychology, this layering of wounds—physical, emotional, interpersonal—is referred to as complex trauma. It is not one event but the interlocking of multiple injuries that makes recovery so difficult. Arizona is not dealing with grief in isolation. She is navigating betrayal trauma, identity trauma, and relational trauma all at once. And this entanglement complicates everything: her ability to trust Callie, to feel safe in her environment, to return to surgery, to reclaim her authority, and to re-engage her former sense of confidence.

There is a chilling moment when Arizona, seated alone, studies her reflection with a mixture of contempt and grief. Her eyes are hollow. Her posture, guarded. It is a scene devoid of dialogue, yet emotionally deafening. The psychological implication is clear—this is a woman who no longer recognizes herself. She is no longer a pediatric surgeon in light-up sneakers. She is a stranger in a body that feels broken. And the most painful part isn't the leg. It's the alienation. The disconnection between who she was and who she's become.

Over time, Arizona begins to re-enter her life. She returns to work. She adjusts to her prosthetic. She tries to re-engage with parenting Sofia. But the internal rupture does not heal on its own. In many ways, she operates in a functional freeze—doing what's expected while remaining emotionally disconnected. This is another core trauma response, often mistaken for healing. Just because someone is performing well again does not mean they are internally restored. Arizona's story reminds us of this psychological truth: external progress can mask internal paralysis. And unless the underlying injury is addressed, the system will eventually collapse again.

The writers do not absolve Arizona of her worst behaviors—her infidelity, her lashing out, her emotional withdrawal—but they do contextualize them. She is not cruel. She is profoundly dysregulated. She is not inherently unfaithful. She is desperately trying to feel something, anything, in a body and life that now feel foreign. These moments of rupture are not just plot points. They are clinical presentations of a person mid-trauma, engaging in maladaptive behaviors that serve, psychologically, to regain a semblance of control.

What ultimately begins to shift in Arizona is not a single decision or turning point, but the slow, painstaking development of integration. She does not erase her trauma. She learns to live alongside it. And this, in the field of trauma psychology, is considered the true work of healing—not returning to who you were, but becoming someone new who includes the wound without being owned by it.

Rebuilding Trust - Parenting, Partnership, and the Long Path Back

Rebuilding a life after trauma is not a solo endeavor, even when it feels isolating. The aftermath always ripples outward, reshaping relationships, unsettling old patterns, and testing the elasticity of love. For Arizona Robbins, healing from the trauma of the plane crash and the loss of her leg was never just about the body—it was about her capacity to re-enter relationships, to allow herself to be seen again, and to trust others with a self she no longer fully understood. This section isn't about a return to normal, because normal no longer exists. It's about the slow reconstruction of safety, the fragile beginnings of new relational architecture, and the quiet, often invisible work of reconnecting with others after rupture.

The most immediate relationship tested is her marriage to Callie Torres. What was once playful, passionate, and grounded in shared ambition becomes a site of grief, tension, and misattunement. Arizona's fury over the amputation—made without her consent—becomes the centerpiece of their conflict. And understandably so. It isn't just about the leg. It's about the decision being taken from her, the violation of bodily autonomy, the helplessness of waking up to a new reality that she never agreed to. For Arizona, Callie becomes both the person she loves and the embodiment of that loss. This duality creates a psychological rift. She cannot lean on Callie for comfort because Callie is, in her mind, part of the injury.

What complicates this further is that Callie does not see herself as the betrayer. She sees herself as the savior. And here we see a classic trauma bond rupture: one partner believes they saved the other, the other feels violated by the very act of saving. Without shared language around trauma and consent, this dynamic becomes almost impossible to navigate. Callie wants gratitude; Arizona wants to scream. And both are valid in their own pain.

In many couples, trauma introduces a mismatch in grief timelines. One person is ready to move forward while the other is still frozen in the moment of loss. Arizona and Callie live this in real time. Callie pushes for normalcy—date nights, sex, family outings—while Arizona withdraws. She is not withholding out of spite; she is protecting what remains of her selfhood. In psychological terms, she is seeking to reclaim agency. To decide when and how she is touched. To move at her own pace. To be seen as a person in pain, not a problem to be solved. Callie, in turn, misreads this as rejection. This misattunement escalates into arguments, distance, and eventually infidelity.

It would be easy to frame Arizona's cheating as moral failure, and it is—by any ethical standard, it causes harm. But to understand it through a psychological lens is to recognize what the act represents. Arizona, at that point in the series, is unmoored from herself. She is fragmented, ashamed, disconnected, and angry. The affair is not about love or desire. It is about reclaiming something—control, identity, sensation. In trauma recovery, it is not uncommon for people to make reckless choices as a way to feel alive or autonomous again. The problem, of course, is that these actions often deepen the very disconnection they are meant to repair.

Arizona's relationship with her daughter Sofia becomes another emotional axis of recovery. Parenthood, unlike romantic partnership, does not allow for complete withdrawal. The child still needs baths, meals, bedtime stories. But even here, Arizona struggles. Her own dysregulation makes it difficult to show up fully. She oscillates between overcompensating—trying to be the fun, perfect mom—and emotionally retreating when the pain becomes too much. These fluctuations mirror the inner turmoil of trauma recovery. She wants to be present, but she is still at war with herself. And presence requires stability she doesn't yet possess.

Yet, it is in the parenting space that we begin to see glimmers of reintegration. Children, unlike adults, respond not to perfection but to attunement. Sofia does not need Arizona to be flawless. She needs her to be there. Over time, Arizona begins to step back into that role—not because she is healed, but because love often coexists with pain. The scenes of Arizona reading to Sofia, carrying her despite physical limitations, and showing up for the everyday tasks of motherhood illustrate a shift: from self-protection to relational re-engagement.

These small, consistent gestures are what psychologists would call "relational repair." They are not grand apologies or sweeping reconciliations. They are acts of showing up. Of being willing to be seen again. Of letting another person back into the emotional field, even when it's terrifying. Arizona's healing is not sudden. It is slow, interrupted, full of setbacks. But it happens in these moments—not in therapy scenes or epiphanies, but in the ordinary intimacy of daily life resumed.

Eventually, Arizona and Callie begin to find a kind of truce—not a return to their former selves, but a recalibration of what they can realistically be to one another. In trauma recovery, there is often a need to re-negotiate relational roles. The person you loved has changed. The relationship you built no longer fits. And the healthiest outcome may not be a romantic reunion, but a stable co-parenting partnership rooted in mutual respect. Arizona and Callie achieve this, not because they resolve everything, but because they stop trying to be who they were. They begin to honor who they've become.

Another thread in Arizona's journey is her re-entry into her professional identity. Surgery, once her sanctuary, now becomes a source of insecurity. Will her body hold up? Will others trust her? Can she trust herself? These questions echo in every scene where she scrubs in, and her colleagues' reactions—some supportive, some doubtful—mirror her own internal ambivalence. But what is psychologically powerful about her return is that it isn't framed as triumphalism. It's tentative. Vulnerable. Earned. And in this, we see a deeper truth about post-traumatic growth: it is not about becoming more powerful. It is about becoming more integrated. Less defended. More whole.

Arizona's long path back is not linear. It is a tangle of grief, resistance, anger, love, and grace. She breaks trust and slowly earns it back. She loses parts of herself and learns to live without them. She shows us that recovery is not about restoration, but about reconstitution. Not about pretending nothing happened, but about learning to live with what did.

This is what it means to rebuild trust after trauma. It is not an act. It is a practice. It is choosing, again and again, to stay in relationship—with others, with your body, with the truth of your experience. Arizona's journey shows us that healing is not always visible. Sometimes it looks like reading a bedtime story when you're still angry. Sometimes it looks like standing in an OR with shaking hands and doing it anyway. And sometimes it looks like letting someone love you, even when you feel unlovable.

* * *

9

Jackson Avery and April Kepner - Faith, Ego, and Existential Crisis

Anatomy of a Collapse

Some love stories don't unravel from a single catastrophic event. They unravel from the slow, agonizing collision of two people trying to hold on to each other while their internal worlds tear apart. Jackson Avery and April Kepner are not merely a case of opposites attracting—they are a case study in existential divergence. Their arc in *Grey's Anatomy* is not only about romance. It is about belief systems, identity crises, unprocessed grief, and the inability to reconcile two different maps of meaning. Together, they are beautiful. They are volatile. And they are doomed—not because they don't love each other, but because they cannot agree on what love is supposed to mean.

From the moment their paths intersect, Jackson and April represent a tension that many relationships carry beneath the surface but rarely confront so directly: the tension between ego and faith, reason and surrender, autonomy and covenant. Their dynamic is charged by differences in worldview. Jackson, raised in wealth and secularism, stands for logic, science, control, and ambition. April, deeply religious, raised with values of purity, sacrifice, and spiritual obedience, represents a different kind of certainty—one rooted in moral conviction and divine purpose. Their early friendship thrives in the friction between those worldviews. But once intimacy and tragedy enter the equation, that friction becomes fracture.

In psychological terms, their relationship is an exploration of existential anxiety—the fear that one's life, choices, or suffering might be meaningless. Each time Jackson and April try to reconcile after a rupture, they are not just trying to love each other better. They are trying to resolve existential dissonance. They are asking, explicitly or implicitly, what holds us together when our fundamental beliefs about life and death, suffering and salvation, differ so greatly? And can a relationship withstand the implosion of a shared narrative?

What makes their story so gut-wrenching is that the love between them is palpable. They see each other. They protect each other. They desire one another deeply. But love, as we are reminded through their arc, is not enough when it lacks coherence. They struggle not because they fail to care, but because their definitions of hope, of God, of loss, and of meaning are incompatible in moments when compatibility matters most. For some couples, differences in belief remain abstract. For Jackson and April, they become existential landmines.

April's faith is not a character trait—it is a psychological anchor. It gives her a framework for moral decisions, for endurance, for how to interpret chaos. When she becomes a trauma surgeon in war zones, her belief in purpose allows her to survive horrors that would shatter others. But it also blinds her. It keeps her from facing certain emotional truths, and it leads her to make decisions that, while consistent with her values, often isolate her from those she loves. Her faith does not protect her from pain—it often exacerbates it by demanding a kind of suffering-as-sacrifice logic that can alienate her from empathy.

Jackson, meanwhile, carries his own unspoken dogma—achievement, excellence, the illusion of control. Though he claims not to believe in anything divine, his ego operates like a creed. He believes in skill, in status, in reason, in the fixable nature of most things. His worldview is threatened not by chaos itself, but by chaos that cannot be solved. He does not understand April's faith-based approach to loss because, for him, loss is a problem to confront—not a mystery to submit to. When tragedy strikes and he finds himself unable to fix what matters most, his identity begins to collapse in on itself. Beneath his confidence is a man deeply afraid of helplessness.

Their marriage becomes a crucible for all of this unprocessed material. They cycle through grief, through betrayal, through periods of silence so deafening it feels like intimacy is no longer possible. What they experience is not merely a communication breakdown. It is a fundamental crisis of shared meaning. When their son Samuel dies—a tragedy so searing it burns through every defense they've built—the cracks in their belief systems become chasms. April turns to God. Jackson turns away. And in that divergence, their marriage begins its final descent.

This is not the story of a villain and a victim. It is the story of two people who love each other and still hurt each other beyond repair. April leaves when Jackson needs her most—not because she doesn't care, but because she is emotionally annihilated. Jackson lashes out with anger and moral judgment—not because he is cruel, but because he is terrified of what they've lost and how far she's drifted. The tragedy of their relationship is not in the death of their son. It's in the failure to reach each other in the silence that followed.

In clinical terms, their story echoes what is often referred to as "existential boundary rupture." This is the point in a relationship where two people can no longer pretend that they are on the same path—not because of small differences, but because their fundamental ways of interpreting suffering, responsibility, and identity are at odds. The collapse that follows is not dramatic—it is slow, almost imperceptible, until it is undeniable. This is what we witness in Jackson and April. Two people looking at the same life and drawing different conclusions about what it means.

Yet, even in the rubble, there are traces of something honest. Something enduring. They never quite stop loving each other. But they learn, painfully, that love cannot always survive the sacred rupture—when the self fractures, when faith and ego no longer speak the same language, and when the very act of being together becomes a trigger for unresolved pain.

Belief and Belonging - When Values Clash with Intimacy

From the beginning, Jackson and April's relationship is structured around a fundamental dissonance that neither of them is ready to name. It's disguised at first by attraction, by camaraderie, by the high-stress intensity of their shared profession. Their connection is genuine, and their early bond is marked by mutual respect and affection. But below the surface, they are operating from entirely different moral operating systems—Jackson from a world of empirical reasoning and personal agency, April from a life grounded in faith, submission, and divine narrative. What starts as difference eventually becomes division, and what begins in harmony eventually exposes the psychological fault lines beneath their intimacy.

April Kepner does not just believe in God. She *relies* on God. Her belief is not merely devotional; it is structural. It gives her order, meaning, and a framework for understanding suffering and responsibility. Raised in a conservative Christian household, April's worldview has been shaped by a strict internalized moral code. Her sense of right and wrong is not subjective—it is derived from external, divinely sanctioned authority. This becomes most evident in how she views sexuality, marriage, life purpose, and forgiveness. Her virginity, her views on premarital sex, her guilt after breaking that vow with Jackson—all of it reflects a psychology of spiritual absolutism. And while that may offer her a sense of clarity, it also sets her up for profound inner conflict when real life does not obey the rules.

Jackson Avery, by contrast, is the embodiment of a secular, intellectual mindset. He is the product of immense privilege and legacy—his family name carries power, and with it comes the expectation of excellence. But Jackson's internal world is not as stable as his exterior confidence implies. His belief system centers around self-determination, evidence, and merit. When he first hears April talk about her faith, it reads to him as naïve, even dangerous. He resists the idea that suffering can be purposeful, that pain can be redemptive, or that anything is outside the domain of personal control.

To Jackson, the world is made of problems to be solved. To April, the world is made of mysteries to be endured. And therein lies their foundational rift.

Their early romantic encounters are steeped in this tension. When they first sleep together, April is thrown into spiritual crisis, while Jackson interprets the moment as intimate and mutual. She spirals into guilt, believing she has betrayed her values, while he is blindsided by her reaction. He doesn't understand why something so intimate and consensual would produce such self-loathing. What he misses, psychologically, is that April's identity is enmeshed with her moral framework. Violating it isn't just an action—it is, to her, a rupture in self.

But this is not a simple case of secular vs. religious. What's fascinating about their story is how each of them becomes both threatened and intrigued by the other's belief system. Jackson is drawn to April's passion, her clarity, her willingness to stand by her convictions. She is unlike anyone he has known, and that difference attracts him. April, for her part, is drawn to Jackson's confidence, his groundedness, and his refusal to be controlled by invisible authority. There is admiration in their differences, but also the seed of unresolvable tension.

The psychological stakes become higher once marriage enters the picture. In a partnership, beliefs are no longer individual—they become the architecture of shared decisions. How do we raise our children? What do we teach them about morality, purpose, and suffering? How do we make meaning when life becomes unbearable? These are no longer abstract debates; they become daily negotiations of values. And Jackson and April quickly discover that they are aligned in love, but divided in philosophy.

One of the most telling conflicts emerges in their discussions about baptism and religion in parenting. Jackson resists baptizing their child, stating that he doesn't believe in God. April is heartbroken by his refusal, seeing it not just as a disagreement, but as a denial of what she believes is necessary for their child's spiritual future. Jackson, meanwhile, feels manipulated—pressured into subscribing to a belief system he does not share. The moment exposes how their respective systems of belonging do not have room for each other. Jackson does not want to lie or pretend. April does not want to compromise on what she sees as sacred truth. The cost of compromise, for each of them, is self-abandonment.

These moments are not petty. They are existential. They reflect what happens when two people who love each other attempt to forge unity from fundamentally incompatible belief structures. April cannot stop believing that there is purpose in suffering. Jackson cannot start believing in a God he experiences as absent. They are not trying to hurt each other—they are trying to protect the integrity of their own minds and hearts. And yet, they hurt each other anyway.

Belief, in psychological terms, serves as a cognitive anchor. It helps individuals manage uncertainty, regulate emotion, and construct identity. When those anchors conflict in a relationship, the emotional safety of the bond begins to erode. Jackson and April begin to experience each other not just as partners, but as existential threats. Jackson sees April's faith as rigidity, dogma, even delusion. April sees Jackson's skepticism as arrogance, spiritual blindness, and a threat to the soul of their family. Neither is wrong from their own vantage point. And that's the tragedy—they are trapped in an irresolvable difference that no amount of compromise can soften.

The intimacy that once flourished in the gap between them becomes poisoned by misunderstanding. Jackson cannot soothe April's fear without betraying his beliefs. April cannot accept Jackson's logic without abandoning her God. Their love begins to suffocate under the weight of their unresolved philosophies. They don't fall out of love. They lose the ability to coexist in each other's inner worlds. And without that, the foundation begins to crack.

In quieter moments, their tenderness re-emerges. They reach for each other. They try to bridge the gap. But the bridge is built on unstable ground. Belief and belonging, in the end, are not incidental to their story. They are its center. And as we will see, when those beliefs are tested by the deepest loss imaginable, the consequences are not just relational—they are existential.

Grief as Identity Disruption – The Shattering Loss of Samuel

There is a grief so profound that it shatters not only the heart but the scaffolding of the self. For Jackson and April, the death of their infant son Samuel marks such a rupture. It is not only the most devastating event in their shared life—it is the moment when the fragile coherence of who they are, what they believe, and why they are together implodes. Up until this point, their differences had been intense but survivable. But the loss of Samuel transforms those differences into irreconcilable fault lines. What happens between them after this loss is not simply the grief of parents—it is the psychological disintegration of two individuals facing existential collapse, side by side but alone.

Grief does not operate on a single track. It is not just sadness. It is a violent reordering of the internal world. It destabilizes one's understanding of time, fairness, purpose, identity, and intimacy. For April, the death of her son is more than a loss. It is a test of her faith. Her theology tells her there is a reason, a plan, a divine order to suffering. But the brutal death of a wanted, prayed-for child defies that logic. Her grief is not only maternal; it is spiritual. She cannot make sense of her loss without unraveling her understanding of God—and yet, she clings to her beliefs even more tightly. This is a familiar trauma response in devout individuals: when loss threatens the belief system, the psyche often doubles down in an attempt to reassert order over chaos.

For Jackson, the loss does the opposite. His lack of belief, once an intellectual position, becomes emotional truth. In his mind, Samuel's death confirms his worst fears—there is no divine justice, no plan, no meaning. This grief annihilates his ability to entertain spiritual possibility. He watches his son die, powerless to intervene, and finds no comfort in April's assertions of faith. Instead, her belief begins to feel to him like denial, like a betrayal of what they have just lived through. He does not want to hear about God's plan. He wants to scream.

This divergence—April's clinging to faith, Jackson's descent into nihilism—is not philosophical. It is neurological. It is trauma in motion.

Each is coping in the only way their worldview allows. But because their worldviews are incompatible, their grief isolates them from each other. April becomes more devout, attending church, seeking spiritual refuge. Jackson becomes more silent, more distant, turning inward. They are grieving in different languages, unable to translate their pain in a way the other can receive.

Psychologists refer to this as "disenfranchised grief"—when the mourner's expression of loss is not understood, validated, or supported by their immediate environment. Both Jackson and April experience this in each other. April feels unseen, dismissed, and spiritually alone. Jackson feels misunderstood, emotionally abandoned, and existentially betrayed. Their home becomes a battleground of unspoken pain, where every gesture—every word, every silence—becomes a referendum on their grief style. Neither is wrong. Both are suffering. But their suffering becomes mutually unintelligible.

In one of the most searing portrayals of this fracture, April eventually chooses to leave. She accepts a position as a trauma surgeon overseas, working in combat zones—an act that reads, on the surface, as noble and brave. But psychologically, it is a flight response. She is not running toward purpose; she is running away from the unbearable weight of home, of memory, of shared loss. The work gives her structure, meaning, and distraction. But it also allows her to avoid the grief that cannot be prayed away.

Jackson, left behind, enters a grief of a different kind. His wife is alive but gone. His child is dead. His belief system has crumbled. And the silence in his home becomes an echo chamber for helplessness. He cannot access April's reasons for leaving. He sees it as abandonment, not salvation. And without the ability to make meaning from the loss, he has nowhere to put his pain. He is a man undone—not by his lack of belief, but by the lack of a framework to metabolize suffering.

The psychological term for what they are experiencing is identity disruption. It is what happens when a core event destabilizes not just one's emotions, but one's very sense of self. April is no longer a mother, but she still carries the weight of that identity in her body. Jackson is no longer the man who could protect his family, no longer certain of his strength. They are grieving not only a child, but their former selves. And as they both try to rebuild meaning in different ways, the person they became in that crucible begins to feel foreign to the other.

This is where their relationship takes on a tragic quality. It is not that they no longer love each other. It is that the people they were when they fell in love have died alongside their son. In the harshest sense, their marriage was designed for a different version of themselves—versions that no longer exist. In the face of trauma, some couples are able to co-create a new identity. Others discover that their new selves cannot coexist. Jackson and April fall into the latter category, not because they are weak, but because grief has rewritten them too deeply.

What remains between them is a painful, aching ambiguity. There are moments of reconnection, of shared parenting, of faint flickers of what once was. But those moments are haunted. They are not signs of healing. They are evidence of what cannot be undone. The grief did not just break them. It made them strangers.

Redemption or Repetition - Can Love Survive the Sacred Rupture

Some wounds do not close. They simply stop bleeding. For Jackson and April, the rupture caused by the loss of their son Samuel, and the existential reckoning that followed, never fully heals. What remains is not restoration, but a kind of scarred familiarity—a recognition of each other as people who once tried to build a life together, failed, and kept orbiting anyway. Their story isn't about resolution. It's about recurrence—two people trying to return to each other, only to find the coordinates have shifted. They navigate grief like a map rewritten in a language neither of them speaks anymore.

After April returns from the war zone, something in her has shifted. She is stronger, or perhaps simply more guarded. The trauma has hardened her in places, and softened her in others. She has seen devastation and survived it.

But survival does not equal healing, and while she may be more composed, she is not more connected. Jackson, too, is changed. He has grown as a father, found steadiness in his surgical career, and learned how to carry grief with quieter hands. But the unresolved chasm between them remains. They move around each other like ghosts, tethered by shared history and parental duty, but unable to fully return to one another in spirit.

There are moments where they try. A kiss, a conversation, a look that says maybe. These moments echo with the memory of their former intimacy—charged, hopeful, suspended in the possibility of redemption. But each time they draw close, the same question emerges, unspoken yet deafening: have we truly changed, or are we just reenacting the old script in softer tones?

Their dynamic exemplifies repetition compulsion—a concept from Freudian psychology describing the unconscious drive to recreate unresolved emotional wounds in new contexts, in hopes of mastering them. Jackson and April keep returning to each other not just out of love, but out of unfinished business. They are trying to rewrite the ending. But because the core rupture has never been truly addressed—because the grief, the betrayal, the existential divergence was never metabolized together—they fall into the same dance. Closeness, misunderstanding, retreat.

Jackson wants clarity. He wants emotional transparency, mutual understanding, and control over the terms of intimacy. April wants faith—faith in forgiveness, in the invisible architecture of something greater than both of them. When they come together, their love still lives between them, but it is burdened by the same incompatibilities that tore them apart. Neither is willing to fully surrender their framework. And love, when yoked to incompatible truths, becomes volatile.

There is a moment when April marries someone else, a quiet yet seismic shift in their story. Jackson watches, not with anger, but with the ache of finality. It is not just that she is choosing another man. It is that she is choosing another story—one that aligns more cleanly with her values, her beliefs, and her need for coherence. Jackson, for all his growth, cannot be that container for her. Not because he is unworthy, but because he is unresolved. He carries a worldview that cannot integrate hers. And at some point, love cannot stretch far enough to span a spiritual divide.

Yet even in this divergence, they remain deeply entangled. Their co-parenting relationship evolves into something tender, respectful, and quietly painful. They support each other. They raise Sofia with care. They hold space, sometimes more gracefully apart than they ever did together. And this, too, is a form of love—mature, reframed, de-romanticized but not hollow. They no longer attempt to force intimacy where it no longer fits. Instead, they learn to honor the parts of themselves that once belonged to each other, without needing to reclaim them.

April's decision to leave her hospital role and devote herself to medical mission work is another defining chapter. It is a decision aligned with her beliefs, her calling, her enduring faith. For Jackson, it is both admirable and destabilizing. He has always respected her conviction, even when he could not understand it. But her departure once again reinforces the distance between them—not geographical, but philosophical. They are not just choosing different lives; they are choosing different answers to the same questions about purpose, suffering, and meaning.

What emerges by the end of their arc is not reconciliation, but peace. Not in the sense of reunion, but in the sense of mutual release. They do not get the happy ending many fans hoped for, and yet what they receive is more honest. They outgrow the version of love that tried to fix everything. They learn that some sacred ruptures do not get repaired—they get respected.

From a psychological standpoint, Jackson and April's journey is one of differentiation. In the early stages of their relationship, each tried to bend toward the other's worldview. April softened her rigidity. Jackson tried to find language for faith. But real growth came only when they stopped contorting. Their eventual strength lies not in blending, but in clarity. They become people who know who they are—and who know that loving someone does not always mean walking the same path.

In a series defined by dramatic twists and declarations of love, the evolution of Jackson and April stands apart. It is not cinematic. It is human. Their story honors the truth that some connections are profound and formative, but not forever. That love can exist inside difference, but cannot always survive it. That sometimes, growing apart is not a failure—it is an act of emotional integrity.

Their love did not fail. It reached its limit. And even within that boundary, something beautiful endured. Not reunion. Not resolution. But reverence. For what they had. For what they lost. And for the quiet, enduring fact that some people remain part of us, even after the ending.

* * *

10

Owen Hunt and Cristina Yang – Love vs. Compatibility

When Passion Isn't Enough

There are relationships that ignite with such force they feel destined. Owen Hunt and Cristina Yang were that kind of pair—fierce, magnetic, drawn together by something deeper than circumstance. Their love was raw, consuming, and urgent, the kind that made everything else fall away. But beneath the fire was a quiet, growing truth: passion does not equal compatibility. And for all their longing and devotion, they were fundamentally mismatched—not in love, but in life.

Cristina Yang is one of the most self-possessed characters in *Grey's Anatomy*. Brilliant, unyielding, and driven by a calling greater than interpersonal connection, she is a surgical visionary who thrives on focus and autonomy. Her identity is not built around romantic partnership or family structure—it is built around excellence, achievement, and mastery of her craft. Owen Hunt, on the other hand, enters the show as a man fractured by war, but yearning for grounding. He wants love, stability, and family. He is drawn to Cristina's brilliance, but also hopes it can soften into a version of partnership that he recognizes—one that includes marriage, home, and children.

Their relationship, from the outset, is a study in emotional chemistry and existential dissonance. They are electric together. But electricity without grounding is dangerous. The intensity of their bond blinds them both to the reality that they want different lives. Not different hobbies. Different lives. Cristina does not want to be a mother. Owen cannot imagine a future without parenthood. And while it would be convenient to frame their downfall around that one divergence, the truth is more complex. Their incompatibility runs deeper, rooted in unspoken expectations, emotional needs they cannot fulfill for each other, and unresolved trauma that spills into the relationship like a silent third party.

Psychologically, Owen and Cristina's arc is a blueprint of relational misalignment. They do not fail because they don't care. They fail because their visions of life are incompatible, and no amount of love can fuse them into alignment. This is a crucial distinction often lost in cultural narratives about romance. Love, we are told, conquers all. But real-life intimacy depends on more than desire. It depends on shared values, emotional regulation, timing, and the ability to co-author a future. Owen and Cristina never co-authored—they co-existed, they collided, but they never truly created a life together that honored both of their needs.

Owen's trauma—layered, raw, and untreated—shapes how he loves. He arrives at the hospital with the nervous system of a soldier, still wired for combat. He moves between tenderness and volatility, between protectiveness and control. Cristina, accustomed to precision and clarity, is drawn to Owen's depth, but destabilized by his inconsistency. She tries, again and again, to support him. But his unprocessed trauma becomes a force she cannot predict or contain. He wants her to be a place of rest. She wants him to be steady. Neither can provide what the other needs.

This becomes most evident in their repeated attempts to domesticate the relationship—to fit it into traditional structures like cohabitation, marriage, and future planning. But each attempt becomes a new battleground. Owen wants normalcy. Cristina wants freedom. They compromise, but the compromises are unsustainable because they are in conflict with core identity.

Cristina agreeing to have children would be a betrayal of herself. Owen giving up fatherhood would feel like erasure. And yet, neither of them can let go—because what they share is not just a relationship. It is a collision of unmet needs, unfulfilled longings, and the hope that maybe, just maybe, intensity can substitute for alignment.

Throughout their arc, the viewer is pulled into the pain of almost. They almost make it. They almost find a way. But almost is not enough when the cost is self-abandonment. Their story is not a failure of love—it is a failure of fit. They each try to become someone they are not, out of devotion to the other. But identity, when suppressed, will always find its way back to the surface. Cristina begins to suffocate under the weight of Owen's expectations. Owen begins to resent the emotional solitude of being with someone who cannot mirror his needs. And so they begin to fracture—not in one clean break, but in a series of emotional implosions that finally make the truth impossible to ignore.

In therapeutic language, this is a relational dynamic built on misattuned caregiving. Each partner is trying to meet the other's needs through a lens of their own pain. Owen wants Cristina to rescue him from his trauma by becoming what he imagines a partner should be. Cristina wants Owen to love her exactly as she is, without asking her to soften or shift. But neither model works, because neither has fully confronted what they are projecting onto the other. They are not healing each other. They are reenacting unresolved fears—Cristina's fear of being consumed, Owen's fear of being abandoned.

Their eventual separation is not just inevitable—it is merciful. For both of them. Because what Owen and Cristina show us, in the end, is that love without compatibility can become a cage. That you can love someone with your whole being and still need to walk away. That freedom is not always the absence of connection, but the clarity of letting go.

Their story does not end in bitterness. It ends in bittersweet recognition—that they mattered to each other, deeply, and that love can be real even when it is not sustainable. For Cristina, the exit becomes a return to self. For Owen, it becomes a reckoning with what he truly needs. And for the audience, it becomes a powerful reminder: sometimes, the most loving thing we can do is admit that love is not enough.

The Soldier's Return - Hypervigilance, Trauma, and Emotional Dysregulation

Owen Hunt arrives at Seattle Grace Hospital like a man still half in combat. His movements are sharp, his eyes wary, his emotional responses either tightly suppressed or violently uncontained. From the first moments on screen, he is marked by the invisible ink of war—trauma etched into his body language, into the way he holds his jaw, into the precision of his surgical technique that contrasts jarringly with the unpredictability of his emotional regulation. He is not just a surgeon. He is a soldier in transition, a man walking back into civilian life with the nervous system of someone still on the battlefield.

This matters because Owen's trauma is not just personal. It becomes relational. Every conversation, every moment of intimacy, every decision is filtered through a nervous system trained for threat detection. In psychological terms, Owen is a textbook example of post-traumatic hypervigilance. His body is always braced for danger, even when none is present. His tone can shift from gentle to explosive without warning. He doesn't intend to harm; he is responding to perceived instability, even when that instability is emotional rather than physical.

Cristina, who thrives on control, precision, and emotional clarity, is both intrigued and destabilized by Owen's presence. She is used to mastering the room. Owen enters not to be mastered, but to be understood—and he offers her something she has rarely encountered: emotional intensity. He is not afraid to feel. He is not afraid to declare. Their attraction ignites quickly, in part because Cristina is so rarely seen. Owen sees her. But what she doesn't realize yet is that being seen by someone who is emotionally volatile carries its own risks.

The psychological profile of Owen in his early seasons reflects symptoms consistent with complex trauma. His time in war has left him not only with PTSD but with a deeply disrupted attachment system. He wants closeness—

desperately—but fears the vulnerability it requires. He seeks emotional connection, yet becomes overwhelmed when that connection triggers his internal chaos. This creates a push-pull dynamic in his relationships, especially with Cristina. He leans in, only to pull away. He offers safety, then becomes the source of instability. He doesn't mean to hurt her. But hurt her he does, again and again, in ways that are shaped less by malice and more by a dysregulated nervous system searching for peace.

One of the most jarring early indicators of this is the scene where, mid-sleep, Owen chokes Cristina in a trauma-triggered flashback. It is horrifying, and the show does not attempt to sanitize it. But it also does not exploit it. What it reveals, instead, is the blurred line between past and present for those living with untreated trauma. Owen is not safe with himself, and therefore cannot be fully safe for someone else. Cristina, to her credit, does not retreat. She seeks to understand. But the psychological toll of being the emotional stabilizer for someone in that much pain begins to take its toll.

This becomes a defining feature of their dynamic: Cristina adjusting, accommodating, interpreting Owen's behavior through the lens of compassion. She wants to be strong enough to handle it. She wants to love him through it. But eventually, she begins to drown in it. Trauma, when unmanaged, becomes a third partner in a relationship—shaping decisions, distorting perceptions, rerouting conflict. Cristina begins to feel not just unseen, but erased. Her needs become secondary to Owen's regulation. Her ambitions, her clarity, her emotional independence—all are gradually compromised in the effort to maintain connection.

Owen, for his part, is trying. He is not emotionally negligent. He is emotionally exhausted. But in trauma psychology, good intentions do not negate impact. His unprocessed pain, his tendency to retreat into emotional control, and his bursts of anger or impulsivity make intimacy with him fragile. Cristina starts walking on eggshells—not in fear, but in fatigue. She becomes responsible not just for her own emotional needs, but for managing his unpredictability. This emotional labor becomes unsustainable.

In moments of calm, their love is evident. They have real tenderness, real humor, real desire. But the volatility lingers beneath the surface. And Owen's need for emotional anchoring becomes increasingly at odds with Cristina's need for autonomy. He wants connection to soothe his dysregulation. She wants space to maintain her clarity. Neither is wrong, but they are psychologically incompatible in their regulation styles. Owen regulates through closeness. Cristina regulates through distance. And each partner begins to experience the other as a source of stress rather than relief.

Owen's journey could have evolved differently if he had committed to serious trauma work—ongoing therapy, nervous system regulation, deep self-examination. But like many trauma survivors, he attempts to power through, to prove his strength through function rather than healing. He returns to surgery, to leadership, to love, without fully rebuilding the internal infrastructure that war dismantled. And so his trauma continues to bleed out, in moments of jealousy, outbursts, and controlling behavior—especially when he feels emotionally out of sync with Cristina.

Cristina's reaction is not coldness. It is protection. Her retreat is often misinterpreted as avoidance, but it is the behavior of someone trying to maintain psychic integrity in the face of someone else's emotional volatility. She is not indifferent to Owen's pain. But she cannot lose herself inside it. And as the relationship continues, she becomes increasingly aware that love alone cannot regulate another person's nervous system. Especially when that person will not take full responsibility for their own healing.

Their dynamic is a sobering reminder of how trauma, when left unprocessed, becomes a relational contagion. It changes not just how someone feels, but how they love, how they interpret conflict, and how they experience closeness. Owen does not abuse Cristina. But he destabilizes her, not through cruelty, but through inconsistency. And Cristina, for all her strength, begins to shrink. Not because she lacks will, but because the emotional cost of staying becomes too high.

Owen's trauma is real. His efforts are sincere. But sincerity is not the same as safety. And in relationships, safety is everything. Love cannot flourish in an emotional climate of confusion, volatility, or fear. It requires grounding. And Owen, though deeply loving, has not yet returned to ground.

The War at Home - Autonomy, Attachment, and the Motherhood Divide

For Owen Hunt and Cristina Yang, the battlefield was never only Owen's past. It was also their present—built not from gunfire and desert trauma, but from kitchen tables, hallway arguments, and the quiet ache of mutual incomprehension. As Owen fought for stability and Cristina fought for autonomy, their home life became the war zone. And the most volatile front of that war was the question of motherhood.

Owen's longing for children is neither shallow nor selfish. It is tethered to his identity, his values, and his conception of a meaningful life. He wants to raise a family, to create what he lost in war—a sense of permanence, legacy, and rootedness. This desire is not abstract. It is visceral. He sees fatherhood not only as a dream, but as a redemptive act. It would give shape to his post-war life, structure to his love, and perhaps even a sense of moral recovery. For him, parenting is not just a want—it is part of his healing narrative.

Cristina, in contrast, has always known who she is and what she does not want. She does not want children. She does not feel ambivalent, nor is she confused. Her clarity is not rooted in trauma, fear, or selfishness—it is rooted in identity. For Cristina, motherhood is not a dream deferred; it is a dream never dreamed. She does not experience a maternal pull. Her calling is surgical excellence, innovation, and professional legacy. Her purpose is the operating room, not the nursery. And this does not make her incomplete. It makes her whole—in her own way.

The tragedy of their relationship is not that one of them is wrong. It's that they are both right. Both are entitled to their desires. But those desires, placed side by side, are incompatible. And because neither can bend without breaking, the issue becomes less a conflict to resolve and more a truth to confront: they are fundamentally unaligned in their vision for life.

When Cristina becomes pregnant, it forces the question into the open. Her decision to terminate the pregnancy is immediate, unwavering, and psychologically coherent with who she has always been. But for Owen, it feels like a betrayal—not just of him, but of the life he had imagined with her. He cannot separate her choice from his pain. And in his reaction, we see the beginning of a deeper fracture—not about abortion itself, but about personhood, respect, and the limits of love.

Owen responds with rage, grief, and withdrawal. He lashes out, not because he doesn't understand, but because he cannot accept. Cristina, for her part, begins to feel not only misunderstood, but fundamentally unaccepted. The conflict isn't intellectual. It's existential. She is being asked to become someone she is not in order to preserve a relationship. And while she loves Owen, she cannot—will not—sacrifice her selfhood to do so.

Their arguments around this issue are some of the most emotionally volatile in the series. Owen accuses Cristina of selfishness. Cristina accuses Owen of trying to change her. And in these fights, we see the slow corrosion of mutual regard. Owen wants something that Cristina cannot give. Cristina wants to be loved for who she actually is—not a version edited for compatibility. Their love becomes a site of grief, because both begin to realize that staying together will cost them something essential.

In psychological terms, this is an attachment crisis. Owen's attachment style, already shaped by loss and trauma, moves toward anxious and controlling behaviors. He tries to hold the relationship together by holding Cristina tighter. He believes that if he can just convince her, appeal to her, she might change her mind. But what he fails to grasp is that her refusal is not stubbornness—it is a boundary rooted in authenticity. Cristina is not resisting Owen. She is protecting herself.

Cristina's attachment, on the other hand, becomes increasingly avoidant—not because she is afraid of intimacy, but because intimacy with Owen now feels coercive. She begins to withdraw emotionally, not out of punishment, but out of necessity. Each time Owen brings up children, or futures she never consented to, she pulls further inward. And what was once an intense, if unstable, connection begins to dissolve into silence and resignation.

The most haunting aspect of this divide is that neither partner is willing to become the villain. Cristina does not demonize Owen's longing for children. Owen does not question Cristina's brilliance or passion. They still admire each other. They still ache for each other. But their conversations grow colder, more circular. Love begins to buckle under the pressure of irreconcilable truth: to be together would require one of them to betray themselves.

This dynamic—where love exists but future compatibility does not—is among the most painful in adult relationships. It defies romantic logic. It violates the cultural script that says love should conquer all. And yet it is a deeply common experience: discovering that your person, your great love, cannot walk with you into the life you need to build.

As this tension deepens, both Owen and Cristina try to compromise. He pretends he might not need children. She pretends she might be able to give him one. But both are lying—to themselves and to each other. And in those lies, the relationship begins to rot. Love without truth is a performance. And performances eventually collapse under the weight of reality.

In time, Cristina stops pretending. She reclaims her clarity. She names, once and for all, that she does not want children and never will. It is not defiance—it is honesty. And for Owen, that honesty is devastating. He is not wrong to want what he wants. But wanting something deeply does not obligate someone else to give it to you. His grief is valid. But it cannot become a mandate.

Their separation is not a dramatic exit. It is an unraveling. A painful, quiet death of what might have been. And what remains is respect. Sorrow. And the kind of love that says: I see you, but I cannot follow you.

Exit Wounds - When Love Leaves a Scar Instead of a Bond

Not all departures are clean. Some leave behind a residue—an emotional imprint that shapes who you become, long after the relationship has ended. For Owen Hunt and Cristina Yang, their separation is not a single rupture but a series of exits, each one cutting a little deeper. The final parting does not occur in the heat of a fight or the cold of apathy, but in that hushed, haunted space where love no longer makes sense and staying would mean abandoning the self.

Their relationship had always been intense, erratic, and charged with contradictions. But as it nears its conclusion, that intensity begins to collapse under its own weight. There is a moment when even they seem to understand—perhaps not consciously, but somatically—that they are done. The battles have been fought. The terms have been drawn. What remains is no longer a life, but a loop: of unmet expectations, attempted compromises, and the slow erosion of intimacy. The love is still there, but it has curdled. And where there was once longing, now there is exhaustion.

Cristina's decision to leave Seattle is not impulsive. It is not reactive. It is the culmination of everything she has tried to preserve—her career, her clarity, her identity. Accepting the opportunity in Zurich is more than a professional step forward. It is an emotional emancipation. It is her way of reclaiming a self that had been increasingly buried under the weight of trying to belong to a life that wasn't hers. She does not leave because she stops loving Owen. She leaves because loving him has started to cost too much.

For Owen, her departure reopens every wound he has tried to keep closed. Abandonment, rejection, the fear that he is impossible to love for the long haul—it all comes rushing back. He is not only losing Cristina. He is losing the story he had written in his mind about what they would be. But this loss is not due to betrayal. It is due to honesty. And that is what makes it all the more painful.

In relationships where trauma and unmet need have shaped the emotional landscape, endings do not always come with clarity. They come with confusion, aching, and the compulsion to make sense of it all. Owen struggles to find that sense. He does not understand why love wasn't enough. He cannot locate where it all went wrong. But the truth is, it didn't go wrong. It simply reached the end of its capacity.

Psychologically, what Owen and Cristina go through is called a rupture of attachment that is not repaired. When bonds break without mutual understanding, the pain becomes unresolvable—not because closure is denied, but because it was never truly possible. They do not part with a shared language for what they endured. They part with parallel truths. Cristina leaves with clarity and direction. Owen remains with grief and questions.

There is a particular agony in watching someone walk away with purpose when you are still sitting in pain. For Owen, that is the final blow. He is left not only with heartbreak but with the sense that his deepest needs—stability, family, emotional intimacy—remain unmet. And yet, Cristina cannot be the one to meet them. To stay would be to compromise the very structure of her being. In the psychology of self-development, this is known as a boundary rupture: when staying in relationship requires the distortion of the self. Cristina chooses preservation over performance. And for Owen, that feels like loss, even if it is a form of mercy.

What remains between them is a kind of scar tissue. Not animosity. Not contempt. Just the ache of knowing that something once beautiful has become impossible. They will never be indifferent to each other. Their love story was too consuming, too formative. But what they shared now belongs to the past. And neither of them, despite their history, belongs in the other's future.

Exit wounds are rarely symmetrical. Cristina leaves stronger, more fully herself, having made a choice that aligns with her inner truth. Owen is left to reconstruct a future that does not include the woman he once believed would be his anchor. And yet, both carry something from the other. Cristina carries the lesson that even the strongest love cannot make you someone you are not. Owen carries the realization that love must include compatibility—not just feeling, but shared direction.

There is no tidy resolution. No grand reconciliation. Cristina walks away not with regret, but with reverence—for what they had, and for what she must now become. Owen stays behind with a life to rebuild. Their story ends not in failure, but in the recognition that love, when misaligned with purpose, can become a wound rather than a bond.

And yet, there is something sacred in the scar. It reminds them both that they were transformed by each other. And even if they could not last, they mattered. Not every great love is meant to be kept. Some are meant to break you open, show you who you are, and then let you go.

* * *

III

Trauma, Death, and the Cost of Caring

In Grey's Anatomy, trauma doesn't just happen—it lingers, rewires, and resurfaces. Plane crashes, mass shootings, addiction, anxiety, and unbearable grief shape the characters as much as love and ambition do. These chapters follow what happens when survival isn't the end of the story, when strong people unravel, and when healing is less about bouncing back and more about learning to live with the scars.

11

Plane Crashes, Shootings, and the Rewiring of the Brain

The Body Keeps the Score, and So Does the Show

Some shows entertain. Others provoke. *Grey's Anatomy* does both, but it also traumatizes—and not by accident. Over its long run, the series has woven catastrophic events into its DNA, using trauma not just as spectacle, but as a mechanism for character evolution. From mass shootings and deadly crashes to sudden deaths and surgical disasters, these moments are not simply plot twists—they are psychological disruptions. They tear at the neural, emotional, and relational fabric of the characters' lives, reshaping who they are and how they move through the world. If *Grey's Anatomy* has a thesis about trauma, it's this: survival changes you, and healing is rarely complete.

The series is relentless in its portrayal of high-intensity emergencies, but what sets it apart is how deeply it allows these events to reverberate. A shooting doesn't end when the bullets stop. A plane crash doesn't conclude with rescue. The trauma seeps into the characters' bodies, their relationships, their decisions. It lingers in silences, in compulsions, in the way hands shake before surgery or eyes scan a room for exits. Where most television resets after a tragedy, *Grey's Anatomy* accumulates. It builds a psychological record. It remembers.

Trauma, by definition, overwhelms the brain's ability to cope. It floods the nervous system, disrupts memory encoding, and alters how one processes time, safety, and self. In trauma theory, it is often said that the body keeps the score—a phrase popularized by Bessel van der Kolk to describe how unprocessed trauma lives in the muscles, in posture, in affect, long after the event itself. *Grey's Anatomy* understands this. It shows characters not just reacting, but rewiring. We see it in Arizona's phantom pain, in Meredith's silence after the drowning, in Cristina's detachment after the shooting. Trauma becomes character.

This chapter is not about episodic trauma—it's about cumulative psychological erosion. One event may start the process, but the cost continues to unfold. Meredith Grey survives drowning, a shooting, a plane crash, the death of her sister, the death of her husband. Each of these moments chips away at the part of her that believed life could be predictable. And the transformation is subtle but deep. She becomes less reactive, more pragmatic, and emotionally harder to reach. It isn't callousness. It's adaptation.

The same is true for Cristina Yang, whose detachment post-shooting is not coldness but a textbook trauma response. She dissociates, unable to operate, unable to speak about what happened. She becomes flat, mechanical. And when she eventually returns to surgery, it is not because she has healed—it is because she has found a way to re-enter her life, even if part of her stays frozen at the point of impact. This is the slow, complex nature of recovery: not a return to normal, but the construction of a new normal that accounts for what has been lost.

The show does not always depict trauma with perfect clinical accuracy. There are moments when recovery seems too swift, or when symptoms conveniently recede for narrative pacing. But overall, it remains unusually attuned to the psychological toll of high-stakes medicine and the cumulative burden of personal tragedy. Trauma in *Grey's Anatomy* isn't a backdrop—it's a co-author of identity.

The plane crash is one of the most vividly depicted traumatic events in the series, not just for its horror but for its aftermath. Arizona loses a leg. Lexie dies. Mark dies. Cristina shuts down. Meredith becomes more armored. Each character who survives does so in body, but not in mind. The physical injuries are immediate; the psychological ones are chronic. This is what trauma does—it outlasts the visible. And the show, in its best moments, refuses to tidy that up.

Acute trauma is often followed by a period of emotional muting—characters move through their days with a kind of surreal detachment, mirroring the real-life symptom of dissociation. This is especially apparent in episodes following mass trauma events. The silence is as telling as the screams. We watch characters sit in hallways, stare at walls, fail to answer simple questions. These moments are subtle but devastating. They reflect the lived experience of trauma not just as pain, but as dislocation. The body is here. The mind is elsewhere.

The show also explores survival guilt with striking consistency. After the shooting, after the crash, after every major loss, someone is left asking: why not me? This question plagues survivors. It interrupts sleep, erodes confidence, and festers quietly in professional environments where appearing competent is essential. For surgeons especially, whose identities are built around control and mastery, trauma introduces a brutal contradiction. You survived, but you couldn't save them. You're alive, but you're not whole. You're back at work, but you're not the same.

There is a psychological realism in how characters are shown returning to the hospital too soon, throwing themselves into surgery, overcompensating with confidence, or emotionally numbing out. These are all trauma adaptations. They don't mean a person is "fine"—they mean the system is trying to stabilize in any way it can. Owen Hunt's hair-trigger anger. April Kepner's emotional shutdown. Jo Wilson's delayed breakdown. These responses aren't plot devices. They're trauma behaviors. And the show, at its best, honors their complexity.

What's especially poignant is how *Grey's Anatomy* portrays trauma recovery not as triumph, but as accommodation. Some characters find healing through purpose—Cristina in Zurich, April in Jordan, Meredith in continued practice.

Others struggle to ever feel fully safe again. But nearly all of them learn to live alongside what happened, rather than overcome it. This is a subtle but powerful shift. In trauma psychology, recovery doesn't mean forgetting—it means integration. It means building a life where the trauma is no longer running the show, but still has a seat at the table.

In the chapters ahead, we'll explore how these traumatic events are used both as narrative accelerants and psychological case studies. The goal is not just to catalog the tragedies, but to understand what they reveal about human adaptation, memory, resilience, and loss. Because in *Grey's Anatomy*, trauma isn't just a detour—it's the path. The characters don't become who they are despite what they've suffered. They become who they are because of it.

Trauma Events as Narrative Devices and Psychological Mirrors

Trauma, when it appears in a television series, often functions as spectacle. It disrupts the narrative, heightens the stakes, and pulls characters into chaos for a few episodes before life neatly resumes. But *Grey's Anatomy* refuses that simplicity. Instead, trauma operates as both catalyst and mirror—a device that not only propels the plot but reveals the deepest truths about the characters involved. The disasters in this show are never just events. They are diagnostic tools. They expose vulnerabilities, histories, coping mechanisms, and the psychological scaffolding that either holds or collapses under pressure.

The hospital shooting, the plane crash, the ferry accident, the bomb in the body cavity, the tunnel collapse, the ambulance explosion—these are not isolated dramas. They are extensions of the characters' internal states. When trauma erupts in the world around them, what surfaces is who they really are: how they regulate fear, how they hold onto control, who they protect, and who they become when the rules vanish. Each disaster acts like a psychological litmus test. Do you freeze or fight? Do you dissociate or rise? Do you let yourself feel, or do you shut down?

Meredith Grey, for instance, is often centered in these crises, not just as a protagonist, but as a case study in psychological endurance. Her trauma arc is cumulative. She nearly drowns. She watches Derek shot in front of her. She survives a plane crash. She is physically attacked by a patient. Each time, her body survives, but something internal shifts. Over time, Meredith becomes more stoic, more pragmatic, harder to penetrate emotionally. The show doesn't portray this as strength or weakness—it portrays it as consequence. She adapts, yes, but adaptation is not always healing. It is sometimes armor.

The narrative use of trauma to accelerate character development is not new, but what *Grey's Anatomy* does differently is insist on aftermath. Cristina Yang's complete emotional shutdown after the hospital shooting is one of the most psychologically grounded responses in the series. Her inability to operate, to engage, or to explain her silence is not dramatized for effect—it is treated as a clinical reality. She is not afraid of surgery; she is no longer emotionally accessible to it. Her detachment is not rejection. It is her body protecting itself from reliving what it cannot yet process. The trauma isn't over. It's just gone internal.

By using trauma as a recurring structural device, the show also challenges the viewer to reconsider who is "strong" and who is "fragile." Owen Hunt, a war-hardened trauma surgeon, unravels in civilian life. Arizona Robbins, cheerful and composed, breaks after losing her leg. April Kepner, a deeply religious woman with a core of moral steel, is shattered by the death of her child. Strength is shown to be context-dependent. The same character who can hold steady in a war zone may collapse under the weight of domestic grief. The show underscores that trauma is not just about what happens—it's about what it disrupts in you.

This becomes especially clear when characters exhibit different responses to the same event. After the plane crash, Arizona responds with anger, depression, and emotional volatility. Cristina shuts down entirely, using work and logic to distance herself from feeling. Meredith goes into hyper-function mode, attempting to hold others together while emotionally compartmentalizing. The show does not offer a single narrative of recovery because there is no such thing. Instead, it depicts trauma as something that hits the same event into different people like stones thrown into separate lakes—each one rippling in its own unpredictable pattern.

Even secondary characters are given space to embody these psychological truths. Jo Wilson's reaction to domestic abuse, for example, is not portrayed as weakness but as delayed reckoning. She spends years functioning well, even thriving, until a confrontation with her past shatters the illusion of normalcy. Trauma, *Grey's Anatomy* reminds us, doesn't always show up on time. It can lie dormant, only to be triggered years later by a word, a face, a situation too familiar.

Trauma events in the show are also used to mirror unresolved personal conflict. The hospital shooting, for example, is not just an act of random violence—it is tied directly to the institutional breakdown, moral dilemmas, and feelings of helplessness that had been simmering under the surface for many episodes. The shooter isn't simply a villain. He is a grieving man whose wife died under what he perceives as negligent care. His pain, while expressed violently and unforgivably, is rooted in loss. This framing complicates the narrative, forcing both characters and audience to confront uncomfortable questions about blame, responsibility, and the limits of empathy.

In this way, *Grey's Anatomy* refuses to let trauma be clean. It uses it to examine the messy, non-linear nature of human psychology. Characters are not given epiphanies wrapped in ribbon. They flail. They regress. They get stronger, only to break again. And the audience is invited not to judge, but to witness—something that mirrors the therapeutic process itself.

The frequency of catastrophic events also serves another function: it calls into question the mythology of control. These are some of the best-trained doctors in the world. They perform miracles on the regular. And yet, when the ground splits open, when the bullets start flying, when the plane goes down—they are powerless. The show subtly but consistently challenges the fantasy of mastery that medicine often relies on. It reminds viewers, and the characters themselves, that control is an illusion, and that being a professional does not inoculate you from being human.

Even more striking is how trauma often shifts the moral center of the characters. After surviving a life-or-death event, priorities change. Marriages are questioned. Careers are rerouted. Friendships are reevaluated. Trauma is not just a narrative detour—it is a point of divergence. Who you were before cannot be retrieved. A new self must emerge. And sometimes, that emergence is liberating. Other times, it is unbearable.

In *Grey's Anatomy*, trauma is not just content. It is transformation. The show teaches that the cost of survival is not always visible. It may show up later, in the way a character avoids eye contact, or cannot sleep, or overcompensates with confidence. These subtleties are part of the show's power. It doesn't just dramatize trauma. It pays attention to how trauma lives on.

Dissociation, Survival Guilt, and the Aftermath of Acute Horror

In the immediate aftermath of catastrophe, something goes quiet inside the mind. For many of the doctors at Seattle Grace, trauma doesn't scream—it stuns. One of the most consistent psychological truths depicted in *Grey's Anatomy* is that the body often survives what the psyche cannot yet absorb. And what follows in the wake of crisis isn't always grief, anger, or even fear—it is blankness. Disconnection. A sudden sense of unreality. This is dissociation, and the series portrays it with unnerving accuracy.

Cristina Yang's response to the hospital shooting is perhaps the show's most acute example. After being forced to operate on Derek at gunpoint while surrounded by death and chaos, she collapses inward. She returns to work but is not present. Her movements are mechanical. Her voice loses affect. She avoids eye contact. She cannot perform surgery. What we witness is not drama. It is textbook psychological shutdown. In the face of overwhelming threat, Cristina's system has done what trauma-exposed bodies often do—it has gone offline. Not in terms of functionality, but in terms of emotional integration. Her cognition continues. Her body functions. But her emotional processing is suspended.

Dissociation is not a weakness—it is a survival mechanism. When the nervous system is flooded beyond capacity, it detaches from sensory and emotional experience. This protects the individual in the short term, but over time, creates a fractured relationship with one's own memory, identity, and emotions. Cristina's detachment, her inability to connect with Owen, her hyper-rationality, all reflect a nervous system in self-preservation mode. She is not choosing to shut down. Her brain is keeping her safe in the only way it knows how.

Survival guilt—also known as survivor's guilt—is another thread that runs through the show's trauma arcs. This is the paradoxical suffering of those who live through events that kill others. Rather than feeling grateful, survivors often feel ashamed, unworthy, or emotionally paralyzed by the fact that they walked away while others did not. Meredith, after the ferry crash, finds herself silently haunted by the faces of those she could not save. Arizona, after the plane crash, not only grapples with her physical loss but with the fact that Mark and Lexie died and she did not. Her fury, her withdrawal, her volatility—these are not mere mood swings. They are expressions of complex trauma laced with guilt.

Jackson Avery, after the bus explosion that kills a child, shows another variation. He throws himself into work, doubles down on control, and becomes emotionally unreachable to those around him. This compulsive competence is not resilience—it is avoidance dressed as mastery. Trauma psychologists recognize this as a form of high-functioning dissociation: the outward presentation of calm hiding an internal world of unrest. Jackson is not okay. But he is succeeding. And in medicine, that distinction often goes unnoticed.

The show is also unflinching in its portrayal of how acute horror—events that are sudden, violent, and destabilizing—can permanently rewire relational dynamics. After the shooting, Meredith and Derek grow closer, but not because they have processed the trauma together. It is because they have survived something that few others understand. Their bond becomes fused with memory, terror, and the fragility of life. This kind of trauma-bonding is intense, but also unstable. It can produce deep intimacy, but it can also create emotional volatility, especially when the unspoken pain becomes too heavy to carry.

In contrast, Cristina and Owen struggle in the wake of trauma. His instinct is to move closer. Hers is to pull away. These opposite responses create friction, not because they don't care for each other, but because they are neurologically out of sync. Owen wants to feel. Cristina wants to forget. And without a shared language for their pain, they begin to view each other not as sources of comfort, but as reminders of what they are trying to escape.

Another striking portrayal of dissociation comes in Meredith's storyline after the drowning. In the episodes that follow, she is subdued, measured, almost eerily calm. Her jokes are flatter. Her energy is reduced. She doesn't talk about what happened. This isn't repression. It's dissociation. The event has fractured her sense of continuity. She is alive, but not fully reconnected with the self who went under. For viewers unfamiliar with trauma psychology, it may look like detachment. But for those who know the symptoms, it is a chillingly accurate representation of what it means to walk through life not fully inside yourself.

Grey's Anatomy also shows how trauma lingers in the body long after the mind thinks it's over. Arizona's phantom pain. Derek's hand tremor. Meredith's miscarriage. These physical symptoms are not isolated. They are somatic expressions of internal chaos. The body, long after the conscious mind moves on, continues to speak. And often, it speaks in symptoms.

What's notable is that the show does not always resolve these traumas. There are no perfect therapy arcs. Some characters get better. Some don't. Some grow. Some unravel. Some do both, in cycles. This is realism. Because trauma recovery is not a straight line. It loops, it retreats, it flares without warning. A character might appear fine for a season, then suddenly collapse emotionally over a minor trigger. Viewers who have lived through trauma recognize this rhythm. It is not dysfunction. It is the long shadow of horror still moving through the nervous system.

The absence of resolution also speaks to another truth: not all pain finds language. Some stays locked in the body, in behavior, in the inability to be touched or the compulsion to work. Cristina may never talk about what the shooting did to her. April may never fully articulate what it meant to lose her son. But the show does not require them to confess in order to validate their experience. It lets the trauma be visible in how they walk, speak, distance, and engage. In this, it offers viewers something rare: psychological honesty without demand for performance.

In the medical world, emotional containment is often seen as professionalism. Surgeons are expected to compartmentalize, to function in the face of horror, to cut without flinching. *Grey's Anatomy* disrupts that myth. It shows what that containment costs. How it fractures intimacy, derails careers, fuels addiction, isolates colleagues. It shows that even the most brilliant minds cannot escape the human need to feel, and the human tendency to shut down when feeling becomes too much.

Acute horror is not a single event. It is a doorway into a different internal landscape. And in *Grey's Anatomy*, those doorways never fully close. Characters walk through them and emerge changed—not always broken, but never the same.

From Shattered to Scarred – What Recovery Looks Like in Real Time

Trauma rarely resolves in a single epiphany. More often, it lingers like a low-grade fever—dull, persistent, altering the rhythm of everyday life. In *Grey's Anatomy*, recovery is not cinematic. It doesn't come in the form of a single powerful speech or a breakthrough therapy session. It unfolds in slow, uneven steps—in the way a character takes off their coat before entering a room, how long they hesitate before returning to the OR, how their voice falters when recalling a name. This is what trauma recovery looks like in real time—not resolution, but adaptation.

Cristina Yang's arc after the hospital shooting is a masterclass in nonlinear recovery. At first, she disappears into silence. Then she returns to work, but with robotic detachment. Her engagement to Owen proceeds, but her presence is dulled. It's not until she finds herself operating during a high-stakes crisis that something begins to return. But what comes back is not who she was—it is a new version of herself, forged in the crucible of survival. Recovery, for Cristina, is not about reclaiming a past self. It's about integrating the fractured parts into something coherent enough to move forward.

This is a central principle in trauma psychology: post-traumatic growth is not about forgetting the pain—it's about creating meaning around it. For many of the show's characters, healing begins only when they stop trying to go back to "normal." Arizona, after losing her leg, doesn't recover by regaining cheer. She recovers by learning to live in a body that no longer feels like hers, by confronting her anger, her grief, and her fractured identity. The prosthetic is not her biggest challenge. The real work is internal—learning to trust herself again, to be touched again, to feel something other than rage or shame.

Jo Wilson's delayed breakdown is another striking example of trauma resurfacing on its own timetable. After functioning for years with buried abuse, her collapse isn't triggered by a major event, but by proximity to her past—her birth mother, her origin story. This mirrors what trauma experts refer to as delayed onset PTSD, where symptoms remain dormant until something in the environment cracks the container. Jo's descent is rapid, but her recovery is painstaking—marked not by dramatic declarations, but by quietly seeking help, taking a leave of absence, telling the truth about what she carries.

Even Meredith, so often the picture of functional trauma, has moments where the mask slips. Her decision to take risks, her streaks of emotional withdrawal, her aversion to loss—all reflect ongoing adaptation. She doesn't collapse, but she doesn't escape unscathed. Her resilience is real, but it comes at a cost: emotional containment, boundaries that harden, and a measured coldness that sometimes reads as strength but is often a shield.

Trauma recovery in the show is also relational. No one heals in isolation. But the support characters receive is rarely clean or perfectly timed. Owen tries to help Cristina, but his own dysregulation interferes. Callie tries to reach Arizona, but her support is complicated by her own sense of betrayal. April finds purpose in war medicine, but it isolates her further from Jackson. These mismatches underscore a psychological truth: support doesn't always mean connection. You can have people who care and still feel profoundly alone in your healing. That loneliness, too, is part of the recovery process.

What *Grey's Anatomy* portrays with unusual grace is the way trauma recovery often includes regression. A character might seem fine, then unravel suddenly. Progress is followed by setbacks. This ebb and flow is not a flaw—it is the rhythm of trauma healing. One day the hands are steady. The next, they shake. One moment the heart is open. The next, it slams shut. And each of these shifts reflects the nervous system learning, failing, adjusting.

The show also captures the exhaustion that accompanies long-term trauma work. Characters don't just heal—they get tired of healing. They get tired of trying to be okay. Amelia's struggle with sobriety and grief reflects this perfectly. Her moments of strength are often interrupted by collapse. And rather than framing this as weakness, the show allows us to see it as part of the cost of survival. Being okay is a job. And some days, the job is too big.

For some characters, trauma becomes the context through which they find clarity. April, shattered by the death of her son, finds meaning in medicine practiced under fire. Cristina, broken by systems and relationships, finds selfhood in Switzerland. These arcs suggest that trauma does not just destroy—it reveals. It strips away what no longer fits. It exposes what was always fragile. And in doing so, it makes room for new versions of self to emerge. This is not redemption. It is reconstitution.

Notably, the show never promises that healing makes people better. Sometimes it just makes them more honest. Miranda Bailey's panic attacks don't make her a weaker leader. They make her more fully human. Richard Webber's sobriety does not erase his regrets. It teaches him to live with them. Meredith doesn't become softer. She becomes sharper. The trauma doesn't vanish. But it is carried with dignity.

What we see in *Grey's Anatomy* is not a parade of broken people fixed by love or therapy. We see layered, intelligent, emotionally complex individuals learning to carry what they cannot drop. And that, in itself, is the show's greatest psychological insight: healing is not a destination. It's a practice. It's a recalibration of self in response to what has been endured.

From shattered to scarred is not a fall from grace. It is the return to self, with the wounds visible, the losses counted, and the soul still—somehow—intact.

* * *

12

The Psychology of Grief in Grey's Anatomy

Every Death Left a Mark

In *Grey's Anatomy*, death is not an interruption. It's a constant. Characters fall in love, make impossible decisions, perform miracles—and then they lose each other. Some are taken by disease, others by trauma, and some vanish with a shocking suddenness that leaves no time to prepare. But unlike most medical dramas, where the dead are mourned briefly before the next patient rolls in, *Grey's Anatomy* sits with grief. It lets loss reshape the living. And in doing so, it offers one of television's most complex portraits of what grief actually looks like—not in theory, but in practice.

Death in this series is never just about who is gone. It's about who's left behind. And the show rarely lets those left behind return to life untouched. There is no easy closure. No reset button. Instead, grief becomes part of the character's ongoing identity. Mark's death changes Callie's emotional center of gravity. Lexie's absence haunts Meredith for seasons. George's loss shatters Bailey's sense of safety. Derek's death forces Meredith to reconsider everything she thought was true about love, permanence, and what it means to raise children alone. These aren't isolated story arcs. They are psychological through-lines that echo long after the funeral fades from the screen.

The emotional realism with which the show handles grief stands in contrast to television's usual impulse to move on. In *Grey's Anatomy*, grief isn't something to "get over." It is something to be lived with, something that reemerges in different forms—anger, withdrawal, silence, compulsive busyness, numbness, overfunctioning, or a single breakdown years later. There are no neatly wrapped resolutions. A death that occurred in Season 5 might resurface emotionally in Season 11. And this is exactly how grief works in the real world: it loops, it flares, it disappears, and it returns.

Grief is also portrayed through its complexity. Not all grief in the series is noble or poetic. Sometimes it's messy. Petty. Even destructive. Jackson and April's agony after losing their baby is not marked by gentle mourning—it is marked by recrimination, escape, and spiritual collapse. Cristina grieves her lost friendships and futures with a detachment that borders on disassociation. Meredith grieves in fragments—often working through someone else's trauma before acknowledging her own. And all of it is real. The show recognizes that people don't grieve in the same ways, or even on the same timelines. They grieve in the languages they know—work, sarcasm, faith, sex, silence.

Some of the most emotionally devastating deaths in the series come with little warning. George O'Malley's demise is so abrupt, so jarring, that even the characters can't process it in real time. Their reactions mirror those of trauma psychologists observing acute shock: denial, confusion, delayed collapse. The death of Lexie Grey is cruel in its abruptness. One moment she is alive and hopeful. The next, she is crushed beneath the wreckage of a plane. And in that violence, we see how suddenly a life can be rewritten—and how slowly the living adapt to the rewrite.

But the grief doesn't stop with major characters. The show gives emotional weight to countless smaller losses: patients who couldn't be saved, parents who outlived their children, strangers who died anonymously but left behind people who were never shown onscreen. There's a reverence in how the show handles death, even when the person dying is barely known to us. The weight is never just in the event. It's in the people who must keep moving after it.

This approach also challenges cultural myths around strength and emotional regulation. In many professions, especially in medicine, grief is considered a private matter—something to be compartmentalized, managed, or ideally, ignored. But *Grey's Anatomy* shows what happens when that grief is swallowed instead of expressed. Bailey's collapse after losing her patient, Webber's retreat into addiction after Adele's death, Arizona's cold fury after the crash—these are not failures. They are the body and mind trying to metabolize pain in systems that were never meant to absorb this much loss.

What the series ultimately offers is not a model of grief that resolves, but one that integrates. The people who die remain part of the living. They return in dreams, in conversations, in choices that would have gone differently if that person were still alive. This is not romanticization. It is psychological truth. The dead don't vanish from our minds simply because the plot has moved on. They become part of the internal landscape—ghosts, not in the literal sense, but in the way they influence who we become.

Every death in the show is a hinge. After it, something closes. Something else opens. And the characters—much like the viewers—must find a way to keep going. Not with closure, but with coexistence. With the memories that hurt and heal in the same breath. With the moments when someone turns to speak and remembers that the person they're reaching for is no longer there.

This is the emotional intelligence of *Grey's Anatomy*. It does not reduce grief to performance. It gives it space. And in that space, it tells a deeper truth: grief is not an interruption of life. It is part of it. It doesn't end when the tears stop. It ends when love ends. And for the doctors of Seattle Grace, that love never does.

Lexie, Mark, George, Derek – The Spectrum of Grief Responses

There is no single shape grief takes in *Grey's Anatomy.* The deaths of Lexie Grey, Mark Sloan, George O'Malley, and Derek Shepherd offer four radically different emotional aftermaths—not just in who died or how, but in what was left behind. Each loss invites a different style of mourning, a different psychological imprint, a different grief pattern shaped by identity, circumstance, and the nature of the relationships that were cut short. In this, the show moves beyond mere sadness. It becomes a study in the many faces of grief—how it lands, who it transforms, and what it asks of the people still standing.

Lexie's death is one of the most abrupt and unjust in the series. Trapped beneath the wreckage of the downed plane, she suffers alone, with only a few final moments of connection before she's gone. The grief that follows is equally fragmented. There is no funeral. No communal ritual. Only silence, shock, and the staggering weight of what might have been. Meredith, Lexie's half-sister, does not collapse outwardly. Instead, she hardens. Her grief takes the form of protective armor—she becomes sharper, more efficient, less open. There is no catharsis, only control. She keeps moving because stopping might mean breaking.

This is a common trauma-adjacent grief response: what psychologists call "instrumental mourning." The mourner focuses on doing—working, managing, controlling—instead of feeling. It's not denial. It's a way to keep functioning when emotion feels like too much. Meredith doesn't suppress her pain. She channels it. But in doing so, she becomes increasingly closed to emotional spontaneity. Love becomes more cautious. Trust more conditional. And underneath her surgical precision is the unspoken ache of a sister never properly mourned.

Mark Sloan's death comes shortly after Lexie's, and with it arrives a different kind of grief: one rooted in complexity. Mark was not universally beloved. He was charming, promiscuous, flawed, occasionally selfish. But in his later seasons, he evolved—becoming a devoted father, a sincere friend, and someone whose love for Lexie grew into something selfless. His death, therefore, stings not just because he died, but because he died *ready.* Ready to be the man he had finally become. This loss reverberates differently among the characters. Callie grieves a partner in co-parenting. Derek grieves a brother-in-arms. Jackson grieves a mentor. The grief is layered, less about the tragedy of sudden loss and more about the tragedy of potential unrealized.

Mark's death also brings up what is often overlooked in grief literature—secondary losses. For Callie, it is not just Mark she loses. She loses the family structure they had built, the sense of stability they shared in raising Sofia. Secondary losses often complicate mourning. You're grieving not just a person, but the entire life that was built around them. The show reflects this in the quiet moments—Callie brushing Sofia's hair alone, Jackson walking past Mark's old OR, Meredith looking over at the place where Lexie once stood. These gestures speak volumes. Grief is not always about crying. Sometimes it's about absence.

George O'Malley's death is marked by suddenness and distortion. He dies heroically, saving a stranger, but the way his death is revealed—unrecognizable in the hospital bed, his identity discovered only when he traces "007" into Meredith's palm—adds a layer of horror that distorts the mourning process. His friends grieve in disbelief. They talk about him as if he might still walk in the door. Their reactions are disjointed, incongruent. Izzie, already on the brink of death herself, sees him in a hallucination. Meredith stares into space. Bailey, who once saw him as a protégé, breaks down not in front of others, but in private.

This is the grief of acute shock, where the mind has not caught up to reality. It's a form of complicated mourning, where the suddenness of the death and the surreal nature of its unfolding interrupt emotional processing. Viewers may notice the delay in grief expression—episodes pass before the full weight settles in. This is psychologically true. Sudden death often creates a lag between fact and feeling. The body registers the loss before the mind does. George's friends can still laugh at a memory of him even as they sit in funeral clothes. That juxtaposition is not a failure of feeling—it is the mind protecting itself.

And then there is Derek. His death is the one that breaks something open—not just in Meredith, but in the tone of the show. Derek was not just a character. He was an anchor—for the hospital, for the love story, for the very structure of the narrative. His loss reorients the emotional landscape entirely. Meredith's grief is vast, but not immediately dramatic. She withdraws, disappears, has her third child in secret. When she returns, she does not speak of Derek in sentimental terms. She does not rehash their romance. She lives in the absence. Her grief becomes embedded in her tone, her pace, her gaze.

This is the grief of identity upheaval. When a partner dies, it's not just their absence that hurts—it's the collapse of the shared life, the disorientation of being singular again after being part of a we. Meredith becomes more pragmatic, more inward. The show resists the temptation to make her collapse in a heap. Instead, it offers the quiet, sustained portrait of a woman rebuilding a self without her other half. She does not idealize Derek. She does not seek to replace him. Her love becomes memory, and her grief becomes structure.

What these four deaths show us—Lexie, Mark, George, and Derek—is that grief is not a singular emotion, but a psychological condition. It reorders meaning. It alters identity. It shifts how people connect, how they perform, how they dream. Each character's response is different, not just because of who they are, but because of who they lost, how they lost them, and what remained afterward.

Grief is not the event. It is the aftermath. And in *Grey's Anatomy*, the aftermath is never forgotten. It becomes part of the storyline, part of the dialogue, part of the body language. Every loss leaves its fingerprint. Every silence is a scar.

Complicated, Delayed, and Disenfranchised Grief

Not all grief is allowed to be visible. Not all pain is legible to others. Some grief gets misread as dysfunction, overreaction, or avoidance. Some never even gets acknowledged. In the world of *Grey's Anatomy*, where professional poise is often mistaken for emotional stability, characters frequently carry silent burdens—grief that doesn't follow the expected timeline, doesn't look the way others think it should, or doesn't have the social permission to be expressed at all. These are the forms of mourning that psychology calls complicated, delayed, and disenfranchised grief. And the series doesn't just depict them—it lives in them.

Complicated grief is prolonged, intense, and emotionally disruptive. It's the kind of sorrow that doesn't soften over time, but calcifies. It interrupts functioning, distorts identity, and embeds itself into daily life. April Kepner, after the loss of her infant son Samuel, becomes a vessel for this kind of grief. Her devastation is not contained by tears or rituals. It is spiritual. It shatters her entire worldview. She leaves her husband, leaves her hospital, throws herself into trauma medicine in a war zone. And while some might read this as noble escape, it is also classic avoidance through overfunctioning. She cannot sit still long enough to feel what the silence would say.

April's grief is complicated because it is unresolvable. The loss of a child violates the natural order. It does not yield to meaning-making, and for someone whose faith was once her anchor, the event causes a spiritual and existential fracture. This is not grief that heals. It's grief that must be integrated into a new self. Her return home is tentative, not triumphant. Her ability to reconnect with Jackson is cautious, conditional. And even when her life stabilizes again, the ache of Samuel's absence never fully leaves. Nor should it. Some griefs are permanent.

Delayed grief, by contrast, often masquerades as resilience. It happens when a person appears to be coping well, functioning, even thriving—until something seemingly unrelated reactivates the original loss. Jo Wilson exemplifies this in her backstory. For years, she presents as competent, assertive, emotionally steady, despite a history of abandonment, homelessness, and abuse. But when she begins to confront her past—her biological mother, the truth about her birth—her long-buried grief erupts. It doesn't arrive politely. It crashes into her life, collapsing her emotional balance.

This is not regression. It's delayed processing. Trauma specialists understand that when survival requires emotional distance, the grief waits. It doesn't go away. It waits until the nervous system is safe enough to release it. Jo's collapse doesn't mean she's broken. It means she's finally safe enough to fall apart. And when she does, her grief doesn't just come from the past—it attaches itself to the present. To her marriage. To her sense of worth. To her fear that she's unlovable. This is what delayed grief does—it doesn't whisper. It roars.

And then there's disenfranchised grief—the kind that society does not validate. In *Grey's Anatomy*, this often shows up in the margins. It's the grief of a friendship rather than a romance, a patient rather than a peer. When Heather Brooks dies—a character with less screen time, fewer connections—her death doesn't receive the emotional weight of others. But Shane Ross, who was with her when she died and arguably contributed to the conditions that led to her death, spirals into a guilt-laced grief that no one else seems to share. His sorrow is private, isolated. He's not offered the same space to mourn. And this isolation accelerates his emotional deterioration.

Disenfranchised grief also appears in the quieter losses: Arizona grieving the dream of future children after her amputation, Webber grieving Adele even before she dies as Alzheimer's steals her piece by piece, Cristina grieving the version of herself she gave up to fit into Owen's life. These griefs are not always about death. They are about identity, about futures foreclosed, about losses that don't come with condolences. In clinical language, these are ambiguous losses—griefs that don't have clear rituals or public acknowledgment. The show gives them room to breathe, even if the characters don't always have words for them.

What unites these grief experiences is not their cause but their complexity. They don't follow stages. They don't resolve on schedule. They aren't clean. And *Grey's Anatomy*, unlike many shows, doesn't rush them. It lets them linger. It lets them hurt. It shows characters avoiding funerals, skipping therapy, or refusing to talk. And instead of judging these choices, it presents them as human. It understands that grief isn't a moral test. It's an emotional reckoning.

There's a moment when Meredith tells a patient that "grief comes in waves," and it's one of the show's most enduring metaphors. Sometimes you're standing on the shore. Sometimes you're underwater. Sometimes it recedes, and you think you're fine—until it hits you again. The show captures this rhythm not just in what characters say, but in what they don't. In the pauses. In the music swells. In the way a character stares into the middle distance as someone else talks about love or loss.

Grief, in *Grey's Anatomy*, is often what's left unsaid. It's in the scenes after the scene. The way someone picks up a coffee mug that used to belong to a friend. The way they hesitate before entering a familiar room. The way they avoid saying a name. These are not narrative filler. They are the texture of mourning. And they remind us that loss is not an event—it is an atmosphere.

Holding the Dead While Living Forward - Ritual, Memory, and Adaptation

In *Grey's Anatomy*, the dead don't disappear. They linger—not in ghostly visions or dream sequences, though those exist—but in behavior, silence, and the quiet rituals that help the living carry on. The show doesn't treat death as the end of a storyline. It treats it as the beginning of a new internal reality for those left behind. Grief doesn't get buried. It gets folded into the rhythm of daily life. And in that choice, the series reflects one of the most emotionally intelligent truths about loss: moving forward doesn't mean letting go—it means learning how to hold what's gone while continuing to live.

This holding is often ritualistic, even when unspoken. Meredith visits Derek's ferry. Bailey touches George's locker. Callie refers to Mark in decisions about Sofia. These moments are not framed with melodrama. They arrive naturally, woven into the characters' environments, suggesting that grief lives in place as much as in memory. The hospital itself becomes a mausoleum of sorts, housing the echoes of those who've walked its halls. It is haunted, not by ghosts, but by presence—what clinicians might call "continuing bonds," a grief theory that suggests we don't lose the dead, we carry them with us.

Traditional grief models emphasized detachment: say goodbye, gain closure, move on. But more recent psychological frameworks validate what *Grey's Anatomy* has illustrated for years—that healing doesn't require severing. It requires integration. Meredith does not forget Derek. She builds a life where his absence becomes a fact, not a wound. Her love for him doesn't vanish when she finds new connection. It stays, tucked into the architecture of who she is.

Adaptation, in this context, doesn't look like overcoming. It looks like adjustment. Bailey returns to surgery after George's death not because she's ready, but because she's needed. She adapts by anchoring herself in the work, a ritual that provides control and clarity in the face of emotional chaos. Cristina adapts by leaving, by reclaiming herself in an entirely new environment. Jackson adapts by throwing himself into his legacy and redefining what it means to do good. Everyone adapts in their own way, and none of these ways are complete. They are partial, cyclical, deeply human.

Rituals of grief in the show are sometimes subtle. The lighting of a candle, the revisiting of a voicemail, the quiet act of saying someone's name. Other times they are formal: memorials, plaques, tributes. But what binds them all is intention. Grief is given time, space, and shape. The dead are remembered not only in sorrow but in action. The choices the living make become rituals of remembrance. Meredith's research. Richard's mentorship. Bailey's mentorship. April's medical missions. All of it says: I carry you with me.

Memory is not always accurate in grief. The show captures this too. The dead are sometimes idealized, sometimes resented. Meredith remembers Derek with longing, but also with anger. Callie remembers Mark as generous and infuriating in equal measure. Webber recalls Adele with devotion, but also guilt. These are not contradictions. They are emotionally honest recollections of real relationships. Memory in grief is fluid—colored by emotion, distorted by time, reshaped by need.

The complexity of remembering is perhaps most visible in how the characters handle anniversaries and triggers. Certain dates, locations, and smells bring everything back. Meredith on the beach. Owen in the ambulance. Arizona boarding a plane. These aren't just callbacks for the audience—they are psychological markers. Triggers that show how thin the boundary can be between now and then, between healing and hurting. The show respects these moments. It doesn't pathologize them. It lets them be real.

Grey's Anatomy also shows how grief is held communally. There are losses that fracture the group—like the plane crash—and ones that draw them together. When Derek dies, the hospital stands still. When George dies, the core cast is altered. In these moments, ritual becomes not only personal but collective. Grief becomes a unifying language, even when it isolates the individuals within it.

But perhaps the most emotionally resonant aspect of grief in the show is how it quietly redefines identity. Meredith is not who she was before Derek. Bailey is not who she was before George. Cristina is not who she was before Burke left or before the shooting that nearly killed her. These losses don't just hurt. They transform. Not instantly, and not without damage. But slowly, they become part of the character's psychological blueprint.

Grief also informs the characters' compassion. When Bailey breaks protocol to comfort a mother whose son is dying, when Meredith stays late with a patient whose husband didn't make it, when Richard sits quietly beside a colleague who can't speak—these are acts shaped by their own proximity to loss. They know what it means to be shattered. And in that knowing, they soften toward others. This, too, is ritual. Compassion born from memory.

In the world of *Grey's Anatomy*, grief is not a hurdle to clear. It is a companion. Sometimes heavy. Sometimes quiet. Sometimes interrupting life when you least expect it. But always present. Always shaping. Always reminding.

The brilliance of the show is not that it glamorizes grief, but that it normalizes its presence. It tells the truth that people don't "get over" loss. They live with it. They change for it. And, if they're lucky, they grow around it. The ones who are gone aren't gone. They're in every decision. Every risk. Every silence. Every love that comes next.

* * *

13

Miranda Bailey - Control, Anxiety, and the Cost of Being the Strong One

Leadership and the Lonely Burden of Containment

Miranda Bailey has long been the backbone of Seattle Grace. Commanding, brilliant, no-nonsense—she is the doctor you want in a crisis and the mentor who will make you better, whether you like it or not. But beneath the formidable exterior lies a reality rarely acknowledged in real life, let alone on television: strength, when unrelenting, becomes its own form of suffering. Bailey doesn't fall apart often. But when she does, it is never just about the moment. It is the result of years spent holding everything—and everyone—together.

Leadership, for Bailey, is not just a role. It is a psychological identity. She was never afforded the luxury of being average. From her early days as "The Nazi," to becoming Chief of Surgery, to guiding interns, managing egos, and navigating institutional failure, she has been a model of excellence. But excellence, especially for a Black woman in a predominantly white institution, is never neutral. It comes with pressure. With surveillance. With the constant awareness that a single mistake will not be read as an individual error, but as a failing of identity. Bailey's strength is not just personality—it is survival.

This chapter examines Bailey not through the lens of her accolades, but through the emotional toll of carrying others while denying herself the space to break. It is about the containment—the holding back, holding in, and holding up—that defines her. In trauma theory, containment refers to the capacity to hold emotional distress without letting it spill outward. Bailey has this in spades. But the psychological cost of being the container is that, eventually, there is no space left for your own grief, fear, or need.

Bailey's anxiety doesn't come out of nowhere. It builds slowly, invisibly, behind competence. It is cumulative. Microaggressions. Life-or-death decisions. Marital strain. Institutional politics. Personal loss. It all sits beneath her surface until the nervous system can no longer accommodate the load. And when her panic attacks begin, they are not weaknesses—they are messages. The body screaming what the mouth cannot say: *This is too much.*

What makes Bailey's arc emotionally resonant is how long she tries to hold it all. Even when she begins to crack, she doesn't ask for help. She diagnoses herself. She self-manages. She doubles down on routines, on control, on logic. This is not pride. It is fear. Fear of being seen as unstable. Fear of being removed from leadership. Fear of what it might mean to no longer be the one everyone counts on. In a system that rewards control and punishes vulnerability, Bailey's anxiety becomes yet another thing to manage—quietly, invisibly, alone.

And yet, her humanity breaks through. In moments of failure, in flashes of doubt, in her marriage to Ben, we see the fragility beneath the authority. Her strength becomes multidimensional—not the absence of fear, but the capacity to function through it. She remains a leader not because she avoids emotion, but because she learns how to live with it. How to bend without breaking.

Bailey's story is a counter-narrative to the myth of the unshakable leader. It reveals that strength can be suffocating, that containment can become isolation, and that the strongest people in the room are often the ones most in need of care. She is a study in the psychology of pressure—how it shapes behavior, masks pain, and defines identity. But she is also a study in resilience—not as bounce-back optimism, but as the long, slow work of making space for one's full humanity.

Internalized Pressure - The Intersection of Race, Gender, and Perfectionism

Miranda Bailey's perfectionism is not ornamental. It is not personality flair. It is armor—worn not to impress, but to survive. From her earliest appearances in *Grey's Anatomy*, Bailey is marked by rigor, control, and excellence. But beneath those qualities lies a deeper psychological architecture built from the realities of race, gender, and professional visibility. She does not get to be "average" without consequence. Her excellence is the floor, not the ceiling. And while her confidence may appear innate, it is actually constructed on a foundation of constant, silent pressure to prove her right to exist in the room.

Bailey is not just a surgeon—she is a Black woman in a historically white, male-dominated institution. This matters. It shapes her demeanor, her leadership style, her refusal to show weakness. In the language of psychology, this is called *minority stress*: the chronic, compounding pressure experienced by individuals who navigate systemic bias while trying to succeed. For Bailey, that means outperforming, over-delivering, outlasting. There is no space for error, because error would not be read as human—it would be read as proof she never belonged in the first place.

This intersection of identity and expectation gives rise to a form of perfectionism that is less about ego and more about protection. Bailey doesn't expect perfection from others because she believes in hierarchy. She expects it because she knows the consequences of imperfection. For her interns, mistakes mean learning curves. For her, they mean scrutiny. Reprimand. Demotion. So she builds herself into a fortress: hyper-competent, emotionally controlled, never visibly shaken. And when others fail to meet her standards, it's not disappointment she feels—it's fear. Fear that their mediocrity will reflect back on her.

This pressure is compounded by her role as a leader. As she rises through the ranks—from resident to attending to Chief of Surgery—her proximity to institutional power increases, but so does her sense of isolation. Leadership, especially for women of color in predominantly white spaces, is often lonely. Bailey must navigate a double bind: if she asserts herself, she risks being labeled difficult. If she softens, she risks being seen as weak. She walks the tightrope of visibility—too much and she's threatening, too little and she's dismissed. The result is a kind of emotional constriction: a narrowed range of acceptable behavior that becomes internalized over time.

Psychologically, this creates a high-functioning but fragile equilibrium. Bailey appears in control, but the cost of that control is immense. She suppresses vulnerability. She internalizes failure. She over-identifies with outcomes. When patients die, she takes it personally. When the hospital is in crisis, she steps in regardless of personal toll. Her identity as a doctor and a leader is not compartmentalized—it is fused. So any threat to her professional competence becomes a threat to her core self.

This is most evident in her reaction to being passed over, doubted, or challenged. She bristles. Not because she lacks humility, but because she knows how precarious her position is. She has worked twice as hard to get half as far, and every oversight feels like erasure. These moments tap into a deeper grief—one that is not always verbalized. The grief of being overlooked. The grief of having to fight for what others are given. The grief of carrying excellence like a burden.

Her perfectionism also bleeds into her personal life. In her marriage, in motherhood, in friendship, she finds it difficult to let the guard down. She struggles to ask for help, not because she lacks trust, but because dependence feels dangerous. Her sense of responsibility is so tightly wound that even delegation feels like abandonment of duty. This is the internalized burden of the "strong Black woman" archetype—a cultural script that praises resilience but punishes vulnerability, that celebrates stoicism while ignoring the cost.

Over time, this internalized pressure takes a toll on Bailey's mental health. She develops anxiety. She has panic attacks. And even then, her first instinct is not to seek support—it's to hide it, to fix it alone, to keep functioning. This is the dark side of perfectionism rooted in survival: it becomes self-silencing.

It teaches you to keep going no matter what. And in doing so, it erodes your capacity to feel safe enough to fall apart.

What Bailey reveals, across seasons, is not just the psychological complexity of a high achiever, but the emotional burden of someone constantly navigating overlapping systems of expectation. Her control is not just about the OR—it's about the space she's had to carve out for herself in a world that did not make room for her. Her high standards are not arrogance. They are self-defense.

And yet, Bailey remains deeply human. She loves fiercely. She mentors tirelessly. She believes in justice, even when the system doesn't. Her resilience is not the absence of injury—it is the determination to keep showing up despite it. She is not bulletproof. She is armoring herself every day against a thousand invisible cuts.

To understand Bailey is to understand that perfectionism is not always a choice. Sometimes, it's what's left when the alternative is being dismissed.

Anxiety Under the Microscope - OCD, Panic, and Emotional Backlog

For most of *Grey's Anatomy*, Miranda Bailey is the emotional thermostat of the hospital. If Bailey is calm, others know they can breathe. If Bailey is rattled, the ground feels less stable. But eventually, that role collapses under its own weight. Because even thermostats crack. And when Bailey's anxiety finally breaks through her composure, it doesn't arrive as a minor inconvenience—it arrives as a full-system alarm. Her panic attacks, obsessive thoughts, and emotional overload are not the unraveling of a weak person. They are the long-overdue consequences of a strong one never allowed to rest.

Anxiety doesn't begin for Bailey in a single moment. It builds through a thousand moments left unspoken. Her need for order, for control, for routine—it isn't quirky. It's protective. Early in the series, these traits are seen as part of her discipline. But with time, they take on a different tone. Her compulsive attention to detail, her intolerance for deviation, her agitation in the face of chaos all point to something deeper than perfectionism.

They suggest underlying obsessive-compulsive tendencies, driven not by cleanliness or ritual, but by the need to ward off disaster. If everything is done exactly right, no one will get hurt. If she stays in control, she can hold the system together. It's not arrogance—it's anticipatory grief.

What unfolds later in the series—particularly when Bailey is triggered by hospital-wide infections and institutional failures—is the surfacing of that backlog. Her anxiety disorder doesn't emerge from nowhere. It is the body's delayed response to years of high-functioning emotional compression. Panic attacks, in this context, are not episodes of irrational fear. They are the body catching up to what the mind has been suppressing. Her heart races. Her vision narrows. Her speech stumbles. These are somatic symptoms of a nervous system finally overwhelmed.

What makes Bailey's struggle with anxiety so clinically resonant is how it hides in plain sight. She doesn't scream or collapse. She doesn't stop working. She doubles down. She increases her demands on herself. She tries to out-organize her own fear. This is a well-documented coping mechanism for high-achieving individuals: manage the unmanageable by trying harder. But of course, that only feeds the cycle. The more control she seeks, the more anxious she becomes when things inevitably slip through her fingers.

Bailey's reluctance to disclose her mental health struggles also reflects a real-world barrier for many professionals, especially those in leadership. She fears stigma. She fears judgment. She fears that her competence will be questioned. This is especially true for physicians, who are trained to treat others, not themselves. Admitting vulnerability feels like forfeiting credibility. So Bailey doesn't talk. She self-diagnoses. She isolates. She hides her panic behind protocol and policy. And all the while, her body is telling her the truth: the container is full.

Her eventual breakdown is quiet but unignorable. She begins to miss cues. She panics at minor disruptions. She obsesses over protocols. And when she does finally step away, it is not out of choice—it is out of necessity. Her nervous system has reached its limit. This is not failure. This is biology. The show, by portraying Bailey's anxiety with this level of nuance, challenges the myth that mental illness looks a certain way. Bailey is not "losing it."

She is human. And the pressure she's carried would break anyone.

Her journey through treatment is not linear. She resists help. She questions herself. She feels ashamed. But gradually, she begins to reframe what strength looks like. It is no longer about perfect control. It becomes about knowing when to step back, when to say no, when to ask for help. These are not easy shifts for someone who has built a career—and an identity—on invulnerability. But they are necessary. Because anxiety doesn't leave because you will it away. It quiets only when it is acknowledged, tended to, understood.

What Bailey experiences also disrupts the binary of mental health and illness. Her anxiety doesn't destroy her capacity to lead. It complicates it. It adds layers to her judgment. It softens her in some places, and makes her sharper in others. She becomes more attuned to others' stress. More willing to delegate. More conscious of what burnout actually feels like. Her anxiety becomes not just a burden, but a lens—a way of seeing the hidden pain in others that she once refused to see in herself.

Psychologically, Bailey's arc is a study in what happens when emotion is deferred indefinitely. There is only so long the mind can compartmentalize, only so much weight the body can carry before it protests. And when it does, the protest is often misread as a breakdown. But in truth, it is a reorganization. Bailey's panic is not the end of her authority—it is the beginning of her emotional integration. She is not unraveling. She is finally being honest.

The most moving part of her anxiety journey is not the treatment or the return to work. It is the moment she speaks the truth out loud. The moment she stops hiding. The moment she says, in her own voice, that she is struggling. That she is afraid. That she is tired. These moments are subtle. But they matter. Because in those moments, Bailey is not just strong—she is free.

Letting Go Without Falling Apart – Bailey's Long Arc to Self-Compassion

Letting go is not Miranda Bailey's instinct. Her identity is built on structure, on accountability, on being the person others rely on when no one else can be trusted. For most of *Grey's Anatomy*, Bailey is the standard. The authority. The solution. But the long arc of her character reveals a deeper journey beneath that reputation—one that has less to do with leading others and more to do with finally learning how to care for herself. The evolution is subtle, spread across seasons, but unmistakable: Bailey moves from control to compassion. From self-containment to self-regard.

Bailey's journey toward self-compassion is not sudden or dramatic. It begins with exhaustion. She starts to recognize that being the glue of every system—home, hospital, marriage, identity—has come at the expense of her internal life. She has spent so much time managing everyone else's needs, emotions, and expectations that her own have been deferred, repressed, or pathologized. And as her anxiety becomes harder to deny, she is finally forced to reckon with a question she's long avoided: *Who takes care of the person who takes care of everyone else?*

The answer, for Bailey, has to become *herself.*

This shift does not come naturally. It threatens her sense of control, her internalized perfectionism, her carefully constructed image of the unshakeable professional. But life, as it does, intervenes with enough force that she cannot outrun the emotional cost anymore. Panic attacks strip away her ability to perform control. Marital strain with Ben reveals her aversion to emotional vulnerability. Institutional failures expose the limits of her authority. And each of these ruptures becomes a mirror—not just showing her where she's overwhelmed, but showing her how little space she's ever allowed herself to rest, soften, or receive.

What Bailey begins to learn—slowly, uneasily—is that letting go is not the same as losing control. She starts by stepping back. Not from medicine, but from the belief that she must fix everything. She begins to recognize that delegating is not incompetence. That rest is not weakness. That asking for help is not failure. These are not abstract lessons. They are felt, practiced, fought for. Because when you've built a life around being invulnerable, opening even a small door to self-kindness feels like threat before it feels like relief.

One of Bailey's most defining traits has always been her sense of duty. But what changes over time is *who* that duty is aimed at. She starts to widen the circle to include herself. She sets boundaries. She becomes more emotionally transparent with Ben. She names her anxiety. She says no when she needs to. These are not grand gestures. But for Bailey, they are revolutions. They reflect a woman learning, after years of self-erasure, that being the strong one doesn't mean sacrificing herself at the altar of everyone else's expectations.

In psychological terms, this is the transition from self-sacrificing perfectionism to integrated self-regard. Bailey doesn't abandon her standards. But she loosens their grip. She stops holding herself hostage to outcomes. She becomes more forgiving of her mistakes, less rigid about identity, more curious about her emotional interior. And this doesn't make her less of a leader—it makes her a better one. Because she is no longer modeling excellence as distance. She is modeling excellence as humanity.

Her relationship with Ben is one of the most telling barometers of this growth. In earlier seasons, she resists emotional dependency, pushes him away, hides her inner chaos. But as she learns to tolerate her own discomfort, she begins to let him in—not as a subordinate, not as someone she needs to manage, but as a partner. She shares more. She explains more. She trusts more. The shift is incremental, but meaningful. Their marriage doesn't become ideal. It becomes real.

Bailey's motherhood also transforms. Not in how much she loves her son, but in how she engages with him. She stops trying to be perfect. She stops trying to shield him from all harm. She begins to model emotional presence over performance. This is no small feat for a woman who was taught that competence is everything. In this realm, too, self-compassion opens the door to deeper connection—not just with others, but with herself.

The hospital continues to rely on Bailey. Crises never stop. But her responses begin to change. She becomes more willing to pause, to ask for second opinions, to admit what she doesn't know. These are quiet revolutions. But they signal something profound: she is no longer leading from fear. She is leading from self-trust.

Self-compassion doesn't make Bailey soft. It makes her fuller. More dimensional. More emotionally congruent. She can still be exacting, still hold high standards. But the edge is gone. The desperation to be impenetrable has been replaced by a more grounded authority—one that makes room for both mastery and mercy.

In the end, Bailey does not become someone else. She becomes more fully herself. And perhaps more than any other character on *Grey's Anatomy*, she shows us what it looks like to lead without abandoning the person behind the title. To admit that the strong one sometimes needs help. That the one who saves others also deserves to be saved. And that power, when it includes softness, becomes something far more sustainable.

Her story is not about burnout. It is about return. Not to who she was, but to a version of herself that includes everything she's carried, everything she's felt, and everything she's finally let go.

* * *

14

Richard Webber – Addiction, Regret, and Generational Cycles

The Mentor Who Carried His Own Ruins

Richard Webber is, in many ways, the institutional soul of *Grey's Anatomy*. He is the one who's been there the longest, the one who's seen the most, the one who made the hospital what it is. To the younger surgeons, he is a mentor, a symbol of tradition, and a moral compass. But beneath that composed surface lives a man fractured by personal failures, haunted by decisions made in secret, and shaped—perhaps more than anyone else on the show—by cycles he could never quite escape. Webber is not just the wise elder. He is the cautionary tale. The man who tried to lead others while never fully forgiving himself.

His authority is grounded in history. Richard has trained nearly every major character in the series. He has set the rules, enforced the standards, and created the culture they either uphold or resist. But that authority has always been complicated by what he hides: his alcoholism, his past infidelities, the marriage he neglected, the love he lost, the daughter he didn't raise. He carries all of it with him into the OR, into his teaching, into the tone of voice he uses when he says, "Do better." Richard doesn't lead from superiority.

He leads from scars.

This chapter is about those scars—what they reveal, how they formed, and what they cost. It's about addiction not as a dramatic arc, but as a psychological mechanism. It's about regret not as a single emotion, but as a lens that reshapes memory. And it's about the legacy of a man who meant to break generational cycles, but in many ways, replayed them.

Richard's most powerful moments come not when he is flawless, but when he is reckoning. When he owns his failures. When he admits what he didn't get right. When he tries—sometimes clumsily, sometimes earnestly—to do better. His mentorship is often a projection of that regret. He pushes others not just toward excellence, but toward integrity, because he knows what it means to live without it. He sees in Meredith the daughter he didn't raise. He sees in Bailey the mentee who surpassed him. He sees in Karev the boy he used to be, before time and loss hardened his edges.

Addiction, in Webber's story, is not portrayed as a moral flaw. It is portrayed as a response. To pressure. To secrecy. To emotional disconnection. To the burden of being the one who always seems fine. Like Bailey, Webber learned to lead by suppressing. Unlike Bailey, his suppression turned outward into behavior that hurt people. And yet, he is never reduced to those behaviors. He is shown as someone always in process, never quite finished, always trying to reconcile the man he is with the man he wanted to be.

The show gives him space to do this slowly. He relapses. He lies. He makes decisions rooted in fear. But he also apologizes. He listens. He rebuilds. He becomes, over time, not just a surgeon, but a man who knows how to sit in discomfort. Who can offer comfort. Who can speak the truth without deflecting. And in this way, *Grey's Anatomy* does something rare: it offers an older character not as a static figure of wisdom, but as someone still learning. Still grieving. Still changing.

Richard Webber's presence in the series is a quiet reminder that leadership does not erase history. It carries it. That the best mentors are often the ones still healing themselves. And that the most meaningful authority is not built on being perfect, but on being honest about the ruins you carry—and still showing up.

Secrets and Shame – The Psychology of a Hidden Life

Richard Webber has always appeared to be a man in control. He wears professionalism like a second skin—polished, composed, unwavering in the face of crisis. But the more we learn about him, the more we see that this control is curated, not natural. It is the product of a life built around carefully managed secrets, unfinished reckonings, and the psychological labor of hiding the most vulnerable parts of himself. Webber doesn't just carry shame. He builds his entire identity around avoiding its exposure.

Shame, as distinct from guilt, is not about what one has done—it's about who one believes they are. And for Richard, that belief is complex. He is not only a recovering alcoholic, but a man who hurt people deeply while appearing to be a moral center. He failed Adele, the woman who stood by him through years of neglect and betrayal. He concealed the existence of a daughter, Maggie, for most of her life. He loved Ellis Grey but didn't leave his wife. He taught generations of doctors while burying the very impulses he warned them against. These are not simply mistakes. They are unresolved legacies. And he carries them not with openness, but with quiet, corrosive shame.

The psychology of secrets is layered. On the surface, they offer protection—control over narrative, delay of judgment. But over time, they become prisons. Webber's secrets create emotional distance. Even when he is kind, he is guarded. Even when he is supportive, he is rarely vulnerable. He keeps people close, but not intimate. He gives wisdom, but rarely asks for help. And in that pattern, we see the psychological toll of self-concealment: isolation disguised as leadership.

His alcoholism is both a symptom and a shield. It first emerges as a way to dull pain, to manage failure, to quiet the noise of contradiction. But even long after he enters recovery, the addiction lives in his nervous system as a shadow. The structure of AA—ritual, confession, accountability—gives him scaffolding, but sobriety alone does not resolve the shame. He still struggles with self-trust. He still fears exposure. And this fear governs much of how he shows up, not just as a leader, but as a man.

Richard's relationship with Adele becomes one of the clearest arenas where shame plays out. He loves her, yet repeatedly prioritizes his ambition over her emotional needs. He lies to her—not with cruelty, but with avoidance. He believes that protecting her from the truth is a form of care. But what he's really protecting is himself—from confrontation, from guilt, from having to admit that he cannot be both the man she deserves and the man he has become. When Adele is diagnosed with Alzheimer's, Richard's grief is laced with regret. He is losing her twice: once to the disease, and once to the past he never atoned for.

His entanglement with Ellis Grey is another long shadow. The relationship is never fully resolved, and perhaps that's the point. It represents the version of his life that might have been. The choice he didn't make. The person he couldn't become. And the child that emerged from it—Maggie—forces him into a confrontation he spent decades avoiding. Suddenly, secrecy is no longer possible. And what follows is not instant connection, but rupture. Maggie is furious. Rightfully so. And Richard, stripped of the narrative he once controlled, is left to reckon with the harm that silence caused. This is the cost of secrets—they don't only protect. They wound.

His mentorship of Meredith is perhaps the most psychologically redemptive relationship he has. She is the living link between the two lives he could never fully reconcile. In her, he sees Ellis. He sees himself. And he tries, with increasing clarity, to offer her what he once withheld from others—truth, presence, care without condition. Their bond is built not just on shared history, but on a mutual understanding of what it means to be shaped by people who couldn't fully show up. He doesn't parent her, but he steadies her. And in doing so, he begins to loosen his grip on the shame that once defined him.

Yet even this growth is uneven. Richard still retreats when overwhelmed. He still guards his pain behind paternalism. He still wears the mask of certainty when what he really feels is lost. But over time, we see something rare: a man who was once ruled by secrecy learning how to stay visible, even when it hurts. We see him apologize more easily. We see him name the past without spiraling into it. We see him begin to believe that he is worthy—not because he was flawless, but because he is still here, still trying, still capable of love.

In psychological terms, this is the movement from shame-based identity to integration. Richard stops defining himself by what he failed to do and begins to define himself by what he is willing to face. His secrets don't vanish. But they lose their power to isolate him. He lets others see the full picture—not because it's tidy, but because it's true.

And in that truth, Richard Webber becomes something more than a mentor. He becomes a mirror. He shows us that healing is not erasure. It is continuity. That the past doesn't have to be rewritten. It only has to be owned. And that a life built around regret can still become a life of repair.

Addiction as Escape from Identity Failure

Addiction, in Richard Webber's story, is never about a lack of willpower. It is about pain management. And more specifically, it is about managing the dissonance between who he thought he was supposed to be and who he knows, deep down, he became. For Webber, alcohol is not a vice he indulges in for pleasure—it is a numbing agent, a way to quiet the psychic noise of shame, regret, and emotional contradiction. His addiction isn't random. It is purposeful, structured, and deeply tied to identity failure.

Richard's public persona is that of the standard-bearer: morally upright, intellectually dominant, professionally unimpeachable. He is the teacher others emulate, the institution others trust. But that version of himself is built on a brittle foundation. Privately, he has compromised his values. He has lied to those closest to him. He has withheld emotional truth from his wife. He has failed to be present for the daughter he didn't acknowledge. The man he wanted to be and the man he is have drifted apart. Addiction, in this context, becomes the bridge between them. It dulls the awareness of the gap.

In psychological terms, this is called *identity incongruence*. It occurs when a person's internal self-image is in conflict with their lived behavior. For someone like Webber—deeply principled, socially respected—this dissonance is corrosive. He cannot fully admit his failures without threatening the core of his self-concept. So instead, he splits. He becomes two Richards: the surgeon who commands a room and the man who drinks alone, in shame and silence. The alcohol is not the problem; it is the attempt at a solution. A chemical way to reconcile what he cannot reconcile emotionally.

What's critical in Webber's arc is how often his addiction is tied to moments of profound relational rupture. When his relationship with Adele deteriorates, he drinks. When he feels eclipsed by new leadership, he drinks. When confronted with his own irrelevance, he drinks. These are not impulsive lapses—they are moments of self-erasure. Drinking, for Webber, is a ritual of disappearance. A way to vanish from the burden of being Richard Webber.

And yet, the show never reduces him to his worst moments. Instead, it explores the terrain of relapse, recovery, and relapse again. Webber is not linear in his healing. He backslides. He denies. He lies to those who care. And in doing so, *Grey's Anatomy* captures something psychologically honest about addiction—it is not an event. It is a pattern. A response to pain. A relationship with relief that becomes a trap.

When Richard enters recovery, it is not triumphant. It is reluctant, shame-filled, fragile. He goes to meetings. He begins to tell the truth. But even sobriety comes with its own crisis: *Who is he, if he's no longer drinking to cope?* Identity, once again, becomes unstable. Because without the buffer of alcohol, he has to feel everything—every regret, every missed opportunity, every hard-earned truth. And feeling all of that, while still leading, still teaching, still mentoring, becomes an emotional marathon.

The show also complicates the recovery narrative by showing how hard it is for others to trust him again. Adele doubts his sobriety. Colleagues look for signs of backsliding. Even those who care about him treat his recovery as conditional. This mirrors real-life dynamics in families and professional environments: addiction doesn't just erode the addict's sense of self—it fractures relational trust. Webber has to rebuild not only his internal world, but his external credibility. And this rebuilding takes longer than he expects. He cannot outwork it. He cannot earn it back quickly. He must simply stay.

One of the most painful consequences of his addiction is the way it isolates him from emotional honesty. Even long after he's sober, Richard remains guarded. The impulse to conceal remains. He still struggles to name his emotions, to accept care, to be fully known. Because addiction was never just a behavior—it was his way of managing the fear of being seen too clearly. Sobriety forces him to face that fear without his usual tools. And what emerges is not always graceful. But it is real.

There are moments, however, when Richard allows the mask to drop. Moments when he speaks plainly about what he's lost. About who he failed to be. About what he's still trying to make right. These moments—fleeting, unvarnished—are where the true recovery happens. Not in abstaining from alcohol, but in reorienting his relationship with the truth. With vulnerability. With self-forgiveness.

And this is where the emotional depth of his story lands: *Addiction was not his deepest failure. It was the symptom of a man who could not yet forgive himself.* Once that forgiveness begins—even in small increments—so does real healing. Richard will never undo the harm he caused. He will never recover the years lost to secrecy or the love that withered under neglect. But he can become someone who stops hiding. Someone who tells the truth in time. Someone who shows up, not as the legend, but as the man.

Addiction does not erase the rest of him. It sharpens the view. And what remains is someone who has loved, failed, tried, and survived.

Repairing the Next Generation - Teaching What You Didn't Learn in Time

Richard Webber's greatest legacy is not a surgical innovation or a policy change. It's not even his tenure as Chief. It's the people. The students. The surgeons who came through his program and became who they were, in part, because of him. If Richard couldn't repair all the harm in his own life, he tried to prevent it in theirs. And in doing so, he lived out one of the most quietly redemptive arcs in *Grey's Anatomy*: the attempt to break a cycle not by undoing the past, but by guiding the future.

This effort is not presented as a mission—it unfolds almost unconsciously. Richard does not make speeches about legacy. He simply invests in people.

He shows up. He holds the line. He encourages. He corrects. He scolds with purpose and protects with steadiness. His mentorship is both structured and emotional. And while the early years cast him as a stern figure—the infamous "Nazi" who expected excellence without exception—what grows over time is a softer, more emotionally attuned leader. One who sees not just talent, but fragility. One who is no longer trying to raise perfect doctors, but whole people.

This transformation happens in part because Richard begins to confront the places in himself where no one ever showed up. No one pulled him aside and said, "You're not okay." No one taught him how to balance identity, ethics, relationships, and medicine without collapse. So he teaches those things to others—not because he mastered them, but because he didn't. He mentors not from superiority, but from the scars of hard-earned wisdom. And in those moments, his most profound teaching becomes this: *You can still become someone others can rely on, even if you were once someone who disappeared.*

His relationships with Meredith, Bailey, Karev, and Jackson each reflect a different version of this repair. With Meredith, he becomes the stable presence Ellis never was. He's not perfect—he withholds the truth about Maggie for too long—but he is steady. He believes in her before she fully believes in herself. He gives her room to be brilliant without demanding she be cold. And he never asks her to be grateful for his mentorship, because he sees her as part of the repair. In teaching her, he heals something in himself.

With Bailey, the dynamic is even more emotionally rich. She becomes the surgeon who surpasses him—technically, administratively, ethically. And rather than clinging to his authority, he yields to her rise with grace. He names her strength. He makes space for her leadership. And in doing so, he rewrites the story that authority must always dominate. His pride in her is unguarded. It's the kind of pride that says, *You didn't just become great—you became what I didn't know how to be.* Their relationship evolves from hierarchy to mutual respect, and in that evolution, Richard models a rare form of generative masculinity: one that finds fulfillment in elevation, not control.

His work with Alex Karev is more subtle. Karev, at first, is the kind of student Richard might once have dismissed: brash, defensive, emotionally aloof. But Richard sees something familiar in him—a young man shaped by scarcity, by the need to protect himself from vulnerability. Rather than write him off, Richard stays with him. He challenges him, supports him, and—perhaps most importantly—trusts him with leadership. Karev's eventual rise to Chief of Surgery is not just a testament to his growth. It is also a reflection of Richard's ability to see possibility where others see disruption.

With Jackson, the mentorship is complicated by legacy. Jackson's lineage looms large—Harper Avery, the foundation, the name. But Richard resists the easy path of projecting resentment or favoritism. Instead, he becomes one of the few people who treats Jackson as someone in formation, not as someone born complete. Their relationship is defined less by warmth and more by structure—expectation, accountability, a kind of paternal challenge that says: *You can't hide behind your last name. You have to decide who you are.* And Jackson does. Slowly, painfully, and in part because Richard never lets him settle for easy answers.

What we see in all these relationships is not just a teacher, but a man quietly attempting generational repair. Richard can't fix what he broke with Adele. He can't go back and raise Maggie. But he can pour into others what was withheld from him. He can offer patience, time, and emotional steadiness where once there was only pressure. And in doing so, he lives out one of the central psychological truths of mentoring: we often teach best the things we learned too late.

This work is not clean. There are missteps. There are moments where Richard lets his shame distort his decisions. But the trajectory is unmistakable. Over time, he becomes a mentor not fueled by image, but by authenticity. And as he begins to value presence over performance, he becomes something more than a teacher. He becomes an ancestor—not just to the hospital's culture, but to its conscience.

Richard Webber may never fully forgive himself for the parts of his life he misused. But his willingness to stay, to keep showing up for others, becomes a form of atonement. Not flashy. Not loud. But lasting. He teaches not just how to hold a scalpel, but how to hold grief. Not just how to save a life, but how to survive your own mistakes. And in doing so, he gives his students—and himself—a second chance.

* * *

15

Amelia Shepherd - Neurosurgery, Addiction, and Self-Destruction

The Beautiful Disaster of a Grieving Genius

Amelia Shepherd enters *Grey's Anatomy* like a storm with a steady hand. She is a paradox—a woman whose surgical brilliance is matched only by her emotional volatility. She is a world-class neurosurgeon and a woman reeling from years of personal loss. She saves lives with immaculate precision and destroys her own with breathtaking speed. If her brother Derek was the golden boy, the blueprint for surgical greatness, Amelia is the haunted variation—just as gifted, but far more broken.

To understand Amelia is to accept contradiction. She is vulnerable and defensive. She is compassionate and erratic. She is a truth-teller and a master of escape. Her presence in the show expands the emotional range of the surgical genius archetype. Unlike Meredith, whose trauma calcifies into control, or Cristina, who intellectualizes her pain into ambition, Amelia lets the damage show. Her struggle is not hidden beneath composure. It is braided into her every decision—raw, unfiltered, often unwise. And yet, even at her lowest, there is something relentlessly honest about her. She doesn't try to be palatable. She tries to survive.

This chapter is not about diagnosing Amelia's dysfunction. It is about tracing the psychological map of someone who has never had the luxury of safety. Amelia's story is shaped by trauma at every turn—early grief, addiction, relapse, professional precarity, and complicated relationships. But what makes her arc so striking is not how much she suffers. It's how fully she feels. How willing she is to name what others repress. And how hard she fights to stay alive, even when her worst instincts threaten to undo her.

From a clinical perspective, Amelia embodies several overlapping patterns: trauma repetition, unresolved grief, substance dependency, and emotional dysregulation. But what sets her apart is her capacity to reflect, even mid-spiral. She knows when she's lying to herself. She knows when she's hurting others. She doesn't always stop—but she rarely deludes herself for long. This kind of meta-awareness is painful. It makes her spirals more tragic, not less. Because she's conscious of her damage, and still, sometimes, she cannot stop it.

Her presence in the hospital disrupts more than the operating room hierarchy. It destabilizes the myth that surgical greatness requires personal control. Amelia is exceptional at her craft—but chaos follows her. And this duality creates tension in every relationship she enters. Some trust her brilliance and tolerate the rest. Others can't separate her past from her present. She is constantly negotiating the question: *Can people love me if they truly see me?* And just as often: *Can I love myself, knowing what I've survived—and what I've done?*

Her grief is her compass. She lost her father as a child, her brother as an adult, her child shortly after birth. She lives with death the way most people live with memory—constantly, with shifting proximity. And that nearness to death makes her both deeply empathic and emotionally combustible. She can sit with a patient's anguish longer than most. But she also combusts when her own pain goes unspoken. Her grief is not linear. It loops. It spikes. It disappears and then floods her without warning. And she builds her identity not around recovery, but around survival.

If addiction was her first escape route, love becomes her second. Amelia moves quickly into relationships, often seeking stability in someone else's arms rather than her own internal ground. Her connection to Owen is intense but unsustainable. Her emotional reactivity, paired with his need for predictability, creates a push-pull dynamic where neither can breathe. And yet, through it all, she remains capable of care—real, deep, often misdirected, but always sincere. She wants to be loved, but she wants to be seen more. And sometimes those two needs fracture each other.

Amelia is also a woman reckoning with control—over her body, her choices, her identity. She resists labels, resists being defined by her past, even as it shapes her. Her decision not to have children is not about fear. It's about clarity. Her resistance to being "fixed" is not defiance. It's self-protection. And in her most grounded moments, she is capable of naming her boundaries in ways that reflect deep growth. But the climb is steep. And she backslides often.

Still, her story is not one of collapse. It is one of reconstruction. Amelia's healing does not arrive with neat arcs or permanent resolutions. It comes in fragments—through therapy, through sobriety, through the brutal honesty of saying *I'm not okay* and still going to work. She is not romanticized. She is not redeemed. She is respected—as someone whose genius doesn't save her from pain, but whose pain deepens her capacity for connection.

Amelia Shepherd is a reminder that brilliance and brokenness are not mutually exclusive. That trauma doesn't disappear just because you've named it. That some lives are not built—they are survived into being. And for all her chaos, all her undoing, what she keeps choosing—again and again—is life. Messy, painful, unglamorous life.

Loss as Origin Story - Childhood Grief and the Addict's Mind

Amelia Shepherd's life doesn't begin with addiction. It begins with grief. Long before the relapse, the breakdowns, the compulsive choices and bottomless guilt, there is a child in a living room who watches her father die. Her father is shot in front of her while reaching for his watch—an object, a gesture, an ordinary moment transformed into the origin point of trauma. That death, brief and brutal, becomes Amelia's psychological blueprint. Not just a memory, but a fracture in the foundation of her nervous system. She doesn't just lose a parent. She loses safety. Permanently.

In trauma theory, early loss—especially sudden, violent, or senseless loss—alters the architecture of the developing brain. It affects emotion regulation, trust, and perception of self in relation to others. Amelia doesn't grow up learning that the world is unpredictable. She learns that it is lethal. That what you love can disappear in an instant. That being present doesn't mean you are protected. And perhaps most damaging, that no amount of need or closeness can prevent loss. This creates what some psychologists call a *trauma-tempered attachment style*—where closeness is both craved and feared, where intimacy is sought but rarely safe.

The death of her father is not an isolated trauma—it is the first in a series of emotional aftershocks. The family system around Amelia does not become safer after the loss. It becomes quieter. More constrained. She grows up in the shadow of Derek, the older brother who becomes a model of excellence and containment. Where Derek channels pain into ambition, Amelia channels it into instability. She is more emotionally expressive, more sensitive, more porous. She is not the golden child. She is the messy one. The risk. And in that designation, a secondary wound forms: the belief that she is too much.

When she turns to drugs, it's not to rebel. It's to disappear. Opioids offer her what trauma stole—a sense of relief, stillness, control. The addict's mind is not looking for chaos. It is looking for predictability. It is looking for the off-switch to a brain that never stops looping danger, grief, shame, and guilt. Amelia's addiction is not glamorous. It's desperate. It's an attempt to turn down the volume on a nervous system still screaming from a childhood that never calmed.

The link between childhood trauma and substance use disorders is well-documented. What Amelia embodies is not just the behavioral component, but the emotional profile: hypersensitivity, unresolved mourning, relational volatility, and a deep, often hidden conviction that she is fundamentally broken. These beliefs are not flaws in judgment. They are symptoms of unprocessed trauma. And because Amelia is highly self-aware, she knows this. But knowing and healing are different animals. Awareness doesn't protect her from collapse. It just makes her collapse more painful.

As Amelia grows into her career, her surgical brilliance becomes both an asset and a shield. Neurosurgery is control, precision, order. It is the antithesis of the chaos she feels inside. In the OR, she is godlike—certain, fluid, unstoppable. But outside the OR, she unravels easily. Conflict overwhelms her. Relationships flood her. The very emotional openness that makes her a compassionate doctor becomes unmanageable in intimate connection. Her self-regulation tools are few. Her emotional literacy is high, but her emotional safety is low. And so, she fluctuates: between vulnerability and retreat, between connection and combustion.

Her identity as an addict is not performative—it's etched into her sense of self. She refers to it openly, but often with shame or resignation. She believes she's damaged, even when she's sober. She believes she's hard to love, even when she's at her best. These are not attention-seeking beliefs. They are deeply held truths that formed long before she ever took her first pill. In addiction recovery circles, this is sometimes referred to as the "shame core"—a set of internalized convictions that fuel the cycle of using, relapsing, and self-loathing. Amelia doesn't just struggle with sobriety. She struggles with the part of her that believes she doesn't deserve it.

The birth and near-immediate death of her infant son is a trauma so profound it nearly erases her. For a brief period, Amelia becomes almost unrecognizable—closed off, numb, unreachable. This grief is not just about loss. It is about reinforcement. It confirms her deepest fear: that she cannot keep love alive. That everything she touches breaks. That grief is her inheritance, and her future. This is not dramatization. It is trauma consolidation. Her past and present meet in that loss, and the result is emotional collapse.

But she doesn't stay there. She never stays down forever. And that is part of her psychology too: resilience, hard-earned, imperfect, and deeply tied to her sense of meaning. She fights for sobriety. She tries again. She fails again. She tells the truth. She hides. She apologizes. She relapses—not just with substances, but with avoidance, projection, emotional sabotage. But she keeps returning to the work. To the meetings. To the friendships. To the impossible task of becoming whole while still grieving what she never had.

Amelia's story doesn't offer a sanitized recovery arc. It offers something more truthful: grief as origin, addiction as adaptation, healing as repetition. She is not cured. She is continually rebuilding. And in her vulnerability—in her brutal honesty about what she has lost and what she still wants—she becomes one of the most emotionally complex characters in the series.

Her genius is real. But so is her grief. And in her most honest moments, she shows us what it means to live as both.

Genius, Mania, and the Intimacy of Collapse

Amelia Shepherd's genius is unmistakable. She is a world-class neurosurgeon, capable of executing some of the most daring, intricate procedures in the history of Seattle Grace. Her intellect is razor-sharp, her instincts nearly infallible in the operating room. But brilliance, in Amelia's world, comes at a cost. Her cognitive power is often inseparable from her psychological volatility. And what begins as eccentricity—speed, intensity, the ability to out-think everyone in the room—sometimes crosses the threshold into mania. In Amelia, we see a version of genius that is unsustainable when left unchecked. Brilliance, when paired with trauma and addiction history, doesn't just illuminate—it burns.

There is an edge to Amelia's thinking, a hyper-verbal urgency that often reads as insight but sometimes flirts with unraveling. This is not unintentional. The show portrays her as someone constantly walking a cognitive tightrope: innovative when centered, dangerous when dysregulated. Her most compelling ideas arrive in moments of heightened energy, confidence, and risk-taking. But those same traits, when untethered from self-regulation, become symptoms of a nervous system in overdrive.

Psychologically, this mirrors traits common in high-functioning individuals with bipolar tendencies or trauma-induced emotional dysregulation. Amelia moves fast, feels fast, speaks fast. Her thoughts leap ahead of the conversation. Her emotional states are intense and brief, shifting rapidly from connection to withdrawal, from confidence to collapse. This volatility isn't dramatized for effect. It's embedded in her emotional profile. And for those familiar with neurodivergent forms of brilliance, or with trauma-induced hyperarousal, it rings true.

The intimacy of Amelia's collapse is part of what makes her breakdowns so emotionally jarring. She doesn't implode publicly. She implodes relationally. Her worst moments often come not in front of colleagues, but in front of people she loves. Her destructiveness is not aimed at patients or staff—it's aimed inward, or at those closest to her, in patterns of avoidance, accusation, deflection, or control. This is the intimacy of collapse. When her fear of abandonment meets her fear of visibility, she lashes out not because she wants to destroy connection, but because she doesn't believe she deserves it.

Her relationship with Owen exposes this most clearly. She wants the safety of love, but she fears the loss of self that love might require. She needs to be known, but when she is known—truly, fully—she panics. Owen, in turn, wants predictability. Stability. Amelia cannot give that, at least not consistently. And the more she tries to perform the version of herself that fits into his world, the more fragmented she becomes. This fragmentation eventually leads to emotional shutdown, and ultimately, to rupture.

Amelia's most revealing moments often come when she is asked to *slow down*. These are the moments she resists the most. Slowing down means feeling. And for someone whose emotional history is layered with grief, guilt, and unprocessed trauma, slowing down is intolerable. So she runs. She fixes. She talks. She solves. She seduces. But when the pace is broken—by a death, by a confrontation, by a partner who won't let her deflect—she collapses.

The tears arrive. The walls fall. And suddenly, the genius becomes the girl again. The one who lost her father. The one who watched her baby die. The one who never believed she was safe.

This intimacy of collapse is especially visible in Amelia's friendships. Her bond with Meredith is one of the more complex emotional threads in the series. Meredith, no stranger to trauma herself, recognizes Amelia's pattern—not just as a sister-in-law, but as someone who knows the architecture of collapse intimately. Their relationship is never easy, but it is real. Meredith holds boundaries. She doesn't coddle Amelia. And in doing so, she becomes one of the few people who doesn't either idolize or infantilize her. She sees both the genius and the ache, and she refuses to let Amelia disappear into either.

There's also a stark contrast between Amelia in the OR and Amelia in her personal life. In surgery, she is clear. Authoritative. Almost transcendent. She enters a kind of flow state that suggests not only mastery, but temporary refuge. The OR is where she is not messy, not unpredictable. It is a space where her mind's speed is a gift, not a liability. But the moment she steps out of that room, the speed turns on her. Her thoughts accelerate. Her fears intensify. And without the structure of medicine, she loses the buffer that holds her anxiety at bay.

What this reveals is the fragility of functional brilliance. Amelia is not faking her competence. But that competence is not stable. It is conditional—dependent on sobriety, on rest, on connection. And when any of those things break down, so does she. The show does not frame this as a personal failure. It frames it as emotional realism. That even the most gifted among us are held together by invisible threads—and when those threads snap, genius alone cannot save you.

Still, Amelia does not vanish into her worst instincts. She fights. She returns. She repairs. The intimacy of her collapse is matched only by the sincerity of her efforts to rebuild. She apologizes when she can. She names her missteps. She returns to meetings. She leans into therapy. And each time she does, she grows—not into someone different, but into someone more congruent. More honest. More at peace with her own contradictions.

Amelia Shepherd is not the cautionary tale. She is the whole story: genius and grief, precision and pain, rupture and return. Her brilliance doesn't redeem her flaws. Her flaws don't erase her brilliance. She contains both, in equal measure. And perhaps that is the most honest depiction of healing there is.

Rebuilding in the Rubble - Recovery as Emotional Reassembly

Amelia Shepherd doesn't recover all at once. She doesn't find clarity in a single decision or heal completely because she falls in love again. Her recovery is not clean. It is not linear. It is lived out in fragments—quiet moments, small steps, and sometimes the choice not to run when every part of her wants to disappear. For Amelia, rebuilding is not about returning to who she was. It's about creating someone new from the remains of who she used to be, with full awareness that some pieces are lost forever.

What makes Amelia's recovery so psychologically compelling is that it does not begin with triumph. It begins with collapse. She admits she's not okay. She walks into meetings after relapsing. She tells the truth even when she doesn't have a resolution. These moments aren't victories in the conventional sense, but they are emotional milestones. Every time she refuses to disappear into shame, she reclaims a bit more of herself. This is what recovery often looks like—not certainty, but continuity. Not breakthrough, but persistence.

Amelia's relationship to recovery is also shaped by grief. She isn't just an addict. She is a bereaved mother, a daughter who watched her father die, a sister who lost her brother, a woman who knows loss intimately. This matters because it makes her reluctant to believe in permanence. Recovery doesn't mean safety to her—it means vulnerability. It means risking something new when the past keeps proving that everything you love can be taken. And so her healing is cautious. Hard-won. Marked by moments of self-sabotage and recommitment.

One of the most honest aspects of her journey is how often she questions her own progress. She doubts herself constantly. She worries she's too much, that she'll hurt people, that she'll ruin good things. These thoughts aren't delusional—they are shaped by lived experience. She *has* hurt people. She *has* disappeared when things got hard. Recovery, for her, means living with that awareness without letting it define her. It means being accountable without collapsing into shame. It means saying, *I did those things. I am still here. I still deserve to try.*

Her relationship with Link offers an opportunity to do that work in real time. He meets her where she is—not by fixing her, but by staying. Even when she stumbles. Even when she falters. Their connection doesn't erase her past, but it gives her space to build something new in the present. Importantly, Amelia doesn't romanticize this. She resists being idealized. She names her past, her patterns, her fears. And in doing so, she makes it clear: love is not her recovery. It's just one part of it.

Amelia also begins to set boundaries, something earlier versions of her struggled with. She says no more clearly. She takes time alone without running away. She defines sobriety not just as abstaining from drugs, but as showing up fully present in her own life. These moments are understated, but they are tectonic shifts. They mark her transition from surviving to participating.

And she begins to find meaning. Not all at once, and not in grand gestures, but in pieces. In her work. In motherhood. In friendship. In her ability to be present even when she's uncomfortable. This is what emotional reassembly looks like. It is not the creation of a new self. It is the stitching together of all the versions of yourself that once splintered under pressure—addict, genius, lover, surgeon, sister, mother—into something whole enough to stand.

Importantly, *Grey's Anatomy* does not sanitize this process. Amelia still struggles. She still gets overwhelmed. But the frequency of collapse lessens. The duration shortens. The recovery quickens. These are the metrics of real healing—not perfection, but the ability to come back. To stay. To regulate. To remain in contact with others even when she's scared. And, most of all, to remain in contact with herself.

Amelia's story is not about redemption. It's about reclamation. She doesn't erase her past. She integrates it. She accepts that her pain will always be part of her story, but not the only part. And through that acceptance, she becomes stronger—not because she stopped being fragile, but because she stopped hiding her fragility.

In the end, Amelia Shepherd remains a paradox. Brilliant and broken. Clear and chaotic. Fierce and afraid. But she no longer sees these contradictions as evidence that she's unworthy. She sees them as evidence that she's human. That she's healing. That she's here.

And for someone who once believed that staying alive was the hardest thing she'd ever do, that is a kind of miracle.

* * *

IV

Legacy, Identity, and Becoming Who We Are

In the final chapters, we explore what Grey's Anatomy has always quietly asked: Who are we, after everything? This section traces legacy, identity, and the lifelong work of becoming—through mentorship, reinvention, ethical dilemmas, and personal reckoning. From aging surgeons to next-generation healers, these stories reveal that becoming isn't a single moment—it's a continual act of remembering who you are, and choosing who you want to be.

16

Being the Only One - Race, Isolation, and Belonging at Seattle Grace

Alone in the Room Full of Colleagues

To walk through the halls of Seattle Grace as a surgeon of color is to navigate more than patients and procedures. It is to navigate presence—the politics of it, the pressure of it, and the loneliness that often accompanies it. While *Grey's Anatomy* has been praised for its diverse casting, the emotional truth of being the only one, or one of few, is embedded into the narrative more subtly than the show's landmark surgeries. You see it in Cristina Yang's silence. In Miranda Bailey's command. In Jackson Avery's ambivalence about legacy. You see it in what they don't say, in what they must suppress just to be allowed to belong.

This chapter is about the psychology of that suppression. About what it costs to perform excellence not just for the sake of medicine, but to justify one's place in the room. It is about racial isolation—not as a dramatic confrontation, but as a constant undertow. For the characters of color in *Grey's Anatomy*, survival often means knowing how to be extraordinary without ever appearing angry, emotional, or unsure. It means excelling while code-switching. It means contorting one's presence to be palatable to the institution, while trying not to disappear in the process.

Representation on television is often measured in numbers—how many, how prominent, how central. But psychological representation asks something deeper: Are the characters allowed to be whole? Are they allowed to be messy, complicated, vulnerable, and still worthy of belonging? *Grey's Anatomy* doesn't always answer this perfectly, but it gestures toward it through the lived experience of its characters. Through what Bailey carries in her posture. Through the edge in Cristina's perfectionism. Through the way Jackson oscillates between pride and erasure.

Race in the series is rarely made explicit. But its influence is always present. In who gets to lead. In who is interrupted. In who is allowed to break down without being labeled unstable. This isn't a story of overt racism. It's a story of structural silence—how people of color move through predominantly white institutions carrying the double weight of their job and their identity. And how that burden, however elegantly managed, shapes the psyche.

To be the only one in a room full of colleagues is not just lonely. It is disorienting. It becomes difficult to trust your reactions, to voice your discomfort, to know whether what you're experiencing is really happening or simply not being acknowledged. This leads to emotional ambiguity—what scholars call *racial gaslighting*—and eventually, to exhaustion. The kind that isn't solved by rest, because it's not about depletion. It's about invisibility.

This chapter explores how *Grey's Anatomy* depicts that experience—not always overtly, but unmistakably. It follows the characters who carry more than their credentials. It traces the emotional and psychological toll of needing to be flawless just to be seen as equal. And it honors the quiet resistance embedded in their excellence: not submission, but survival. Not assimilation, but endurance.

Because in the world of *Grey's Anatomy*, as in life, being the only one means learning how to carry your whole self in a space that only wants to see part of you—and still choosing to stay.

Cristina, Miranda, and Jackson - Performing Excellence to Survive

Cristina Yang, Miranda Bailey, and Jackson Avery represent three of *Grey's Anatomy*'s most accomplished and complex characters—and all three are people of color navigating an institution built to question them. While their personalities, training paths, and internal struggles differ greatly, they share a quiet, relentless drive toward excellence. Not because they are innately more ambitious than their white counterparts, but because they know what is at stake if they are not.

This is not performance for glory. It is performance for survival.

Excellence becomes their currency—an unspoken contract with the institution that says: *If I am exceptional, you will let me stay.* This is a psychological pattern familiar to many marginalized professionals, particularly in high-stakes environments. Social psychologists call it *stereotype threat*—the internalized fear that one's performance will confirm negative assumptions about their group. For Cristina, Bailey, and Jackson, this creates a double burden. They are not only striving to succeed. They are striving not to fail in ways that would invite judgment, suspicion, or erasure.

Cristina Yang is perhaps the clearest example of how brilliance can be weaponized as armor. From the moment she enters the hospital, she is focused, ruthless, and hyper-competent. But underneath that drive is a deep sense of vulnerability. As an Asian woman in a majority-white, male-dominated surgical program, Cristina knows that her right to be there is always conditional. She cannot afford doubt. She cannot afford emotional display. She cannot afford failure. So she channels everything into mastery. Her sarcasm, her dismissiveness, even her aversion to emotional intimacy are not flaws in character—they are psychological defenses. To survive, she becomes the best. And to protect herself, she makes sure no one sees how much it costs.

Cristina is not allowed to be mediocre. She's barely allowed to be human. And she knows this. It shapes her from her earliest scenes to her final departure. Even in her most personal relationships—with Burke, with

Owen—she negotiates identity through excellence. If she cannot be seen for who she is, she will be seen for what she can do. And though her exit to Zurich marks a new chapter, it is not a retreat from pressure. It is a shift in control—her excellence, her terms.

Miranda Bailey's relationship to performance is different in tone but just as urgent. From the beginning, she carries authority. She is "The Nazi," the resident with no time for mistakes or emotion. But this identity—like Cristina's—is also armor. Bailey's standards are impossibly high, not just for others, but for herself. She is a Black woman in a system that rewards obedience and punishes disruption. Her control is not just personality—it is protective strategy.

Bailey cannot afford to appear uncertain. Her authority is hard-won and fragile in the eyes of those above her. Every mistake she makes is amplified. Every moment of emotion is a potential liability. Her perfectionism is not vanity—it is survival instinct. She leads through discipline because softness could be interpreted as weakness, and weakness as confirmation of stereotype. Even when she rises to Chief of Surgery, she remains acutely aware of what is being seen, what is being judged, and what she must hide.

And yet, Bailey is deeply emotional. She loves her patients. She mentors with real care. She grieves. She panics. But she shows these things selectively, and only after earning the right to do so. Her eventual diagnosis of anxiety is not a character twist—it is the logical consequence of decades spent performing stability in an environment that gave her no room to fall apart. Her excellence, like Cristina's, is not only about drive. It is about containment. To be the strong one, to be the only one, is to constantly suppress the need to be held.

Jackson Avery's experience is shaped less by being an outsider and more by being perceived as a symbol. As the grandson of Harper Avery, Jackson walks into the hospital with inherited status. But that legacy is double-edged. He is constantly read through the lens of privilege—assumed to be coasting, to be unearned. As a biracial man in a white-dominated hierarchy, his position is frequently misunderstood. He must not only prove his talent, but differentiate himself from the institution he represents.

Jackson's struggle is not just about race—it is about the complexity of representation. He wants to lead with integrity. He wants to be respected on his own terms. But he is burdened by expectations from every direction: to be exceptional, to be grateful, to be progressive, to be compliant. In private, he is often frustrated, lonely, angry. His facial expressions may be composed, but the emotional labor is constant. He is never allowed to just be another doctor. He is always *the* Avery. Always *the* example.

What unites Cristina, Bailey, and Jackson is not just their excellence. It is the unrelenting need to prove that their excellence is the only thing keeping them safe. They do not have the luxury of imperfection. They are judged not just as individuals, but as representatives. And that representation, while groundbreaking on screen, comes with enormous psychological weight.

The most poignant moments in their arcs are the ones where they let the mask slip. Cristina admitting that she doesn't want a child—not because she lacks empathy, but because she knows herself too well. Bailey collapsing in a hospital room, her hands shaking, the burden finally visible. Jackson walking away from a legacy that never truly saw him. These are not moments of failure. They are moments of truth. Moments when performance gives way to presence. And in those moments, the characters cease to be symbols. They become fully human.

Because for the only one in the room, survival is never just about being good. It is about being undeniable. And the cost of that performance, no matter how well managed, is always carried in the body.

Tokenism, Code-Switching, and the Exhaustion of Representation

Representation is often celebrated as progress. A person of color in a position of power, a queer character at the center of a story, a woman leading with authority. But *Grey's Anatomy*—without always naming it—often gestures toward the psychological toll of representation when it is solitary. When you're not just present in the room, but *the only one like you* in the room. Tokenism, code-switching, and the exhaustion of having to carry both visibility and caution at the same time quietly haunt characters like Cristina Yang, Miranda Bailey, and Jackson Avery.

Tokenism isn't just about underrepresentation—it's about symbolic inclusion without structural support. It is the experience of being allowed to be there, so long as you don't challenge too much, ask too much, or remind others of what makes you different. And in an institution like Seattle Grace, where white leadership and culture remain dominant even amid apparent diversity, the characters of color often feel this pressure without ever naming it directly. They are expected to be exemplary, emotionally restrained, and unshakably professional—not just for themselves, but for the illusion of progress they symbolize.

Miranda Bailey experiences this most acutely. As a Black woman in leadership, she cannot afford public error. Her policies must be airtight. Her demeanor must be calm, even in the face of chaos. Her competence must not only meet the standard, it must exceed it. But the burden of perfection is isolating. There is rarely another Black woman in the room who shares her vantage point, no one to debrief with after microaggressions, no one to validate her weariness. Even when she earns the title of Chief, she remains alone at the top—held up as a model, but rarely held emotionally.

This is the emotional reality of tokenism: success does not equal safety. Being seen does not mean being supported. Bailey's anxiety doesn't emerge in a vacuum—it emerges after years of over-functioning in an institution that expects her to represent diversity while punishing the humanity that inevitably comes with that role.

Cristina Yang navigates tokenism differently, through silence and control. Her Korean-American identity is rarely addressed explicitly, and yet it subtly shapes every part of her experience. She is often read as hyper-competent, emotionally cold, even robotic—tropes deeply linked to racialized perceptions of Asian professionals. Cristina plays into these expectations at times, because doing so protects her. She is allowed to lead, allowed to excel, allowed to be heard—but rarely allowed to be messy. Rarely allowed to be emotional unless it's strategic. The toll of that containment is never fully spoken, but it lives in her avoidance of vulnerability, in her refusal to explain herself, in her preference for solitude.

Cristina rarely code-switches verbally, but she constantly code-switches emotionally. She reads rooms with precision, calculating when it's safe to speak, when it's time to defer, when sharpness will be respected and when it will be punished. Her intelligence is not just surgical—it is social. It's survival. And the tragedy is that very few people in her environment even recognize the sophistication of this labor.

Jackson Avery carries the burden of tokenism in a different way—through legacy. As the grandson of Harper Avery and one of the few Black men in the hospital hierarchy, Jackson is both overrepresented in name and underrepresented in solidarity. He stands in for privilege even when he feels none. His ideas are sometimes dismissed, his authority questioned, his confidence mistaken for entitlement. And because of his lineage, his discomfort is often ignored. He can't complain without being seen as ungrateful. He can't speak up without seeming combative. He is visible, but not seen.

Code-switching, for Jackson, isn't about language or tone. It's about identity. He adapts to the expectations of the room—cool-headed, neutral, deferential—while internally managing the dissonance of feeling both insider and outsider. He is Avery, but he is also "other." And when he tries to lead with clarity or emotion, he finds that too much expression makes others uncomfortable. Like Bailey and Cristina, Jackson learns that authenticity, while idealized rhetorically, is dangerous when you don't fit the dominant mold.

The exhaustion of all this is cumulative. It shows up not as grand declarations, but in micro-movements. In the pauses before speaking. In the smile that doesn't reach the eyes. In the way these characters so often retreat to solitude, not because they don't want connection, but because connection in a space that only partially welcomes them is exhausting. Over time, this exhaustion becomes a kind of emotional debt—owed to the self, but rarely repaid.

What *Grey's Anatomy* does, at its best, is let this tension live on screen without resolution. It doesn't always give the characters the space to name what they're feeling. But it shows it. And for viewers who've lived similar dynamics, the recognition is powerful. The long stares. The silences. The precise professionalism. The way Bailey tightens her jaw before a board meeting. The way Cristina disappears into her work. The way Jackson scans a room before he speaks. These are not just character traits. They are survival responses.

This is the unspoken contract of being the "only one." You may get to be there. But you must stay calibrated. Pleasant, professional, productive—and never too much of anything else. And while others may see that as success, what it often feels like is pressure without end.

Quiet Resistance – Agency, Anger, and Emotional Integrity

Not all resistance is loud. Not all revolution looks like confrontation. In *Grey's Anatomy*, the characters of color who navigate tokenism and institutional pressure do not always rebel with speeches or walkouts. Instead, they resist by surviving with their emotional integrity intact. They resist by saying no in spaces where they're expected to say yes. They resist by protecting their selfhood in systems that expect them to perform, comply, and assimilate. And while their acts may appear quiet from the outside, they are psychologically profound.

Cristina Yang's resistance is surgical. Literal and symbolic. She knows that her worth lies in her precision, her innovation, her fearlessness in the OR—but she never allows that brilliance to be co-opted for someone else's agenda. She turns down promotions, walks away from legacy-defining surgeries, and eventually leaves Seattle altogether—not because she isn't capable of staying, but because staying would mean shrinking. Cristina does not yell. She simply walks. She refuses to become what the institution wants her to be. Her exit is not a failure. It is a radical act of self-definition.

Her resistance also lives in her refusal to adopt the emotional language expected of her. She doesn't soften when prompted. She doesn't feign vulnerability to comfort others. This isn't detachment—it's a refusal to translate herself for a system that never asked others to do the same. She will feel what she feels, on her terms. And in a world that tries to dictate who gets to show emotion and when, that defiance is a form of integrity.

Miranda Bailey resists in even subtler ways. She rarely disobeys rules, but she often redefines them. She doesn't storm out of rooms—she stays and alters the tone. She adapts the institution around her, not the other way around. Her resistance is in her longevity, in her refusal to burn out despite the weight of tokenism and the cost of containment. She keeps showing up. She keeps mentoring. She keeps holding the line. But the most powerful moment in Bailey's resistance comes when she finally stops hiding her anxiety.

When she tells the truth—that she is not okay, that she cannot keep functioning at the same pace, that even the strongest have a threshold—she fractures the myth of the invulnerable leader. She makes space for other people of color to show up as full humans, not just as symbols of resilience. Her truth is not weakness. It is protest against a culture that equates perfection with worth.

Jackson Avery's resistance is more conflicted, but equally meaningful. Raised inside the legacy of Harper Avery, Jackson carries institutional power even as it isolates him. But over time, he begins to separate his sense of self from his family name. He challenges the Foundation. He questions the system. He uses his platform to speak about race, justice, and medical equity—even when others resist. This is not performative. It is vulnerable. Jackson risks being seen as ungrateful, divisive, difficult. He risks disrupting the very privilege that once protected him. But he does it anyway.

His resistance also lives in his choice to redefine success. He steps back from power when it no longer aligns with his values. He chooses purpose over prestige. And in doing so, he models a different kind of masculinity—one that is allowed to change its mind, to feel deeply, to lead from humility instead of dominance. He becomes, slowly and imperfectly, someone who lives with emotional congruence. Not because the world made it easy—but because he stopped waiting for permission.

Across all three of these characters, resistance is never just about the institution. It's about the self. It's about protecting what is most at risk in high-pressure, high-visibility environments: one's internal compass. It is about refusing to contort oneself so thoroughly that the original shape is lost. And it is about trusting that dignity, even when invisible, is worth holding onto.

This kind of resistance often goes unnoticed by the characters around them. But viewers see it. Viewers feel it. Especially those who know what it is to perform excellence in a space that wasn't built with them in mind. The quiet resistance of Cristina, Bailey, and Jackson says: *I am here. I will not be reshaped by your discomfort. I will not trade my soul for your approval. I will do the work, and I will do it as myself.*

That is not weakness. That is endurance. That is agency. And in a system that tries to reduce people to roles, that is a radical form of being.

* * *

17

LGBTQ+ Representation and the Psychology of Visibility

To Be Seen Is To Be Disrupted

Visibility is often mistaken for acceptance. But in psychological terms, visibility—especially for queer people in environments historically shaped by heteronormative norms—isn't always a relief. Sometimes it's a rupture. Sometimes it marks the first moment you realize that who you are is no longer protected by privacy. Visibility isn't just about being seen. It's about being interpreted, surveilled, mythologized, and, at times, rejected.

Grey's Anatomy has offered some of network television's most emotionally nuanced portrayals of LGBTQ+ characters. But beyond the screen-time and romance plots, the show has quietly dramatized one of the most psychologically complex experiences of queer life: the tension between authenticity and safety. What does it mean to live fully in your truth when your truth may alter how people see you, speak to you, touch you, trust you, or leave you?

Coming out, in this world, is never just a personal decision. It is a psychological exposure. A reorientation of relationships. A recalibration of power. And for characters like Callie Torres, Arizona Robbins, and Levi Schmitt, the stakes of that visibility are never abstract. Their identities shape not only how they are loved, but whether they are seen as credible, competent, or even worthy of empathy.

To be out in a high-stakes professional environment is its own kind of emotional labor. It's one thing to navigate heartbreak, jealousy, or betrayal; it's another to do so while carrying the added pressure of representing your entire identity category. A straight character's emotional volatility is read as human. A queer character's may be misread as political. Their decisions are often not just personal—they're interpreted as cultural statements. This is the unseen weight of representation.

This chapter explores LGBTQ+ identity not just as a demographic box, but as a lens on selfhood, relationships, and belonging. It traces how *Grey's Anatomy* captures the complexity of queer presence within a system that both celebrates and constrains it. And it does so through characters who are never reduced to symbols. They are messy, real, proud, ashamed, defiant, afraid. They long for love and fear abandonment. They want to be understood without having to educate everyone around them.

What the show dares to suggest—without always saying it aloud—is that visibility is powerful precisely because it's disruptive. It interrupts assumptions. It destabilizes norms. It forces people to re-see what they thought they understood. And that disruption is not always comfortable, even for the person doing the revealing.

But comfort, as *Grey's Anatomy* has always shown, was never the goal. The goal is truth. And truth, when fully lived, can be both liberating and deeply, deeply costly.

Coming Out as Emotional Unveiling

Coming out is often framed as a moment of declaration—public, powerful, final. But in psychological reality, it is rarely a single moment. It is a process. A series of revelations, recalibrations, and emotional negotiations that unfold over time. In *Grey's Anatomy*, coming out is not just a statement of sexual orientation—it is a relational turning point, an internal confrontation, and often, an emotionally disorienting act of unveiling. What the show portrays, often with quiet precision, is that to come out is not just to say *I am this*. It is to ask, *Will you still hold me once you know?*

For Callie Torres, one of the show's earliest and most central LGBTQ+ characters, coming out is not linear. Her journey is marked by denial, curiosity, resistance, joy, and pain. She doesn't step into her queerness with full confidence. She steps into it with conflict—with herself, with her family, with the cultural and institutional scripts that once told her who she was supposed to be. Her attraction to Erica Hahn isn't portrayed as a bold sexual awakening—it's portrayed as a psychological rupture. It forces her to confront not just who she desires, but who she believes herself to be.

Callie's coming out is particularly rich because it unfolds within the context of faith, tradition, and familial expectation. When she finally tells her father, the rejection is swift, controlling, and deeply rooted in a theology of shame. This is not a caricature of homophobia—it's a depiction of love that cannot accommodate change. And the emotional fallout is devastating. Callie isn't just losing her father's approval. She is losing a sense of belonging to a version of herself that once felt stable.

This is what makes coming out so psychologically intense—it's not only about revealing yourself to others. It's about surviving their response. And when that response is rejection, silence, or shock, the person coming out must not only cope with grief, but also with self-doubt: *If you can't love me now, was I ever really loved?* The show does not answer that question. But it allows Callie to sit in it. And that honesty makes her arc emotionally resonant.

Arizona Robbins' journey is different. She is out from the beginning—confident, secure, playful. But that doesn't mean her identity is without psychological weight. Arizona's visibility as a lesbian is not something she wrestles with internally. Instead, she wrestles with how others react to her—with the hospital's assumptions, with patients' discomfort, and with the ways her queerness becomes both a source of pride and a frequent obstacle to professional neutrality. She doesn't hide. But she also doesn't get to forget.

This distinction matters. While Callie's arc is about *becoming*, Arizona's is about *being*—and the emotional labor of existing in a system that tolerates difference while still expecting conformity. Her queerness is both incidental and defining. It's not the problem. But it's never irrelevant. And the tension between normalization and hypervisibility becomes part of her emotional landscape.

Levi Schmitt's story brings a different layer entirely. His coming out is not loud or politically framed. It's tentative, tender, and deeply rooted in self-permission. When Levi falls for Nico, it's not the beginning of a love story—it's the beginning of *undoing everything he thought he had to be to belong.* For Levi, the fear isn't just about others rejecting him. It's about being seen as different at all. About breaking the code of invisibility that made him feel safe in his ordinariness.

Coming out for Levi is less about sexuality and more about shame. He isn't ashamed of being gay—he's ashamed of being *seen.* Of taking up space. Of disappointing his mother. Of stepping outside the version of himself that made life manageable. This is where *Grey's Anatomy* gets it right: the deepest fear is not always external rejection. Sometimes, the deepest fear is having to meet yourself without the camouflage.

In each of these characters, coming out is shown as an act of emotional unveiling. Not just identity disclosure, but self-exposure. The moment when you say, *This is who I am,* and then wait in the raw space between expression and response. Sometimes that response is love. Sometimes it is silence. Sometimes it is loss. And always, it changes everything.

Because once you've been seen, truly seen, you can't go back to pretending. And whether that visibility brings belonging or loneliness, it brings truth. And truth, for all its discomfort, is the beginning of freedom.

Callie, Arizona, Levi - Pride, Rejection, and Internalized Narratives

For queer characters in *Grey's Anatomy*, identity is never a static label—it's a lived, layered experience shaped by love, rejection, desire, and self-concept. Pride does not arrive cleanly. It is often forged through tension, disappointment, and the painful process of shedding internalized narratives about what it means to be acceptable. Callie Torres, Arizona Robbins, and Levi Schmitt each embody different aspects of this negotiation, and through them, the show quietly dramatizes how visibility is inseparable from vulnerability, and how pride is often born not in acceptance, but in defiance.

Callie's story arcs through some of the most emotionally brutal and redemptive terrains of the series. After coming out, she is not embraced by her family—instead, she's financially cut off by her father, dismissed by her mother, and shamed by the religious framework that once offered her belonging. This rejection is not just painful—it's destabilizing. Callie has always been someone who values connection, tradition, and approval. So when those structures crumble, her sense of self falters.

What emerges in Callie isn't immediate pride—it's fragmentation. She questions her decisions. She leans into relationships for stability. She over-corrects to prove that she's still worthy. And yet, slowly, quietly, a new self begins to form—one that is less dependent on external approval and more rooted in lived experience. Pride doesn't arrive as a parade. It arrives as resolve. In choosing to stay with Arizona. In choosing to raise a child in her own way. In choosing to be visible without needing to be validated.

But even then, Callie's pride is not without ambivalence. Her relationship with Arizona is full of love, but also marked by power struggles, betrayal, and complex negotiations about autonomy and desire. Callie wants to be loved fully—but sometimes, she still chases being chosen. Her queerness doesn't resolve her insecurities. It intensifies them, at least for a while. Because every relationship becomes a mirror: *Am I too much? Not enough? Still lovable now that I've changed?* And while her strength grows, her need for reassurance never entirely disappears. This is psychologically honest. Queer pride is often layered with residue from early rejection. The self-esteem doesn't rebuild overnight.

Arizona, in contrast, appears sure of herself from the beginning. Her identity is not questioned—she walks into the hospital openly gay, confident, and flirtatious. She is not ashamed. She is not in hiding. But as her story unfolds, we see that confidence does not insulate her from pain—it only postpones its exposure. When she loses her leg in the plane crash, her identity fractures—not because of her sexuality, but because of her sense of self as whole, desirable, in control. Her trauma reopens questions about worth and visibility: *Am I still lovable? Still sexual? Still me?*

And in the tension with Callie over these questions, Arizona's pride begins to harden. She becomes defensive, irritable, increasingly volatile. Her identity, once held with ease, becomes something she protects aggressively. And this shift reveals something essential: when a marginalized person feels unstable in one part of their identity, it reverberates through all of it. Visibility becomes fraught. Intimacy becomes threatening. What once felt like authenticity now feels like exposure.

Levi Schmitt's journey stands apart, shaped by quiet repression and a long-standing fear of being different. When we first meet him, he is shy, clumsy, eager to please. He is a character defined by avoidance—not of others, but of himself. His coming out is not only about sexuality. It is about the collapse of the mask. And when he finally does fall for Nico, the exhilaration is quickly followed by anxiety. Levi doesn't know how to exist while being seen. He doesn't know how to carry his desire publicly. Every look, every touch, every assumption from others feels like a test.

What Levi internalizes, even before anyone says it, is that visibility could cost him respect. He struggles with feeling "too gay" or "not gay enough." He feels judged for his awkwardness, for his inexperience, for the way his queerness doesn't fit neatly into confidence or charisma. These are the narratives many queer people internalize long before they speak a word about their identity—that to be acceptable, one must be polished, articulate, stylish, bold. Levi is none of these things. And that makes his journey more difficult, and more real.

Over time, he begins to assert himself—not with bravado, but with clarity. He confronts his mother's resistance. He stops shrinking. He steps into love not because he believes he's perfect, but because he believes he's worth showing up for. His pride is not glamorous. It is grounded. And in that, it reflects a quieter form of queer strength—the kind that builds slowly, patiently, and in direct resistance to shame.

Each of these characters teaches us something different about identity. Callie shows how pride can rise from rejection. Arizona shows how confidence can still hold fragility. Levi shows how tenderness is a form of courage. And all of them remind us that visibility is not a fixed state. It is a relationship—between self and society, between desire and dignity, between fear and freedom.

Pride, in *Grey's Anatomy*, is not rainbow-colored confidence. It is self-permission. It is survival. And, ultimately, it is the right to be fully known—without apology.

The Long Road to Wholeness - Visibility as Healing and Risk

In *Grey's Anatomy*, visibility is never just an external event—it is an internal reckoning. To be seen is not only to be recognized. It is to be known, misinterpreted, judged, loved, or rejected. And for the LGBTQ+ characters on the show, visibility is always double-edged. It offers the chance to step into wholeness, but also opens the door to new vulnerability. The emotional arc is not about arrival. It is about endurance—living through the questions that follow the moment someone says, *This is who I am.*

The road to wholeness, for Callie, Arizona, and Levi, is not about perfection or resolution. It is about the long, messy, uncertain work of integrating identity across every part of life—professional, romantic, familial, and internal. Callie doesn't become whole because she comes out. She becomes whole because she continues to fight for her right to love and be loved, even when that love doesn't always go smoothly. She builds a family. She remakes her life after heartbreak. She redefines herself after being told she was no longer wanted. And she does all of it while refusing to shrink back into invisibility.

This is what healing looks like—not becoming bulletproof, but becoming real. Callie does not lose her capacity for doubt. But she learns to trust her own choices. Even when they lead to pain. Even when they don't end in happy-ever-after. She doesn't need her queerness to make her exceptional. She simply refuses to let it make her ashamed.

Arizona's journey is more circular. Her trauma—physical and emotional—fractures her sense of self. Her queerness, once held with joy and clarity, becomes complicated by grief and resentment. She struggles with the aftermath of the plane crash, with losing her leg, with losing Callie. And for a time, her visibility hardens into defensiveness. She pushes people away, makes impulsive decisions, clings to control. Her identity does not protect her from pain. But it eventually helps her find her way back.

Because for Arizona, wholeness is not about returning to the woman she was. It's about accepting the woman she became. One who knows injury and recovery, love and loss. One who carries both confidence and caution. She finds peace not by reclaiming the past, but by making space for a future she defines on her own terms. Her queerness is no longer a performance or a defense. It is simply her life.

Levi's path to wholeness is the most delicately drawn. He begins invisible, unsure of himself, unsure of whether he even *wants* to be seen. His sexuality is not something he hides intentionally—it's something he's never allowed himself to consider fully. When he comes out, it's not with flair. It's with trembling hope. His pride builds not in declarations, but in micro-movements: standing his ground, asking to be treated with respect, insisting on honesty. He slowly stops apologizing for taking up space.

But visibility comes at a cost for Levi, too. The moment he's seen, he feels surveilled. He wonders if colleagues are re-evaluating him. He internalizes doubts, not because he lacks integrity, but because he has spent so long trying not to stand out. The show captures this tension beautifully. He doesn't suddenly become bold or radiant. He becomes real. He is scared, soft-spoken, occasionally awkward—and still worthy of love, dignity, and leadership.

This is where *Grey's Anatomy* pushes past superficial representation. It doesn't just show LGBTQ+ characters living out and proud. It shows them navigating the psychological fallout of living in a world that politicizes their identity, even when all they want is to exist. It shows them loving and losing not because they are queer, but because they are human. It honors the fact that visibility can be healing, but that healing is slow. And fragile. And always incomplete.

Visibility is risk. It asks: *If I show you who I am, will you still stay?* But it also invites possibility: *If I stay true to myself, maybe I will find people who love me for all of it.* In this way, visibility becomes a threshold. Not a conclusion, but an opening. And for Callie, Arizona, and Levi, stepping through that threshold is not about being brave in the way the world often demands. It's about being brave enough to stop hiding from themselves.

To be seen, then, is not just about identity. It is about self-relationship. It is about the inner gaze—the part of you that knows, accepts, forgives, and stands by who you are, even when others don't. Wholeness is not granted by society. It is claimed, breath by breath, decision by decision. And it is lived out not in statements, but in staying. Staying with yourself. Staying visible. Staying open.

Intersectional Invisibility - When Identity Is Multiplied, Not Divided

To be queer is never just to be queer. Identity is never experienced in clean, isolated categories. It is layered, entangled, context-bound. And in the world of *Grey's Anatomy*, where characters arrive with complex histories, inherited expectations, and embodied contradictions, queerness is often just one thread in a much more intricate weave. Yet, despite the show's long-standing emphasis on diversity, the intersection of queerness with race, class, religion, and gender is rarely explored in full. The result is a subtle, yet powerful form of invisibility—not erasure, but simplification.

Callie Torres embodies this tension more than any other character. She is not just a queer woman—she is a Latina, a daughter of religious tradition, a former heiress of familial expectation. Her queerness cannot be separated from her Catholic upbringing, from the cultural emphasis on family honor, or from the coded silence around sexuality that permeates many conservative and Latinx households. When her father cuts her off after she comes out, it is not only an emotional severing. It is a cultural rupture. She is not just losing financial support—she is losing access to the version of daughterhood that once made her feel included. And yet, this cultural weight is rarely named explicitly in the show. The pain is portrayed, but the layers go unspoken.

This omission matters. It reflects a broader cultural pattern in media where queer characters of color are either minimized or flattened into singular narratives. Callie is granted space to explore her sexuality, but her Latinidad becomes background noise. Her struggle is framed as personal when it is deeply cultural. Her father's rejection is cast as theological conservatism, but it's also about community shame, generational expectations, and the invisibility of queer Latinas in positions of power. That complexity never fully lands—not because the show ignores it, but because it stops just short of saying it out loud.

Levi Schmitt's queerness also intersects with multiple invisible burdens. He is Jewish, middle-class, socially awkward, and emotionally repressed—not the sleek, charismatic gay archetype often favored in television. His sexuality is not his only secret. His entire selfhood is organized around avoidance. His Jewish identity is quietly acknowledged but never integrated into his struggle with coming out, even though many queer Jewish people wrestle with religious ambivalence, inherited guilt, or family-centered expectations of marriage and legacy. Levi doesn't come out into a void—he comes out into a family system and a cultural framework that prizes cohesion and duty. And like Callie, he pays a relational cost.

Levi's softness, his lack of polish, his inability to be confident even after he comes out—all of these traits challenge the dominant media image of the "acceptable" gay man. He is not stylish, not assertive, not immediately embraced. His visibility is not glamorous. It's fragile. And that, in itself, is deeply intersectional. He embodies what happens when queerness collides with insecurity, social anxiety, and a background that didn't prepare him to assert himself in any domain, let alone sexual identity.

Then there's Casey Parker, introduced in Season 15—the show's first openly transgender doctor. His presence is brief, but it's notable. He's confident, competent, integrated into the staff without sensationalism. This is progress. But his arc is underdeveloped. The potential to explore the complex realities of being trans *and* a medical professional—navigating patients, colleagues, paperwork, and microaggressions—is never fully realized. Casey is visible but not central. He is a signpost of inclusivity, not a lens into the lived experience of trans embodiment in professional spaces. His identity is acknowledged, but his inner life remains out of reach.

That absence is not just a missed narrative opportunity. It reflects the limits of representational politics in a long-running show still built around cisgender, largely white, emotionally controlled characters. When queerness intersects with other forms of difference—race, gender identity, neurodivergence, economic class—the complexity is often trimmed down for legibility. The audience is offered one axis of identity at a time. But no one lives that way.

What would it mean for *Grey's Anatomy* to fully explore intersectional queerness? It would mean allowing Callie to speak directly to the tension between faith and love, between family loyalty and authenticity. It would mean exploring Levi's Jewish identity not as trivia, but as a shaping force in how he relates to shame, secrecy, and duty. It would mean letting Casey have a storyline beyond his transness—not to erase it, but to embed it in the whole of his life. It would mean allowing queer identity to be messy, contradictory, and deeply shaped by other social forces.

The silence around these intersections mirrors a real-world psychological phenomenon: when marginalized people are asked to represent only one aspect of their identity, they are forced to compartmentalize. They become legible at the cost of complexity. And this compartmentalization carries emotional consequences. It creates what theorist Kimberlé Crenshaw called "the basement of rights"—a space where those with overlapping marginalized identities are seen less, supported less, and left out of both mainstream and minority-centered protections.

For viewers living at these intersections, the partiality of representation is felt. Queer people of color. Queer people of faith. Queer people with disabilities. These lives don't fit neatly into narrative containers. They are often seen as "too much" for television. Too hard to explain. Too risky for ratings. And yet, these are precisely the stories that matter most. They reflect the actual texture of queer life—not as a monolith, but as a mosaic.

To honor queerness fully, a show like *Grey's Anatomy* must be willing to complicate it. Not just through romance, but through psychology. Through cultural specificity. Through the acknowledgment that sexuality is never lived in isolation—it is braided into every part of the self. When that complexity is embraced, representation becomes more than a checkbox. It becomes a mirror.

In real life, queer people are not just navigating coming out. They're navigating systemic bias, cultural norms, inherited shame, economic precarity, and the pressure to be palatable. Media that sanitizes that complexity in the name of visibility offers only partial liberation. It says, *You can be seen—if you fit the role we've written for you.*

Grey's Anatomy has taken bold steps toward inclusion, especially in later seasons. But inclusion alone is not the goal. Integration is. And integration means allowing queerness to be shaped by, and in dialogue with, all the other truths of a character's life.

The hospital itself is a perfect metaphor for this. It is a place of specialization—different departments, different tools, different roles. But the patient? The patient contains it all. The same body that suffers holds grief, rage, love, memory, and resilience. The same is true for identity. We are not departments. We are systems. We are intersections. And when media honors that truth, it does more than represent us. It dignifies us.

* * *

18

Who Gets to Break Down? Gender, Mental Health, and Representation

Strong Women, Stoic Men, and the Hidden Rules of Breakdown

In the high-stakes world of *Grey's Anatomy*, breakdowns are inevitable. But not everyone is allowed to fall apart the same way. Some collapses are framed as human, others as weakness. Some are met with sympathy, others with suspicion. What begins to emerge—quietly, insistently—is a pattern shaped not only by personality or plot, but by gender. The show, perhaps unintentionally at first, reveals the unspoken rules about who gets to lose control and still be respected. Who is permitted to feel publicly. Who is forgiven. Who is feared. And who, even in emotional ruin, is still seen as strong.

This chapter explores the intersection of gender and psychological expression. It looks closely at how characters across the gender spectrum are portrayed when they break down—how men are often rewarded for delayed vulnerability, while women are punished for showing it too soon or too fully. It examines how emotional stoicism in men is romanticized, while the emotional labor of women is expected, unthanked, and pathologized when it falters. And it traces how these portrayals mirror real-world biases in how we read emotion, strength, and mental health.

At the center of this exploration is the question: *Who is allowed to not be okay?* The answer, within the culture of Seattle Grace and the broader television landscape it reflects, is complicated. Women can cry—but only in private, and only after they've proved their strength. Men can break—but only after long silence, and only if the pain doesn't threaten their authority. And when these boundaries are crossed, the consequences aren't just narrative. They're psychological. Characters are either elevated or diminished depending on how well they conform to the emotional rules assigned to their gender.

The show doesn't resolve this tension, but it reveals it. In the quiet exhaustion of Miranda Bailey, who holds the hospital together until her body gives out. In the slow deterioration of Alex Karev, whose violence and withdrawal are tolerated far longer than any woman's would be. In Meredith's grief, which is revered when stoic but questioned when raw. In George's emotional sensitivity, which is seen as weakness rather than depth. In Owen's spirals, which are treated as crises to be managed, not truths to be honored.

Grey's Anatomy allows many of its characters to struggle. But who gets empathy, who gets narrative space, and who gets framed as unstable or heroic in the process—those are decisions shaped not just by story arcs, but by gendered expectations of emotional performance.

This chapter is about those expectations. About the rules we don't say aloud but feel deeply. And about what happens when a character dares to break them. Because in the world of medicine—and in the world at large—how we are allowed to break down often determines whether we ever get to fully heal.

Cultural Scripts and Emotional Permission

In any environment—professional, familial, cultural—emotions are not just felt. They are regulated, permitted, and often policed. Certain feelings are allowed; others are penalized. But who gets to feel what, and how freely, depends not only on personality, but on gender. The characters in *Grey's Anatomy* don't just experience mental health challenges; they navigate emotional permission. They move through a world where the scripts for feeling are unevenly distributed—where women must earn the right to cry, and men are rewarded for holding it in until the perfect, redemptive moment.

This unevenness isn't unique to Seattle Grace. It reflects broader cultural norms. From a young age, girls are socialized to manage emotion—expressing enough to be relationally attuned, but not so much as to be seen as hysterical. Boys, on the other hand, are often taught to withhold—praised for stoicism, encouraged to "man up," and subtly punished for softness. These gendered norms don't dissolve in adulthood. They become embedded in how we interpret behavior, in ourselves and in others.

In *Grey's Anatomy*, these patterns are everywhere, often unspoken but deeply felt. Meredith Grey, the show's narrative center, is a woman marked by trauma, loss, and emotional endurance. Her pain is rarely performed. It simmers under the surface, managed through control, sarcasm, and overwork. When she does break down—when she falls apart after Derek's death or lashes out in grief—it is dramatic but fleeting. She returns to function quickly, a quiet message that even in collapse, women must remain composed. Her emotional regulation becomes part of her appeal. She is allowed to hurt—but only if that hurt is elegant.

Contrast this with Alex Karev. His volatility is not just tolerated—it's integrated into his identity. Alex can lash out, withdraw, scream, throw punches, and still remain beloved. His pain is framed as depth. His aggression is excused as trauma. He's allowed to be messy, reactive, even destructive—because as a man, his breakdowns are not read as instability. They are read as the cost of survival. The cultural script for men in pain is indulgent. They are seen as complex, tortured, tragic. Their emotions, when finally expressed, are seen as proof of growth.

Cristina Yang, by contrast, is not given such grace. Her emotional restraint is interpreted not as strength, but as coldness. Her unwillingness to cry, her distaste for sentiment, her hyper-focus on achievement—these are treated as obstacles to intimacy. She is constantly asked to be softer, to open up, to perform vulnerability in ways that align with feminine expectations. But when she does express emotion, it's often received with discomfort or disbelief. When she breaks down after her abortion, or freezes in the aftermath of the shooting, it shocks those around her—not because she's incapable of feeling, but because her emotions don't follow the script assigned to women.

Bailey, too, lives inside this contradiction. She is the model of strength, control, and composure. But her emotional permission is tightly circumscribed. She can be angry—but only when it's professional. She can be nurturing—but only when it's contained. Her anxiety, when it emerges, is both humanizing and pathologized. She is expected to lead with steadiness, and when she falters, the silence around her pain is louder than the pain itself. Bailey's panic attacks are not just medical—they are psychological consequences of emotional over-regulation. But rather than being treated as the logical outcome of chronic containment, they are framed as deviation from her usual excellence.

The scripting is also evident in how grief is portrayed. George O'Malley's sensitivity, his kindness, his emotional accessibility—all qualities that would be praised in a female character—are often used to diminish him. He is mocked by peers, underestimated by patients, and rarely taken seriously by women he loves. His emotions are visible, but they are not valued. Masculine vulnerability, when not wrapped in aggression or redemption, is still seen as weakness. George doesn't lash out. He feels deeply. And in that quiet feeling, he becomes invisible.

This is the paradox: women are allowed to express—but only in socially sanctioned ways. Men are not allowed to express—until they do, and then they are celebrated for it. Owen Hunt's breakdowns—frequent, angry, sometimes violent—are always framed as symptoms of trauma. His erratic behavior is met with concern, not judgment. His suffering gives him complexity. But when Amelia Shepherd, also traumatized, breaks down, it is seen as instability. Her pain must be named, managed, and medicalized. She is not allowed to be chaotic and still be competent. She must either be healing or broken. There is no in-between.

Levi Schmitt offers yet another version. His emotional softness, his indecision, his tears—these make him the subject of mockery, especially early in his arc. He is a man, but not a traditionally masculine one. And so his emotionality is read as immaturity. He must toughen up, grow into himself, prove he can contain what others find too exposed. Only once he develops confidence—once he controls his emotional display—is he taken seriously. Visibility is not enough. He must also conform.

The rules are clear. You may cry, but not too soon. You may grieve, but only gracefully. You may be angry, but only if it's righteous and brief. These rules are written into the body language, the reactions of colleagues, the framing of the camera. They are not spoken. They are enacted. And they reflect a wider cultural discomfort: we do not know how to hold people who break outside the script.

This is what makes the most subversive moments in the show so important. When Meredith collapses in the OR. When Cristina screams in her apartment. When Bailey sobs in a supply closet. When Alex cries in front of a patient. These are moments that defy the rules. Moments where breakdown becomes declaration. *I am not okay, and I am still here.* The show doesn't always linger in these spaces. But it shows them. And in doing so, it invites the audience to reconsider what we expect from people in pain—and why.

Cultural scripts are powerful. They shape not only how we perform our own emotions, but how we interpret the emotions of others. And until those scripts are rewritten, certain people will always be more allowed to fall apart—and more likely to be held after they do.

When Masculinity Silences Pain - Karev, George, Owen, Webber

The men of *Grey's Anatomy* are not emotionless. They are wounded. They are afraid. They are grieving. But in nearly every case, their emotional lives are filtered through the narrow framework of masculinity—a framework that does not forbid feeling, but represses its open expression until it becomes either explosive or redemptive. Alex Karev, George O'Malley, Owen Hunt, and Richard Webber represent four distinct versions of how masculinity intersects with emotional suppression, and how deeply that suppression shapes their psychological arcs.

Alex Karev is perhaps the most misunderstood male character in the early seasons. Introduced as a brash, callous intern with a cruel streak and no time for empathy, Alex seems, at first, like a walking stereotype of toxic masculinity. But over time, it becomes clear that his behavior is not rooted in confidence—it's rooted in terror. Raised in a home filled with abuse and addiction, Alex learned early that softness invited danger, that emotion was a liability, and that the only safe position was hardness. His arrogance is camouflage. His cruelty is armor.

This is the masculine script at its most dangerous: a worldview in which protection means detachment and survival means shutting others out. Karev's journey toward emotional maturity is slow and halting because he doesn't just have to unlearn bad behavior—he has to unlearn the belief that vulnerability equals destruction. Every moment of tenderness—his friendship with Izzie, his mentorship of interns, his quiet support of Meredith—is a moment of risk. And yet, he takes them. Not all at once. Not without backsliding. But he begins to show that masculinity does not have to mean emotional starvation.

Yet the system around him reinforces the old script. His pain is overlooked because he's tough. His breakdowns are excused as volatility. When he punches someone or walks out mid-shift, there are consequences, but rarely questions. Rarely does anyone say, *Are you okay?* Instead, the question is always, *What did you do?* The emotional context is erased. And in that erasure,

Karev's pain becomes his responsibility alone—never something others are invited to hold.

George O'Malley, by contrast, is gentle, warm, and emotionally expressive from the beginning. He cries. He doubts himself. He wants love, and he says so. But this very openness, this emotional transparency, becomes a liability. George is mocked, underestimated, passed over romantically and professionally. His masculinity is constantly questioned—not because he lacks competence, but because he lacks traditional performance cues. He is not dominant. He does not posture. He leads with care.

George's arc is a slow, devastating study in how emotional openness in men is read as weakness unless paired with status or strength. He saves lives. He stands by friends. He sacrifices for others. But he is rarely rewarded for these traits. The show mourns him when he dies—but it never quite makes space for him while he's alive. His softness is never reframed as courage. His pain is never given the space to grow into wisdom. And in that omission, *Grey's Anatomy* reflects a brutal cultural truth: that emotionally sensitive men are often invisible until they're gone.

Owen Hunt's pain, by contrast, is loud. He arrives on screen already broken—wracked with guilt, disassociated from emotion, and trapped in the aftershocks of war. His PTSD is real and raw, but the way it manifests often aligns with what society finds palatable in male suffering: rage, withdrawal, silence, self-destruction. Owen rarely cries. He rarely confesses. His breakdowns are almost always somatic—clenched fists, erratic behavior, dissociative states. And because his pain is coded as masculine, it is often treated with seriousness and sympathy.

But Owen's pain is not more valid than George's. It is simply more familiar. His suffering is legible because it aligns with what we expect from traumatized men. He is given narrative space to unravel. His symptoms are explored. His triggers are discussed. He is loved despite his volatility. But rarely is he held accountable for the emotional labor he places on the women around him—Cristina, Amelia, Teddy—who must absorb his turmoil without always being believed themselves.

This is the masculine script of righteous damage: when a man's pain is seen as heroic, even when it harms others. And the tragedy is that Owen's suffering is genuine. But because it is expressed through dominance and collapse, rather than reflection and care, it becomes cyclical. It doesn't heal. It consumes.

Richard Webber represents a more internalized version of masculine suppression. He is calm, composed, deeply respected. But beneath the surface is a man drowning in unspoken shame—over his alcoholism, over his infidelity, over the daughter he didn't raise, over the love he betrayed. Richard's pain is buried beneath decades of silence. And when it emerges, it comes out sideways: in secrets, in relapse, in retreat.

Richard's version of masculinity is quieter, but no less constricting. He is the wise mentor who rarely asks for help. The leader who keeps his own wounds private. And this, too, is a kind of emotional denial. He teaches others how to be excellent, but he does not teach them how to fall apart. Because he never learned how to do it himself.

What unites Karev, George, Owen, and Webber is not simply that they suffer—but that the world around them assigns different meanings to that suffering. Karev is feared, George is dismissed, Owen is justified, Richard is revered. The scripts are uneven. The emotional permissions are unequal. And the result is that men are often left to manage their breakdowns alone, or worse, to weaponize them.

There are moments of rupture—Karev crying, George leaving surgery after a patient dies, Owen finally naming his PTSD, Richard admitting his addiction. But these moments are framed not as continuations, but as exceptions. They are emotional episodes, not emotional lives.

To rewrite these scripts, *Grey's Anatomy* would have to allow male characters to live in their vulnerability, not just visit it. To show their pain not as a detour, but as part of their identity. And to offer them the same emotional grace it often reserves for women: the space to feel, to falter, and to come back without explanation.

Until then, masculinity will continue to silence pain—not by forbidding it, but by allowing only certain forms, in certain doses, with certain consequences.

Women Who Crack - Meredith, Amelia, and the Path to Softness

If the men of *Grey's Anatomy* are often bound by the script of silence, the women are bound by the paradox of performance. They are expected to feel—but only the right emotions, at the right time, in the right amount. They must be resilient but not cold, vulnerable but not needy, expressive but never hysterical. Meredith Grey and Amelia Shepherd, two of the show's most psychologically rich characters, walk this tightrope constantly. Both have lived through enormous trauma. Both have broken down in private and public. But only one is allowed to crack and still be framed as strong. The other must constantly justify her collapse.

Meredith Grey is the axis of the show—a woman built from absence, intellect, and a series of personal catastrophes. From the beginning, she carries grief like a second spine: her father's abandonment, her mother's psychological instability, a suicide attempt in college, the death of her soulmate, and the burden of being exceptional in a world that expected her to disappear. Meredith is a survivor in every sense of the word. But her survival comes at a cost: she must remain emotionally composed in the face of loss that would shatter most people.

Her breakdowns are episodic—moments of rupture that quickly resolve into function. When Derek dies, she disappears. When her mother dies, she swims until her body gives out. When a patient reminds her of past pain, she lashes out or retreats. But she always returns. She always resumes the rhythm of competence. This pattern is not just character development—it is the cultural script of the strong woman. She may cry, but she will also lead. She may scream, but she will be right. Her pain is visible, but never disqualifying.

The grace given to Meredith is rare. She is allowed to be complex, distant, grieving, and even cruel at times—without losing the respect of her peers or the loyalty of the audience. Her emotional guardedness is read as depth. Her sharpness is forgiven. This is not to say she doesn't suffer. She does. But the way her suffering is received matters. She is protected by her centrality, by her narrative importance. Her cracks are seen as texture. Her darkness is interpreted as depth.

Amelia Shepherd, by contrast, does not receive the same narrative protection. Her pain is louder. Her emotions are messier. Her breakdowns are more frequent, more visible, and more difficult to predict. And as a result, her suffering is often framed as instability. Where Meredith's collapse is framed as tragedy, Amelia's is seen as volatility. Where Meredith is allowed to retreat into silence, Amelia's silence is interpreted as disconnection. She is not granted the same room to hurt without consequence.

This difference is not accidental. Amelia's character threatens the neat categories we use to contain women's pain. She is brilliant, impulsive, emotionally intense, and often self-sabotaging. She cries in public. She lashes out. She relapses. She apologizes and repeats the pattern. Her arc is one of rupture and repair, but the rupture is so uncontained that others often fail to see the repair. Her pain is not elegant. It is raw. And for that reason, it is more often pathologized than empathized with.

The cultural script around female emotion demands polish. Meredith fits within its margins. Amelia exceeds them. And this has consequences. Amelia must constantly re-earn trust. Her brilliance is questioned when she cries. Her judgment is scrutinized when she reacts. Her romantic relationships are destabilized by her emotional openness. She is, in short, punished for not curating her pain into something digestible.

And yet, it is precisely this refusal to perform her pain that makes Amelia psychologically important. She does not present a sanitized version of trauma. She shows what it means to live with emotional scars that are still healing. She shows what it looks like to tell the truth about grief, addiction, and mental illness—not as obstacles to overcome, but as realities to live with. Her vulnerability is not an aesthetic. It is a function of her survival.

The show occasionally allows her moments of grace—therapy sessions, conversations with Meredith, acts of courage in the OR—but they are always hard-won. Amelia's path to softness is not natural. It is resisted. She does not trust calm. She does not trust stillness. But when she begins to soften—not for others, but for herself—the shift is seismic. She sets boundaries. She pauses before reacting. She admits she does not always know what she feels. These are not narrative peaks. They are internal revolutions.

Meredith and Amelia, together, reveal the duality of being a woman in emotional pain: one can be mourned and admired, the other must fight to be seen as competent while still being honest. The difference is not in their strength, but in how their strength is read. Meredith's pain is palatable. Amelia's is not. Meredith gets to be mythic. Amelia must prove herself over and over.

But in the end, both crack. And both come back. And in their different paths to emotional integrity, *Grey's Anatomy* tells a deeper truth: there is no correct way to suffer. There is no neat arc of healing. Some women cry alone. Some scream in public. Some disappear. Some show up anyway. And every version is real. Every version is human.

The task, then, is not to determine whose breakdown is more justified. It is to expand our scripts. To allow for softness without suspicion. To honor rage without recoiling. To see in women's pain not a liability, but a record of survival. A sign that they have been carrying more than anyone saw—and have, somehow, still made it to morning.

* * *

19

Medical Hierarchies, Ego, and Identity Performance

When the Scrubs Become the Self

In the world of *Grey's Anatomy*, identity is more than backstory—it is behavior. And no behavior is more ritualized, more coded, or more psychologically revealing than what happens inside the hospital's hierarchy. Titles are everything. Intern. Resident. Attending. Chief. Each rank comes with a new script—how to speak, how to stand, who to defer to, who to discipline. But beneath the clinical language and surgical hierarchy lives something much more primal: a constant, often unconscious performance of self-worth. In this system, the scrubs don't just cover the body. They begin to shape the self.

This chapter explores how the hierarchy of medicine becomes a psychological scaffold—and sometimes a trap. Characters don't just seek competence. They seek identity confirmation. Validation. Belonging. And in doing so, they begin to perform not only procedures, but personas. They adopt the posture of power long before they feel it. They reject emotion not because they don't feel, but because they've learned that feelings threaten rank. In this hospital, to be respected is to be efficient. To be promoted is to be detached. And to rise is to become someone new—or at least pretend.

But the costs of that performance are immense. Ego, over time, is not just arrogance. It is insulation. It is what builds up around the wound of not feeling good enough, fast enough, or safe enough. For characters like Cristina Yang, Miranda Bailey, Alex Karev, and even Meredith Grey, climbing the ranks isn't just about skill—it's about proving to themselves that they are not as broken, small, or invisible as they once felt. And the higher they climb, the more difficult it becomes to separate who they are from the roles they inhabit.

The hospital structure intensifies this confusion. Seattle Grace isn't just a workplace—it's a world where performance is constant, surveillance is unrelenting, and authority can vanish with a single mistake. Promotions are sometimes punishment. Praise can isolate. A botched surgery or a blown diagnosis doesn't just risk a patient's life—it threatens the self-image that's been meticulously constructed to hold back fear.

What the show reveals—sometimes explicitly, sometimes through long arcs of self-doubt and implosion—is that medical hierarchies are not neutral. They shape personality. They reward certain temperaments and repress others. They create environments where confidence becomes currency, even when it's hollow. And for many characters, especially those already grappling with trauma, loss, or disconnection, the hierarchy becomes both a refuge and a cage.

This chapter is about that duality. About how ego becomes both survival strategy and burden. About how identity, once fused with professional status, can make breakdown feel like erasure. And about how, in a system designed to produce excellence, the most difficult task is often learning how to be human again. Not just a doctor. Not just a title. But a person—with uncertainty, limits, and a selfhood that exists even after the badge is taken off.

Competition, Collapse, and the Myth of Competence

Hospitals are built on hierarchy. The structure is both visible—white coats, pagers, job titles—and internalized. From day one, interns are trained not just to become doctors, but to internalize where they belong in the food chain. Competence isn't just about skill. It becomes a performance of worth. And in the high-pressure world of Seattle Grace, that performance is often mistaken for identity.

This is the myth of competence: that being good at your job means you're okay. That precision equals stability. That success means you've outgrown your wounds. But *Grey's Anatomy* repeatedly shows how brittle that illusion is. Beneath the veneer of mastery lies fear. Anxiety. Self-loathing. Exhaustion. These doctors aren't striving just to succeed. They're striving to feel safe—safe from judgment, from shame, from the fear of being ordinary.

The competition among interns is framed early and often as necessary. It's what filters out the weak. It's how the best rise. But the pressure is rarely productive. It doesn't make people better. It makes them desperate. Cristina operates on patients to beat others to the punch. Meredith cuts her own stitches to prove she's ready. Alex torpedoes his own relationships in pursuit of surgical supremacy. Izzie, George, even Bailey in her early days—they are not just trying to be great doctors. They are trying to feel like they matter.

This is the psychological trap of institutional hierarchy: the belief that excellence will fill the hole left by insecurity. That if you just earn enough accolades, win enough surgeries, outshine enough peers, the quiet self-doubt will disappear. But it doesn't. Because the structure doesn't validate self-worth—it replaces it. It teaches you to seek external confirmation in place of inner coherence. And in that gap, identity becomes fragile.

When collapse comes, it rarely announces itself. It hides beneath sarcasm. It shows up in skipped meals, in sleepless nights, in quiet panic behind bathroom doors. But eventually, the system cracks. The collapse is not about a single case gone wrong. It's about the slow erosion of the self behind the scrubs. And when that self finally speaks up, it often sounds like resignation: *I can't do this anymore. I don't know who I am without this. I don't remember why I started.*

Cristina Yang embodies this collapse with particular clarity. She is the most competent surgeon in her cohort—but her competence is not the antidote to pain. It is the mask. She drives herself mercilessly because the hierarchy offers her what people never did: structure, predictability, measurable worth. But when she freezes during surgery after the shooting, the illusion shatters. Her breakdown is not about the trauma alone. It's about the realization that even her mastery cannot protect her from herself. That excellence does not immunize you from collapse.

Bailey's collapse comes later, but it's just as telling. She is the one who holds everyone else up. She sets the rules, maintains order, offers discipline and stability. But beneath that strength is terror: that if she falters, everything will fall. Her breakdown, marked by anxiety and panic attacks, is the body's rebellion against years of emotional suppression. It is not a failure of competence. It is a failure of the myth that competence is enough.

Alex Karev's arc is built entirely on the pursuit of this illusion. He wants to be respected. To be the guy others count on. To shed the label of "the jerk" and replace it with "the doctor." And for a time, he succeeds. He becomes a trusted pediatric surgeon. He mentors others. He takes on leadership. But the trauma remains. The abandonment issues. The anger. The fear of never being enough. And eventually, he leaves. Not because he can't handle the job—but because the job can't save him from himself.

The myth of competence is seductive because it feels like control. It offers a measurable path: do more, know more, save more, rise higher. But it's a trap. It teaches doctors to equate their humanity with their productivity. And when life intrudes—when someone dies, when a marriage falls apart, when grief hits—the mask doesn't hold.

What *Grey's Anatomy* shows, often quietly, is that collapse is not weakness. It is the body and mind calling out for integration. It is the moment when the performance of competence no longer protects the person inside. And that person, once revealed, is rarely what others expected—softer, more uncertain, in need of care.

But here lies the potential: when a character collapses, they often find what the hierarchy could never give them. Community. Clarity. Permission to rebuild. Cristina finds it when she steps away from the OR and begins to feel again. Bailey finds it when she admits she's not okay. Alex finds it when he chooses love over prestige. Meredith finds it over and over as she confronts loss, not with stoicism, but with eventual softness.

Collapse is not the end of the arc. It's the truth that interrupts the performance. And from that interruption, something more real begins.

The myth of competence tells us that hierarchy builds identity. But the reality is that identity built on hierarchy alone cannot withstand collapse. True integration—the kind that survives even when titles are stripped away—begins when the person behind the scrubs is finally allowed to emerge.

The Doctor as a Persona – Self-Worth Through Status

To become a doctor in the world of *Grey's Anatomy* is not just to master medicine—it is to adopt an identity. The hospital doesn't merely train surgeons; it molds personas. Over time, the white coat becomes less a uniform and more a second skin, a role that offers both protection and peril. For many characters, particularly those who come to Seattle Grace with unresolved wounds, the title of "Doctor" becomes a psychological anchor—something to cling to when everything else feels uncertain. It's a way of saying, *I matter. I belong. I am not the broken thing I feared I was.*

But when identity fuses too tightly with status, the distinction between role and self begins to dissolve. Characters who once wore the title with purpose begin to rely on it for self-definition. They introduce themselves not as Meredith or Cristina or Karev, but as *Dr. Grey*, *Dr. Yang*, *Dr. Karev*. The hospital is not just a place of work—it is the stage where their value is either affirmed or denied, depending on performance, rank, and perception. And the emotional cost of this fusion is profound.

This dynamic begins early in training. Interns are immediately thrust into a culture of hierarchy, where being respected means speaking with confidence, moving with certainty, and concealing doubt at all costs. Vulnerability is interpreted as incompetence. Slowness is seen as weakness. Errors are not only clinical—they're moral failings. And so, the performance begins: a daily enactment of authority, even when fear is the dominant internal state.

Cristina Yang is a prime example of the doctor persona at its most consuming. From her first days at Seattle Grace, she knows what she wants—to be the best. But excellence for Cristina isn't about ego. It's about identity stabilization. If she can be the best surgeon, she won't have to deal with the disarray inside—her fear of closeness, her discomfort with emotion, her unresolved grief. She builds herself around her title, not because it makes her feel superior, but because it gives her a version of herself that feels durable.

This persona allows Cristina to bypass vulnerability. She doesn't need to be liked if she can be respected. She doesn't need to be emotionally fluent if she can be technically brilliant. But the longer she holds onto that mask, the harder it becomes to access herself outside of it. The breakdown she experiences after the shooting is not just a reaction to trauma. It is a rupture in self-definition. She can no longer be who she was in the OR. And if that identity is gone, what is left?

For Alex Karev, the doctor persona is a redemption narrative. He grows up in chaos—poverty, abuse, neglect. Becoming a surgeon is not just upward mobility. It's self-reinvention. He takes on the swagger, the detachment, the clinical sharpness that allows him to function without being seen too clearly. To be Dr. Karev is to escape Alex, the boy who had nothing and expected no one to stay. But the performance wears thin. His need to be respected hides a deeper terror: *If I stop being useful, will I still be worthy?*

This is the emotional trap of persona-based identity. When worth is contingent on performance, the person becomes invisible. Alex isn't just afraid of failure—he's afraid of what failure would reveal: that without the status, he might return to being nobody. His arc softens when he starts to build relationships based on presence, not productivity. Pediatrics becomes his access point to authenticity. The kids don't care about his resume. They care that he shows up. And for a time, so does Jo. But the tension between title and self remains. He's always looking over his shoulder, wondering whether the identity he built will hold.

Miranda Bailey, too, struggles with persona. Early on, she wears authority like armor. She is The Nazi, the enforcer, the one who never wavers. This is not natural—it is constructed. A survival adaptation in a system that would overlook a soft-spoken Black woman. Bailey doesn't just become strong. She becomes *bulletproof.* But over time, the cracks appear. The pressure to uphold her title becomes suffocating. Her anxiety builds. Her perfectionism turns inward. And the role that once protected her begins to trap her.

Bailey's journey toward integration is hard-won. She doesn't abandon her role—she reclaims it. She learns that being Dr. Bailey doesn't mean denying Miranda. That leadership doesn't require emotional suppression. But this lesson takes years. And during that time, the emotional labor she performs is enormous. Every day, she must be both symbol and person. Every day, she must over-function just to be read as competent. The persona sustains her power. But it also erodes her joy.

Even Meredith Grey, for all her narrative centrality, wrestles with this collapse of role and self. After Derek's death, she disappears—not just from the hospital, but from her identity. Who is she, if not Dr. Shepherd's wife, if not the brilliant surgeon ascending the ranks? The answer comes slowly, through loss and repetition. She builds a new version of herself not around achievement, but around presence. Around motherhood. Around quiet competence. Her identity as a doctor remains, but it is no longer her only self.

This is the heart of the dilemma: when the scrubs become the self, failure becomes existential. A botched surgery isn't just a mistake—it's a threat to identity. Being passed over for promotion isn't just disappointment—it's erasure. And leaving medicine, as Cristina eventually does, isn't just a career decision—it's a radical act of self-reclamation.

The hospital's hierarchy amplifies these dynamics. Every title is a rung on the ladder of worth. Interns feel like ghosts. Residents compete like gladiators. Attendings hold the keys to the future. Chiefs play politics to maintain power. And somewhere along the way, many forget what brought them there in the first place: the desire to heal. To help. To matter. Not to be seen as gods—but as people who make a difference.

When ego fuses with role, empathy becomes harder. Doctors begin to protect their status more than their patients. They snap at students. They make decisions to preserve image, not integrity. And yet, beneath the bluster is always someone who once believed that this work could make them whole.

What *Grey's Anatomy* reveals, episode after episode, is that no title can substitute for a stable sense of self. That being "Dr. So-and-so" may open doors, but it cannot quiet shame. The doctor persona is powerful—but it is not peace. And when characters begin to shed that persona, when they start to speak and love and choose as themselves, not as their role—that's when real healing begins.

Burnout, Breakdown, and Rehumanization

The culture of Seattle Grace—and by extension, the larger world of medicine—demands sacrifice. It demands your time, your presence, your composure, your identity. And over time, that demand extracts something subtle but essential: your humanity. Burnout on *Grey's Anatomy* is not just exhaustion. It is the slow erosion of the self beneath the role. It's the point at which the doctor can no longer remember who they were before the hierarchy asked them to become invincible.

Burnout isn't a side story in *Grey's Anatomy*—it is the atmosphere. You see it in the hollow eyes of residents sleeping in on-call rooms, in the way characters flinch when pagers go off, in the increasing sense that to rest is to fall behind. Burnout becomes a badge of belonging. You are tired because you care. You are angry because you're good. You are emotionally numb because you're doing your job right.

But this story cannot sustain itself indefinitely. Eventually, the performance collapses. The persona breaks. And what comes next is not always ruin—but rehumanization.

Miranda Bailey's burnout is perhaps the clearest and most relatable. For years, she held the hospital together—mentoring, correcting, planning, managing. She didn't rest; she led. And that leadership came at the expense of her nervous system. The panic attacks she eventually suffers are not random—they are the body's final protest against a life of emotional containment. Her mind was never broken. But her balance was. Her identity had become so deeply tied to function that when function faltered, there was nothing left to catch her.

Bailey's path to rehumanization begins with telling the truth. *I'm not okay.* That phrase, spoken by a woman who has spent her entire career being the one everyone else leans on, is revolutionary. She doesn't fall apart in public. She simply stops pretending. She allows the emotional cost of excellence to be seen. And that act reclaims her humanity. She is no longer just a leader. She is a person with limits, tenderness, and a right to care.

Cristina Yang, too, burns out. But her burnout is quieter, colder, more internal. After the shooting, she dissociates. She continues to operate, but she is no longer there. Her brilliance remains, but her selfhood is absent. She gets married, she takes fellowships, she checks all the boxes of success—but none of it lands. Because the part of her that once lit up in the OR is now extinguished. Not because she doesn't love surgery, but because the system used her love until it became obligation.

Cristina's rehumanization comes when she finally chooses herself. Not her status. Not her partner. Not the hospital. Herself. She walks away—not from medicine, but from the belief that her value is conditional. Her exit is not a collapse. It is a declaration: *I am not just what I can do for you.* And in that departure, she reclaims the part of her that was slowly disappearing beneath the weight of being exceptional.

Even Alex Karev, often portrayed as the rough-edged survivor, shows signs of burnout that go unnoticed because of how well he hides them. He is irritable, dismissive, emotionally distant. But beneath the surface, he is exhausted—of fighting for belonging, of managing his triggers, of pretending that being needed is the same thing as being loved. His sudden departure from Seattle is jarring to fans, but psychologically, it is consistent: Alex didn't leave because he stopped caring. He left because he couldn't keep caring from that place. Because caring had become performance. And that performance had become a prison.

Meredith's burnout builds slowly, over years. It doesn't arrive with collapse. It arrives with detachment. With the gradual loss of joy. With the increasing sense that her life is happening *to* her, not *with* her. And when she nearly dies from COVID, the show literalizes the dissociation she's carried for years. The beach she visits in her dreams is peaceful, tempting, free from urgency. It is the emotional life she's long denied herself. And when she returns, it is not to the same role. It is to a new sense of clarity: that being a doctor cannot mean erasing the person.

Burnout, in this series, is not just an individual problem—it's a systemic inevitability. The hospital rewards over-functioning, punishes pause, and equates identity with usefulness. And the characters absorb those messages until they begin to vanish beneath them.

But rehumanization is always possible. Not easily. Not quickly. But always.

It begins with saying no. With stepping back. With crying, or resting, or admitting you're scared. It continues with friendships, mentorship, love, reflection. With remembering why you entered the system in the first place. And it takes shape when a character begins to act not out of obligation, but out of alignment—with who they are, and what they actually want.

When Bailey says she can't be Chief if it costs her health. When Cristina chooses Zurich because it feels right, not because it's impressive. When Karev writes that letter explaining that he found peace, even if others don't understand. These are moments of rehumanization. Not glamorous. But whole.

To heal from burnout is to remember that your worth was never in your title. That your softness is not your weakness. That rest is not a betrayal of excellence. And that you were a human being before you were ever a doctor.

The hierarchy doesn't teach this. But survival depends on it.

* * *

20

The Hospital as a Psyche - Seattle Grace as a Metaphor for the Inner Life

Dreamscape in Scrubs

For nineteen seasons, Seattle Grace has existed not only as a hospital but as a world unto itself. It is a place of routine and rupture, of precision and chaos. Patients flow in and out, lives are saved and lost, surgeons come of age and come undone. But beyond its function as a dramatic setting, the hospital operates on a deeper, more symbolic level. It is not just the backdrop for these characters' growth—it is the container of their psychological life. And in many ways, it becomes a living metaphor for the self.

This chapter explores Seattle Grace as a dreamscape. A psychic landscape. A map of trauma, memory, identity, and transformation. The hallways are not just places of movement—they are pathways through emotional thresholds. The elevators are not just modes of transport—they are liminal spaces where truth slips out. The operating rooms are not just technical arenas—they are rituals of control in a world that constantly reminds the characters how little they can actually control.

In Jungian terms, a hospital like this one becomes a *symbolic container*—a structured space where the ego, the shadow, the persona, and the self all play out through relationships, crises, and choices. It is a place of ego inflation and ego death. Of projection and integration. Each wing, each floor, each season reveals a different aspect of the collective unconscious—not only of the characters, but of the audience that sees themselves reflected in these crises.

Over time, Seattle Grace morphs with the inner lives of those who inhabit it. As the characters evolve, so does the hospital. It survives shootings, mergers, earthquakes, plane crashes, lawsuits, leadership turnovers, and literal name changes. It is perpetually being rebuilt. And that rebuilding is not just architectural. It mirrors the ongoing process of psychological repair that each surgeon undergoes. The place never stays the same—because the people inside it cannot.

The hospital also enacts repetition compulsion—another psychological truth made spatial. Time and again, the characters return to the same rooms, the same decisions, the same heartbreaks, hoping for a different outcome. Trauma doesn't disappear. It replays, reconfigures, reasserts itself until it's fully seen. And within this repetition is the opportunity for integration. Seattle Grace becomes a place where the ghosts don't just haunt—they teach.

What makes *Grey's Anatomy* distinct among long-running dramas is that the hospital never becomes just scenery. It breathes. It holds memory. It holds contradiction. It holds the characters in their worst and most luminous moments. And like the psyche, it holds it all without collapsing. It is not always safe, but it is always familiar. A strange paradox of constancy and crisis. A mirror for the inner work no one has time to do—until they have no choice.

This final chapter is not about the hospital as a building. It is about the hospital as metaphor. About how place and psyche intersect. About how trauma lives in rooms and relationships. And how healing is not something that happens after the hospital—it happens inside it, in fleeting moments, under fluorescent lights, between alarms, in silent elevators, and in the quiet recognition that *this place knows me*—and I've survived it.

Trauma on Every Floor - Mapping the Psyche onto Physical Space

Seattle Grace is not just a hospital. It is a geography of memory. A container of pain, resilience, and transformation. Every floor, every hallway, every break room holds the imprint of what happened there—and those imprints function much like the markers of trauma in the human psyche. Just as a traumatic memory is not neatly filed away but carried in the body, the characters in *Grey's Anatomy* carry their personal histories in the physical spaces where those histories unfolded. The hospital becomes a living map of what they've endured, survived, and sometimes refused to process.

Trauma in this setting is not just thematic—it is structural. You can trace it spatially. The OR where Cristina froze after the shooting. The stairwell where Meredith grieved in silence. The maternity ward where April delivered her dying child. The elevator where Derek first kissed Meredith. These locations are not just cinematic touchpoints. They are psychic zones. They are encoded with emotion. And like trauma itself, they do not lose their charge with time. Every time a character re-enters a familiar room, a dormant memory is activated. Every trauma leaves a residue, and the building remembers.

This is what it means to map the psyche onto physical space. In psychological terms, the hospital becomes a symbolic extension of the characters' internal world. Each floor mirrors a different domain of experience: the surgical floor is the realm of control, the ER is chaos and urgency, the on-call rooms are intimacy and isolation, the boardroom is power and judgment, and the lobby is performance—the face presented to the world. When characters move through these spaces, they are not just navigating the building. They are moving through layers of selfhood.

The trauma that lives in these rooms does not announce itself—it waits. The psyche does the same. A hallway may look neutral, but step into it after a loss and it becomes loaded. The hospital simulates this perfectly. A character may walk through a familiar corridor and suddenly be overwhelmed—not because the setting changed, but because they changed in it. In trauma theory, this is known as *state-dependent recall*—the phenomenon where past emotional states resurface in the environments where they were originally encoded. Seattle Grace is a textbook case.

Meredith's experience encapsulates this dynamic. She knows the hospital better than anyone. And yet, there are places that unnerve her. The scrub room where she once begged Derek to stay. The OR where she almost drowned in her grief. The trauma bay where George died. These are not neutral spaces. They are emotional landmines. Meredith's composure often falters not because she forgets, but because she remembers too much. The environment doesn't allow her to disassociate. The walls are saturated with what she's lived.

But the trauma is not only individual—it is collective. When the hospital is attacked during the mass shooting, every corner becomes charged. For weeks afterward, characters flinch at loud noises, freeze in hallways, lose time in the middle of tasks. The trauma rewires the building just as it rewires the brain. Suddenly, Seattle Grace is no longer a place of healing—it is a site of survival. And no one moves through it the same way again.

Cristina Yang's departure from surgery after the shooting is a spatial trauma response. The OR, once her sanctuary, becomes a threat. She can't operate in the place that almost cost her life. Her decision is not a failure of strength. It is a neurologically and emotionally accurate response to a nervous system overwhelmed by stored terror. It takes time—and environmental change—for her to return to her former sense of competence. And even then, the space is never neutral again.

These examples highlight a fundamental truth: trauma localizes. It lives in the body, yes, but also in place. And the hospital, as a recurring set piece, allows us to see that process in action. When a character avoids a room, they are not being dramatic. They are practicing spatial self-protection. When they return to that room, sometimes years later, and pause before entering, we are watching psychological exposure therapy in real time.

There's also a kind of emotional haunting that pervades the show. Past residents echo in the halls. Lexie, George, Mark, Derek—they are gone, but never fully absent. The hospital holds their memory. Their deaths don't just affect the characters who loved them. They affect the texture of the hospital itself. Every new cohort enters a space that is already saturated with past narratives. And in that saturation, we find a truth about how trauma layers: the psyche remembers not just what happened to *you*, but what happened around you.

Even spaces designed for neutrality—conference rooms, elevators, patient rooms—take on emotional charge. Bailey breaks down in a supply closet. Owen has a panic attack in an empty stairwell. Meredith kisses goodbye to multiple versions of her life in the same corridor. The psychological realism here is acute: we do not choose where we feel. We feel where we've felt before. And the hospital, with its repetitive choreography of crises and coping, becomes the embodiment of this loop.

The metaphor deepens when we consider how the hospital is altered, damaged, and rebuilt over time. The shooting, the fire, the merger with Mercy West, the plane crash, the administrative overhauls—these events don't just change the logistics. They reflect the fracturing and integration of the collective psyche. Trauma hits. The walls collapse. The system breaks. And then begins the long, grueling work of reconstruction. Just like therapy. Just like healing. Just like the brain recovering from loss.

Seattle Grace—or Grey Sloan, depending on the season—is ultimately a metaphor for what it means to survive within yourself. The chaos of the ER mirrors the chaos of the trauma response. The sterile, orderly ORs mirror the part of us trying to stay composed. The staff lounge, the on-call rooms, the stairwells—these are the liminal spaces where the real emotions slip through. They are the dream sequences in the structure. And in this way, the hospital operates like a subconscious—dense with symbols, layered with memory, always active beneath the surface.

To watch these characters move through the hospital is to watch them move through themselves. Each hallway is a neural pathway. Each patient a projection. Each elevator door a threshold between ego and shadow, between persona and truth.

Seattle Grace is not just where these characters become doctors. It's where they learn who they are when everything else falls away.

Rooms of Memory, Guilt, and Transformation

In *Grey's Anatomy*, rooms don't just hold patients—they hold stories. And more than that, they hold memory. The trauma room isn't just a trauma room; it's where George O'Malley flatlined. The OR isn't just an OR; it's where Cristina Yang reclaimed herself after being frozen by PTSD. The maternity wing is where April Kepner delivered her dying son. These aren't merely physical spaces. They are emotional echoes. They hold the psychic weight of what occurred within them, much like the rooms in our own lives that have absorbed memory and now silently replay it in our bodies when we return.

This phenomenon—where place becomes emotionally charged through lived experience—is as much psychological as it is narrative. These rooms don't change. The lighting, the layout, the equipment all stay the same. But the characters do. The person who walks into the OR the day after losing a patient is not the same person who operated there a week before. And so, each reentry becomes a reckoning. A chance to confront not just the task at hand, but the residue of what happened last time.

Memory lives in the repetition. Meredith Grey performs dozens of surgeries in the same rooms, walks the same halls day after day, and yet the meanings attached to those spaces evolve with her. The room where she first scrubbed in with Derek becomes, over time, the room where she says goodbye to him. The memories are stacked—joy, fear, grief, strength—and those emotional layers change how she inhabits the space. This is a form of psychological anchoring: a way the self ties place to experience, and then carries both forward.

But it isn't just memory that lives in the rooms—it's guilt. And guilt, in *Grey's Anatomy*, is not an occasional emotion. It is a constant undercurrent. Doctors do everything they can, but outcomes are never guaranteed. Mistakes happen. Judgment fails. Time runs out. And when it does, the room becomes a kind of altar. A place where remorse lives, replayed again and again in the minds of those who were there.

Richard Webber knows this intimately. For him, the hospital is a mausoleum of past choices. The room where he performed surgery while hungover. The hallway where he didn't tell Adele the truth. The corridors where he mentored, misstepped, and tried to teach what he himself hadn't yet learned. Each space becomes a mirror. He cannot escape himself in these halls—he can only learn to coexist with the man he was in them.

For April Kepner, the hospital becomes the site of spiritual collapse and rebirth. After the loss of her son, she doesn't just mourn at home. She mourns at work. She carries grief into every trauma room, every hallway, every interaction. She operates as if trying to repay a debt—to God, to her child, to the order she can no longer believe in. The rooms she once walked with naive optimism become spaces of existential doubt. And yet, it is within those same rooms that she eventually rebuilds a different kind of faith—not in outcomes, but in presence. In staying. In holding space, even when nothing can be fixed.

Amelia Shepherd, too, lives in a constant loop of transformation within the hospital. She begins as Derek's sister—a brilliant, volatile shadow of her brother—and ends as a woman who has learned how to sit with her own pain without running. The OR, the break room, the patient rooms—these become places where she disassembles and reassembles herself over and over. Each relapse, each revelation, each hard-won choice leaves a mark. And so the space becomes charged with evolution. Not only with what she's done, but with who she's become.

There's a particular kind of intimacy that arises when trauma and transformation happen in the same physical place. It's disorienting, but also grounding. The OR doesn't judge you. It doesn't forget. And because it doesn't change, you get to measure your own growth against its consistency. Cristina, once frozen in fear, eventually commands the room. Meredith, once defined by grief, becomes the calm in every crisis. Amelia, once unpredictable, becomes reliable. The rooms are the same—but the surgeons aren't. And that contrast is what makes the transformation visible.

But the transformation isn't just about skill. It's about integration. The hospital becomes a place where compartmentalization eventually gives way to wholeness. Where characters stop pretending that their professional and personal lives are separate. Where breakdowns happen mid-surgery, where confessions happen mid-shift, where the walls between persona and person dissolve—not catastrophically, but truthfully.

In some ways, the hospital serves as a kind of therapeutic space—not because it's calm or supportive, but because it relentlessly exposes whatever remains unresolved. There is no hiding here. If you're not dealing with your grief, it will find you on the operating table. If you're suppressing fear, it will show up in your hands. If you're pretending to be okay, the body or the patient or the pager will call your bluff. And in this constant confrontation, the work of transformation begins.

This is why leaving the hospital is so hard for some characters—not just because they're giving up a career, but because they're stepping out of the container where their emotional life was held. Where they failed, forgave, fell in love, fell apart. The hospital is their mirror, their crucible. To walk away from it is to walk away from a version of themselves they spent years building—and breaking.

The rooms of Seattle Grace hold more than stories. They hold emotional residue. They hold silence. They hold the breath that catches in a doctor's throat after they've saved a life, or lost one. They hold the decisions that haunt and the ones that heal. They are not just places where things happen. They are places where people change.

Memory. Guilt. Transformation. These aren't separate arcs—they're threads braided into the physical space. And through those rooms, *Grey's Anatomy* reminds us that healing is never abstract. It's as tactile and real as the place where you first broke open.

The Collective Patient - The Hospital as Shadow, Symbol, and Self

Hospitals are designed to treat patients—but in *Grey's Anatomy*, Seattle Grace often feels like the patient itself. Its walls bleed. Its systems malfunction. Its staff breakdown. It absorbs trauma and dysfunction and healing, not only in its medical capacity but in its emotional and symbolic one. It is, in many ways, a reflection of the characters who inhabit it: brilliant and broken, resilient and overwhelmed, continually reconstructing itself after being shattered.

In Jungian psychology, the *shadow* represents the parts of the self that are denied, repressed, or unintegrated—often those that carry fear, shame, grief, or rage. The hospital, over time, becomes an externalized shadow for its surgeons. It holds the secrets they won't speak aloud, the losses they never fully grieved, the darker impulses they try to bury beneath professionalism and perfection. And just as the shadow always returns until it is integrated, so too do the traumas of Seattle Grace—shootings, disasters, ghosts of patients past—reappear, again and again, forcing confrontation.

It is no accident that the hospital is where the worst things happen. Derek's death. The mass shooting. The plane crash fallout. It is also where many of the most personal crises unfold—infidelity, addiction, breakups, panic attacks. The space itself does not separate the personal from the professional. It fuses them. It reflects the reality that trauma is not compartmentalized. And neither is healing.

Over time, the hospital begins to resemble a symbolic psyche. The ER becomes the amygdala—reactive, urgent, filled with the fight-or-flight panic of fresh trauma. The OR is the prefrontal cortex—precise, practiced, orderly, often removed from feeling. The on-call rooms and stairwells are the subconscious—private, chaotic, and often where the truth emerges. And the boardroom is the superego—the internalized voice of expectation, punishment, image management. The entire building becomes a working metaphor for the internal mind of someone managing too much, too fast, with too little room for stillness.

And then there is the collective patient—not a single person, but the hospital itself as a living being. The hospital gets sick. Its power goes out. Its systems fail. It breaks down under pressure. It's attacked. It's understaffed. It's mismanaged. And when this happens, we see how the institution is not separate from its people—it *is* its people. The characters project their own needs, fears, and ambitions onto the hospital's body, much as we project our inner lives onto our environments.

When Bailey tries to hold the hospital together during personal crisis, she is not just managing the hospital—she is trying to regulate her own inner world. When Meredith becomes Chief of General Surgery, she is not just earning a new title—she is finally integrating authority and empathy, power and presence. When Cristina leaves Seattle Grace, she is not just walking away from a job—she is shedding a self that no longer fits the truth she's grown into.

In this way, the hospital serves as both a setting and a mirror. It reflects back to each character their own developmental arc. Sometimes it betrays them. Sometimes it cradles them. It never forgets. The call rooms where affairs began later become places of heartbreak. The ORs where heroes were made later become chambers of loss. The quietest rooms hold the loudest memories. And as each new generation enters, they inherit not only the physical space—but the emotional weight of everything that came before.

The hospital also carries an archetypal energy. It is the Temple. The place where transformation happens. In religious myth and psychological theory alike, the temple is not safe because it's peaceful—it's safe because it's *set apart.* A threshold space. Neither the outside world nor the internal world, but something in between. That's what Seattle Grace becomes. Not merely a hospital, but a liminal space—between life and death, between breakdown and breakthrough, between who you were and who you're becoming.

The characters rarely say this aloud. They joke. They grieve. They blame the hospital for their misfortunes. But beneath that, they all know: this place changed them. This place *saw* them. Not just at their best, but in their most fractured, least present, most human states. And the hospital, for all its dysfunction, held them through it. It became a shadow they couldn't run from, and in not running, they found pieces of themselves they didn't know they still carried.

Seattle Grace—Grey Sloan Memorial—is the collective patient. And healing that patient has never been about flawless leadership, or new wings, or shiny equipment. It has been about showing up. Again and again. Stitching wounds. Sitting through discomfort. Holding space for grief. Naming what went wrong. And refusing to walk away from the parts of the system—or the self—that still need care.

In the final analysis, the hospital is not just a metaphor for trauma. It is a symbol of transformation. A psyche in motion. A living story of how people grow not in spite of pain, but through it. Not by escaping the place where they were broken—but by staying long enough to become someone new.

* * *

Epilogue

Why We Keep Watching – The Mirror, the Myth, and the Medicine

There is a strange comfort in returning to *Grey's Anatomy*. Even after nineteen seasons, even after the cast has turned over and the names on the walls have changed, the feeling of the show remains the same. We still recognize the pulse beneath it. The show has become something more than television—it has become a place. A place to revisit when we are in need of story, of catharsis, of familiarity in a world that continues to fray at its edges.

But what is it we're really returning to?

We're not just watching scalpels and storylines. We are watching ourselves—fragmented, longing, defended, soft. In every heartbreak, every surgical triumph, every messy love, we see versions of who we've been and who we fear we might become. The brilliance of *Grey's Anatomy* is not that it's a hospital drama. It's that it's a psychological mirror—an endless series of emotional case studies about what it means to be human under pressure.

The operating table is a metaphor. The hallway confrontation is a stand-in for every moment we couldn't say what we felt. The on-call room isn't just about sex—it's about disarming. About the quiet places where people drop their personas and show themselves raw. The hospital, the patients, the staff—it's all a landscape we've come to understand not just narratively, but neurologically. *Grey's Anatomy* has taught us how to feel our way through stories we weren't given language for.

What began as a soapy medical drama grew into something far more emotionally instructive. For many viewers, the show provided an early emotional education. It was where you first saw someone grieve messily. Where you witnessed the psychological aftermath of assault, addiction, burnout, or death—not just as plot points, but as textured experiences with real-time consequences. These weren't morality plays. These were trauma responses, attachment patterns, recovery attempts. And they were framed through character, not diagnosis. That distinction is essential.

We don't love Meredith because she's perfect. We love her because she survived without needing to become unrecognizable. We don't love Cristina because she softens. We love her because she *refuses* to, and still earns love anyway. We don't admire Bailey because she never cracks. We admire her because when she finally does, we feel the weight of every year she held it together.

Grey's Anatomy teaches us, implicitly, that survival isn't clean. That healing isn't always visible. That people carry their wounds into the workplace, into their marriages, into their friendships—and that sometimes the best we can do is notice, name, and try again. There is a profound kindness in how the show handles emotional breakdowns. Not always perfectly, not always evenly, but consistently with the message that emotional failure is not the end. That collapse is a beginning.

This message matters because we live in a world that doesn't often extend that grace. We are asked to perform, to rebound, to demonstrate progress and wellness on a timeline. But *Grey's Anatomy* rarely demands this of its characters. It lets them circle. It lets them avoid, backslide, sabotage. And eventually, it lets them heal—not because they've achieved moral growth, but because they've learned how to stay present through discomfort. That's a deeper lesson than resolution. That's a model for how we can show up in our own lives.

There is also something mythic in the show's structure. The characters rotate, yes. The setting shifts. But the core themes repeat—loss, belonging, ambition, betrayal, reparation. In this way, the show mimics the psyche. It loops. It revisits old wounds in new bodies. It offers the same lesson until it's finally integrated. We don't just watch the show. We participate in it emotionally. We forecast outcomes. We rehearse arguments. We mourn people who were never real because what they symbolized was *so* real. The longing, the collapse, the wish for one more minute.

In many ways, *Grey's Anatomy* offers a cultural holding space. It lets us metabolize emotions we were never taught to name. It gives us a structure—weekly, seasonal, consistent—within which we can practice empathy. We grieve the characters we once dismissed. We fall in love with those we once overlooked. We watch ourselves grow through how we respond to them. That's not just storytelling. That's emotional development.

And the show's emotional accessibility is its own kind of medicine. Few series have made psychological realism feel so familiar, so unthreatening. Trauma isn't always named as such, but it is everywhere—coded into the way characters speak, react, isolate, forgive. What *Grey's Anatomy* understands, and what this book has sought to explore, is that trauma isn't always the explosion. Sometimes it's the silence after. The way someone walks a hallway. The way someone says *I'm fine* when they aren't. The way they hold a body, or refuse to.

Every major character on this show has endured some form of identity rupture. They've lost children, lost limbs, lost lovers, lost selves. And yet, their survival isn't positioned as triumph. It's portrayed as maintenance. As work. As showing up again even when it's painful. This is perhaps the most psychologically responsible thing the show has done: it removed the fantasy of emotional closure. It replaced it with the slow, nonlinear reality of emotional repair.

And for all its romantic messiness and narrative dramatics, *Grey's Anatomy* remains a show about repair. Not just of the body—but of trust, of faith, of connection. It is about what it takes to continue in a world where things are not fair, not tidy, not logical. It is about being human in the wake of loss—and still letting people close.

The psychological insight offered by *Grey's Anatomy* is not prescriptive. It doesn't hand out lessons like afterschool specials. Instead, it makes space for contradiction. Meredith is both brilliant and avoidant. Cristina is both loyal and unwilling to stay. Owen is both a trauma survivor and emotionally destructive. Bailey is both a caretaker and emotionally exhausted. These are not conflicts to be resolved. They are truths to be held.

That's what the show offers us: a model of internal pluralism. A reminder that people are not one thing. That the self is not fixed. That who we are is often defined not by certainty, but by what we can hold without disowning. And in that model, viewers are invited to reconsider how they judge themselves.

There's also the question of why we stay. Why we continue to return to a show whose characters often suffer so much. And the answer is simpler than it seems: because they survive. Because they grow. Because even when they do not end up where they thought they would, they keep choosing connection. That's the real emotional arc. Not the wedding. Not the career victory. But the willingness to remain in the room with one another, to say, *I see you,* and stay.

We watch *Grey's Anatomy* because it doesn't lie to us about what pain looks like. And it doesn't flinch when showing what healing really costs.

In this way, the show becomes more than entertainment. It becomes ritual. For some, it is grief therapy. For others, emotional rehearsal. For many, it is a weekly return to a world that—despite its chaos—makes more emotional sense than their own.

Seattle Grace is not just a hospital. It is a symbolic container for everything we are afraid to say in real life: *I'm not okay. I'm still angry. I wish you hadn't left. I don't know how to let go. I need more time. I'm not ready to forgive you. I want to come home but I don't know how.*

And every season, it lets us hear those things aloud—through someone else's voice, someone else's face. It reminds us that feeling doesn't make us weak. That care isn't unprofessional. That longing is not pathology. That love, however messy, is always the thread that pulls us through.

We keep watching not because *Grey's Anatomy* has answers—but because it has mirrors. And sometimes, seeing yourself reflected is the beginning of remembering that you are, in fact, still here.

* * *

About the Author

RJ Starr is an Academic Psychologist, Professor, and Author whose work explores the emotional and existential challenges at the heart of human life—how we make meaning, shoulder responsibility, and stay grounded in times of uncertainty. Known for a voice that is both thought-provoking and deeply accessible, he invites readers into greater self-awareness, emotional clarity, and purpose. When not teaching or writing, he reflects on the inner lives we carry and shares his insights with audiences around the world.

You can connect with me on:

https://profrjstarr.com

www.ingramcontent.com/pod-product-compliance
Lightning Source LLC
LaVergne TN
LVHW052304200926
848481LV00002B/462